WHO'S YOUR CITY?

WHO'S YOUR CITY?

*How the Creative Economy Is Making
Where to Live the Most
Important Decision of Your Life*

RICHARD FLORIDA

BASIC
BOOKS

A MEMBER OF THE PERSEUS BOOKS GROUP
NEW YORK

Designed by Timm Bryson

Library of Congress Cataloging-in-Publication Data
is available for the hardcover edition:
ISBN: 978-0-465-00352-5
Paperback ISBN: 978-0-465-01809-3

10 9 8 7 6 5 4 3 2 1

For Rana

If everything that exists has a place, place too will have a place, and so on ad infinitum.

—Aristotle

How in the image of material man, at once his glory and his menace, is this thing we call a city.

—Frank Lloyd Wright

The large towns and especially London absorb the very best blood from all the rest of England; the most enterprising, the most highly gifted, those with the highest physique and the strongest characters go there to find scope for their abilities.

—Alfred Marshall

Contents

Part IV: Where We Live Now

1

THE QUESTION OF WHERE

————

I'M NOT EASILY SHAKEN. I LIKE TO THINK OF MYSELF AS A guy who can take just about anything in stride. But when I was asked to appear on the *Colbert Report* in July 2007, I felt my stomach drop. Just a few months prior, I'd told my wife, Rana, how nerve-racking it would be to do an interview with Stephen Colbert. It's the one show that puts butterflies in my stomach. His technique of disarming mindless punditry through smart and edgy commentary is brilliant, but tough to fend off. He has an uncanny ability to stay in character—that now-famous bloviating right-wing talking head who grills his guests at a rapid-fire tempo, leaving them dumbstruck. I'm a regular watcher of the show and big fan, so I've seen how embarrassing it can be for guests who can't keep pace. But after some persuading from Rana and my team, I decided to give it a shot.

I took along some backup, Rana, my colleague David Miller, and his wife, Emily, all accompanied me on the high-speed Acela train from Washington, D.C., where we then lived, to

New York and eventually to the studio. Waiting in the green room, I was pumped up by energizing conversation with my friends and some *Colbert Report* staff. We were quite the contrast to Stephen's other guest, Senator Ben Nelson, who was prepping with his Hill staffers across the hall. At one point, the producer had to close the door to our green room to contain all the noise we were making.

As the minutes ticked by, my heart began racing. I started to sweat, and I couldn't help pacing the dressing room and the hall outside. I felt so nervous that when an assistant producer came over to brief me on the segment, I was literally speechless. That may have made them doubt their choice of guests. Stephen came in quickly to say hello. He reminded me that while he was going to stay in character, I should focus on playing it straight and getting my ideas across.

After makeup, they sent me out into the studio. The whole place felt electric. Then the music cranked up, blaring the Sex Pistols' "God Save the Queen." Great choice. It brought back the heart-thumping feeling I'd had long ago, playing lead guitar with my band.

It's now or never, I said to myself. I planted my feet, took several deep breaths, and with the music pumping, found my zone. I reminded myself to have fun, and to make sure Stephen and the audience knew I was in on the joke. It wasn't hard to relax during Stephen's introduction to the segment. I was busting a gut just listening to him start:

"For all the good news, there was some bad news last week. The National Association of Realtors forecasted that the slump in home sales and prices would be deeper and last longer than previously expected, all the way into 2008 . . .

"But a disturbing new study has found a solution to the housing slump: Live next to gay people. The study's author measured changes in income and property values using something called the Bohemian-Gay Index.

"Now while that may sound like another name for the San Francisco phone book, folks, it is BAAAD NEWS! This study found that artistic, bohemian, and gay populations increase housing values in the neighborhoods and communities they inhabit. According to that, I guess people these days want a house with a view of some goateed beatnik playing his bongos while he smokes a clove cigarette and chisels a sculpture of k. d. lang.

"The theory is that tolerant communities, where homosexuals are likely to reside, nurture an open-minded culture of creativity, which can lead to innovations like Google, or YouTube, or ShirtlessHunksBaggingGroceries.com.

"Well, personally, I don't believe that the value of my twelve-bedroom Tudor will go up just because a couple of opticians move in next door. Oh yeah, a lot of opticians are gay. . . ."

He introduced me to the audience, and then we were off. "Should I be following gay people around to see where they're living?" Stephen asked.

When I answered, "Yes," he shot back, "Good. I do it already. Now I have a reason."

After three to four minutes of back and forth, he ended the segment with this zinger. "You know what I think, sir? I think you are a gay, bohemian artist who just wants to sell his house."

To which I replied, trying as best I could to keep from laughing, "You know, we just sold our house on Sunday, my wife and I, to move to Toronto!"

Colbert had zeroed in on a controversial finding of my research: the relationship between housing prices and concentrations of gays and bohemians. Is it possible that a single factor—like a certain group of people —could make or break an area's housing market, much less determine its economic potential or its residents' happiness? True to his character, Colbert scoffed at the idea that he should be following gay populations around in order to find the best housing markets or most creative labor markets.

But the point had been made. Where we live is increasingly important to every facet of our lives. We owe it to ourselves to think about the relationship between place and our economic future, as well as our personal happiness, in a more systematic—if different— way.

The Biggest Decision of All

If someone asked you to list life's biggest decisions, what would you say? If you're like most people, you'd probably start with two things.

The first, I call the "what factor." Most of us will say that one of the key decisions in life is figuring out what you want to do for your career. Even if money can't buy happiness, many people believe that doing work you love is likely to give you a prosperous and fulfilling life. My father drilled that notion into me. "Richard," he would say, "you don't have to end up in a factory like me, working hard and punching a clock for modest pay. You need to be a lawyer or doctor, so you can do something important and make good money."

Many would add that an essential prerequisite to financial and career success is getting a good education and attending the right schools. Graduate from Harvard, MIT, Stanford, or Princeton, so goes the theory, and the rest will take care of itself. A good education is the means to a great job, a solid financial future, and a happy life. My parents, like so many others, were education fanatics. Even though they struggled to make ends meet, they put my brother Robert and me in Catholic school—which required not only tuition but also regular contributions to the local parish—and impressed upon us day and night the importance of studying hard, getting good grades, and going to college. They inspected our report cards and gave us rewards for good marks. Like so many other hardworking and devoted parents of modest means, they saw education as the key to upward mobility.

Others, meanwhile, will argue that while jobs, money, and schooling are surely important, the most critical decision in life is picking the right life partner—someone who will support you in all your endeavors and love you unconditionally along the way. Those who study human psychology agree: Loving relationships, their studies find, are key to a happy life.[1] My mother knew this intuitively. She turned down many college-educated suitors to marry my dad, a factory worker and World War II veteran with an eighth-grade education. "Richard," she would say, "it was the best decision of my life by far. Sure, some of those other guys made more money. But love is what is really important. I was madly in love with your father every day of my entire life."

Without question, both of those decisions—the what and the who—mean a great deal to our lives. But there is another decision that has an equal, if not greater, effect on our economic future, happiness, and overall life outcome. The question of *where*.

Maybe this seems so obvious that people overlook it. Finding the right place is as important as—if not more important than—finding the right job or partner because it not only influences those choices but also determines how easy or hard it will be to correct mistakes made along the way. Still, few of us actually look at a place that way. Perhaps it's because so few of us have the understanding or mental framework necessary to make informed choices about our location.

The place we choose to live affects every aspect of our being. It can determine the income we earn, the people we meet, the friends we make, the partners we choose, and the options available to our children and families. People are not equally happy everywhere, and some places do a better job of providing a high quality of life than others. Some places offer us more vibrant labor markets, better career prospects, higher real estate appreciation, and stronger investment and earnings opportunities. Some places offer more promising mating markets. Others are better environments for raising children.

Place also affects how happy we are in other, less palpable ways. It can be an island of stability in a sea of uncertainty and risk. Jobs end. Relationships break up. Choosing the right place can be a hedge against life's downsides. I hate to dwell on the negative, but you need to think about this. It's always terrible to lose a job, even worse to suffer a breakup with a significant other. As bad as those are, however, they are substantially worse if you also happen to live somewhere with few options in the job market or the mating market. It's exponentially easier to get back on your feet when your location has a vibrant economy with lots of jobs to choose from, or a lot of eligible single people in your age range to date.

The point is, where we live is a central life factor that affects all the others—work, education, and love—follow. It can make or break existing work arrangements and personal relationships. It can open new doors. And regardless of what kind of life we envision for ourselves—whether we aspire to make millions, have a family, or live the way of a bachelor—choosing where to live is a decision we all must make at least once. A good number of us will make it multiple times. The average American moves once every seven years. More than 40 million people relocate each year; 15 million make significant moves of more than 50 or 100 miles.[2]

The stakes are high, and yet, when faced with the decision of where to call home, most of us are not prepared to make the right choice. If you ask most people how they got to the place they live now, they'll say they just ended up there. They stayed close to family or friends, they got a job there, or more commonly, they followed an old flame. Some don't even see that there's a choice to be made at all.

Still, the miracle of our modern age is that we do have a choice. For the first time ever, a huge number of us have the freedom and economic means to choose our place. That means we have an incredible opportunity to find the place that fits us best. But this remarkable freedom forces us to decide among a large number of options. Today there are many types of communities out there, all with something different to offer.

The key is to find a place that fits you—one that makes you happy and enables you to achieve your life goals. For some people, career and wealth are big components of their happiness, but that is far from everybody. Many of us know people who left good jobs and prosperous careers in law or engineering to do something they truly love. Others move back to their hometown after college to help run the family business or to be closer to family and friends. These people usually know very well what they are giving up, and they make their choices knowingly. They prefer family and community to wealth. And many people are very happy where they are. These people may well know the real value of community better than others. What they value about place is the opportunity to live their lives in the towns and among the people already familiar to them.

The thing to remember is that when it comes to place, like most other important things in life, we can't have it all. There are real tradeoffs to be made. Many people who move for their careers will give up the joy of being near family and lifelong friends. Those of us who choose to stay close to family and friends may give up economic opportunity.

Before I go any further, I want you to think hard about the following questions.

1.   How do you like the place you're living now? Is it somewhere you really want to be? Does it give you energy? When you walk out onto the street—or the country lane—in the morning, does it fill you with inspiration, or stress? Does it allow you to be the person you really want to be? Are you achieving your personal goals? Is it a place you would recommend to your relatives and friends?

2.   Have you thought about moving? If so, what are the top three places on your radar screen? What do you like about them? Specifically, what do you think they offer you? How would your life be different in these places?

3.   Have you ever sat down and compared where you're living now to those places? Honestly, have you given this a fraction of the thought and energy you've given to your job and career prospects, or if you're single, to your dating life?

If you have, you are part of a very small minority. For such an important life decision, it's remarkable how few of us explore all the options or sufficiently ponder all of these questions.

Maybe that is because we're not fully informed. It's a mantra of the age of globalization that where we live doesn't matter. We can work as efficiently from a ski chalet in Aspen or a country house in Provence as from an office in Silicon Valley. It doesn't make a difference as long as we have wireless and a cell phone.

But impressive new technologies notwithstanding, the so-called death of place is hardly a new story. First the railroad revolutionized trade and transport as never before. Then the

telephone made everyone feel connected and closer. The automobile was invented, then the airplane, and then the World
Wide Web—perhaps the quintessential product of a globalized
world. All of these technologies have carried the promise of a
boundless world. They would free us from geography, allowing
us to move out of crowded cities and into lives of our own bu-
colic choosing. Forget the past, when cities and civilizations were
confined to fertile soil, natural ports, or raw materials. In today's
high-tech world, we are free to live wherever we want. Place, according to this increasingly popular view, is irrelevant.

It's a compelling notion, but it's wrong. Today's key economic
factors—talent, innovation, and creativity—are not distributed
evenly across the global economy. They concentrate in specific
locations. It's obvious how major new innovations in communications and transportation allow economic activity to spread out
all over the world. What's less obvious is the incredible power of
what I call the *clustering force*. In today's creative economy, the
real source of economic growth comes from the clustering and
concentration of talented and productive people. New ideas are
generated and our productivity increases when we locate close
to one another in cities and regions. The clustering force makes
each of us more productive, which in turns makes the places we
inhabit much more productive, generating great increases in
output and wealth.

Because of the clustering force, cities and regions have become the true engines of economic growth. No wonder these
locations continue to expand. Today, more than half the world's
population lives in urban areas. In the United States, more than
90 percent of all economic output is produced in metropolitan
regions, while just the largest five metro regions account for 23
percent of it. And cities and their surrounding metropolitan corridors are morphing into massive *mega-regions*, home to tens of

millions of people producing hundreds of billions and in some cases trillions of dollars in economic output. Place remains the central axis of our time—more important to the world economy and our individual lives than ever before.

As the most mobile people in human history, we are fortunate to have an incredibly diverse menu of places—in our own countries and around the world—from which to choose. That's important because each of us has different needs and preferences. Luckily, places differ as much as we do. Some have thriving job markets, others excel at the basics, like education and safety. Some are better for singles, others for families. Some are more about work, some play. Some lean conservative, others liberal. They all cater to different types, and each has its own personality, its own soul. The different personalities of places seem like hard variables to get a handle on—but it's not impossible. We've mapped them, and you can find the maps in Chapter 11.

It's not just that places' personalities are different. What we need from a place also shifts with each stage of our life. When we're young, just out of school and single, many of us want a place that's stimulating, offering lots of jobs and opportunities for career advancement, great nightlife, and a vibrant "mating market" filled with single people to meet and date. When we get a bit older, and certainly when we marry and have children, our priorities change. We want a place that offers good schools, safe streets, and better lives for our families. And when the children go off to college and leave the house, our needs and interests change yet again.

At each of these turning points, and at many others along the way, a growing number of us have the opportunity to choose a place that truly fits our needs.

But how do we begin to think about that choice? Some fifty years ago, the brilliant economist Charles Tiebout outlined a powerful framework for identifying the tradeoffs involved in choosing our place.[3] Tiebout argued that communities specialize in the bundles of services or "public goods" they offer—such as education, police, fire, parks, and what not. Different bundles of services and different qualities of services come with a price, paid as taxes. So when we choose a place, we're not only selecting a physical location—we're also picking the bundle of goods and services that will be available to us there. As Tiebout famously argued, people will "vote with their feet," selecting the particular community which offers goods and services compatible with their particular preferences and needs. Some people prefer great schools and are prepared to pay for them. Single people, or those whose kids are out of the house, will value schools much less: they are more likely to desire nice restaurants, world-class beaches, great golf courses, and lower taxes. Tiebout's model provides a basic logic for thinking about what we value in our communities. When given a wide range of choices, we need to identify our key needs and priorities and then find a place that meets them at a price we are willing and able to pay.

Speaking of price: The place we live is one of the biggest ticket items of our lives. Some people want the thrill, excitement, and opportunity that big cities like London or New York offer. But understand that those things can come with a hefty price tag. Living in these cities, and others such as San Francisco, Amsterdam, Boston, Chicago, Toronto, and Sydney, has become extraordinarily expensive. People who work in finance may find that the cost of living in New York or London is offset by the economic success they can achieve there. The same might be said of filmmakers who choose to move to Los Angeles or fashion designers who need to be in Milan or Paris—and other places at the top of the pecking order in their given industries.

But what if you work in a different kind of field where there is no go-to location, or if you're the kind of person who simply doesn't aspire to be at the very pinnacle of your industry. Then there are plenty of other, lovely places out there where you can live for a fraction of the amount. It's absolutely essentially that you weigh your career goals against the quality of life you'd like to achieve.

I wrote this book to help you pick the place that's right for you. I'll share with you more than twenty-five years of personal research, as well as the work and findings of many others.[4] I've structured my advice around three key ideas.

1. Despite all the hype over globalization and the "flat world," place is actually more important to the global economy than ever before.
2. Places are growing more diverse and specialized—from their economic makeup and job market to the quality of life they provide and the kinds of people that live in them.
3. We live in a highly mobile society, giving most of us more say over where we live.

Taken together, these three facts mean that where you choose to live will greatly affect everything from your finances and job options to your friends, your potential mate, and your children's future.

The first part of this book tackles the big picture. It looks at how and why place continues to matter to the global economy. It provides maps and statistics that chart the reality of globalization and the function of mega-regions, the new economic units of what I call the "spiky world."

The second part addresses how where you live affects your economic situation—the new realities of the job market, trends in the housing market, real estate appreciation, all of which are real pocketbook issues. It shows how economic advantage accrues in some places more than others, details the new migration of talented and skilled people to a small set of regions, and documents the forces driving the ups and downs of the housing market. It also describes the trend toward the clustering of jobs—high-tech in Silicon Valley or Austin, finance in New York, filmmaking in Hollywood, music in Nashville.

The third part confronts what is perhaps the biggest trade-off we need to consider when picking a place to live: how to balance our career goals against our lifestyle and other needs. It looks at the relationship between where we live and our ability to live happy, fulfilled lives. It draws from a large-scale survey of 28,000 people that I conducted with the Gallup Organization. This study, the Place and Happiness Survey, found that location is as relevant to a person's well-being as are his or her job, finances, and interpersonal relationships.

The fourth part looks at how our needs and preferences for where we live evolve and change as we go through three of life's main stages—when we're young and single, married with children, and as empty-nesters after our children have left the house. This section features new rankings my team and I developed of the best places for each of these main stages of your life.

The last chapter gets practical. It provides the basic tools you need to identify the place that's best for you. Even if you're ecstatic about where you currently live, this chapter will help you better understand what you truly desire and need. If you're thinking about a move, it provides a detailed guide of what to look for and where to look for it. By the end of this book, you'll better understand the critical role of place in today's global economy, and how to maximize your chances for a happy and fulfilling life by picking the place that's right for you.

PART I

WHY PLACE MATTERS

2
SPIKY WORLD

———————

·

T HE WORLD IS FLAT, SAYS *New York Times* COLUMNIST
Thomas Friedman.[1] Thanks to advances in technology the
global playing field has been leveled, the prizes are there for the
taking, and all of us are players—no matter where on the surface of the earth we may reside. "When the world is flat," Friedman writes, "you can innovate without having to emigrate."

It's an old idea with a long history. Since the turn of the twentieth century, commentators have been writing about the leveling effects of trade and technology that make place
unimportant. From the invention of the telegraph and the telephone, the automobile and the airplane, to the rise of the personal computer and the Internet—many have argued that
technological progress has eroded the economic significance of
physical location.

The same prophecies persist today. In 1995, *The Economist*
proclaimed the "Death of Distance" on its cover. "Thanks to

technology and competition in telecoms," journalist Frances Cairncross predicted, "distance will soon be no object." Four years later the same magazine proudly announced the "Conquest of Location": "The wireless revolution is ending the dictatorship of place in a more profound way."[2] The new communications technologies were proving to be the "great levelers" in an increasingly globalized world. Place, we've been led to believe, is no longer relevant. We should feel free to live wherever we please.

I've spent the better part of the past decade trying to come to grips with those theories, to square provocative concepts with the facts. With the help of my research team, I've sorted through mounds of studies, statistical evidence, and counterevidence on the critical role of place in the global economy, which the next two chapters will detail. The bottom line?

By almost any measure, the international economic landscape is not at all flat.

"There are many advantages that children can enter this world with—including intelligence, physical power and agility, good looks and caring parents," wrote UCLA economist and global trade expert Edward Leamer in a devastating review of *The World Is Flat* in the highly respected *Journal of Economic Literature:* "It also matters where you live."[3] And while theoretically we can choose to live virtually anywhere, the reality of the global economy is that certain places offer far more opportunity than others.

The most obvious challenge to the flat-world hypothesis is the explosive growth of cities and urban areas worldwide. More and more people are clustering in urban areas—and there's no evidence to suggest that they'll be stopping anytime soon. The share of the world's population living in urban areas increased from just 3 percent in 1800 to 14 percent in 1900. By 1950, it had reached 30 percent. Today, this number stands at more than

50 percent. In the advanced countries, three-quarters of people live in urban areas.[4]

Population growth isn't the only indicator that the world is anything but flat. In this chapter, I'll show detailed maps that illustrate the extreme concentrations of economic activity and innovation. In terms of both sheer economic horsepower and cutting-edge innovation, today's global economy is powered by a surprisingly small number of places. What's more, the playing field shows no sign of leveling. The tallest spikes—the cities and regions that drive the world economy—are growing ever higher, while the valleys—places that boast little, if any, economic activity—mostly languish.

To be sure, globalization is powerful. Places that never had a chance to participate in the world economy are now seeing some action. But not all of them are able to participate and benefit equally. Innovation and economic resources remain highly concentrated. As a result, the really significant locations in the world economy remain limited in number.

The reality is that globalization has two sides. The first and more obvious one is the geographic spread of routine economic functions such as simple manufacturing or service work (for example, making or answering telephone calls). The second, less obvious side to globalization is the tendency for higher-level economic activities such as innovation, design, finance, and media to cluster in a relatively small number of locations.

When thinkers like Friedman focus on how globalization spreads out economic activity (its centrifugal force, so to speak), they miss the reality of this clustering (the centripetal force). Michael Porter, Harvard Business School professor and expert on competitive strategy, dubs this the "location paradox": "Location still matters," he told *Business Week* in August 2006. "The more things are mobile, the more decisive location becomes."

And "this point," he added, "has tripped up a lot of really smart people."[5]

The mistake they make is to see globalization as an either-or proposition. It's not. The key to our new global reality lies in understanding that the world is flat and spiky at the same time.

The World at Night

I'm a big fan of maps. The ones on the following pages were developed by Timothy Gulden, a researcher at the University of Maryland's Center for International and Security Studies. They depict global economic activity on a fine spatial scale. When previous versions of these maps were published in the *Atlantic Monthly* in October 2005, they generated quite a stir.[6] Since then, we have updated them to reflect more comprehensive data. Based on traditional measures of population density and new measures of global economic production and innovation, these maps show the striking location-based *spikiness* of globalization. There are roughly two or three dozen places that dominate the global economy.

Figure 2.1 charts population distribution across the globe. It is based on existing data that my team and I collected in order to identify the world's mega-regions (which I'll discuss in more detail in Chapter 3). The most populous region is India's Dehli-Lahore, which is home to more than 120 million people. There are eight regions with more than 50 million people; another twelve are home to 25 to 50 million; and thirty-three more have between 10 and 25 million people.

Of course, population density is a rudimentary measure of economic activity that does not fully convey the vast gulf separating the world's most productive regions from the rest. Sometimes, relatively small cities like Helsinki can be immensely rich in per capita output. Conversely, some enormous urban

FIGURE 2.1 POPULATION IN A SPIKY WORLD

MAP BY TIM GULDEN

SOURCE: LANDSCAN GLOBAL POPULATION DATABASE, OAK RIDGE NATIONAL LABORATORY

settlements like those of the developing world do not generate a lot of economic output and remain quite poor. So it is important to identify mega-regions not just in terms of their population but also in terms of their economic output.

Unfortunately, there exists no single comprehensive information source for the economic production of the world's regions. A rough proxy is available, though. Our second map shows a variation on the widely circulated illustration of the world at night, with higher concentrations of light and thus higher energy use—and, presumably, stronger economic production—but in greater relief (see Figure 2.2).

To build these maps, Gulden used data from the U.S. Defense Meteorological Satellite Program at the National Oceanic and Atmospheric Administration (NOAA). He charted contiguous lighted areas, noting the sources behind the emissions—lit homes, powered factories, illuminated streets, and lively entertainment districts. Using a series of spatial and statistical techniques, Gulden was able to estimate the amount of economic activity from the amount of light emanating from these areas. I call Gulden's measure light-based regional product, or LRP for short.

Once Gulden had derived his estimates, he calibrated them against published figures on economic output of U.S. metropolitan regions and against World Bank estimates of Gross Domestic Product by country. He then overlaid the light-based estimates with detailed population estimates from Oak Ridge National Laboratory to verify that the method produced plausible estimates of economic activity. Finally, Gulden checked his estimates of LRP against GDP estimates by William Nordhaus and his team at Yale University.[7] The final result, shown as Figure 2.2, shows our estimates of light-based regional product for every square kilometer on the globe for the year 2000.

FIGURE 2.2 ECONOMIC ACTIVITY IN A SPIKY WORLD

MAP BY TIM GULDEN

SOURCE: U.S. DEFENSE METEOROLOGICAL SATELLITE PROGRAM

As this map shows, the world economy takes shape around a couple dozen mega-regions. As the next chapter will detail, two of them produced more than $2 trillion in economic output— Greater Tokyo ($2.5 trillion) and the giant mega-region stretching from Boston through New York to Washington, D.C. ($2.2 trillion). These two mega-regions would rank as the third and fourth largest economies in the world, about the same size as Germany: only the United States and Japan are larger. Four more mega-regions produce more than $1 trillion in output— the great mega that runs from Chicago to Pittsburgh ($1.6 trillion), Europe's Am-Brus-Twerp ($1.5 trillion), Japan's Osaka-Nagoya region ($1.4 trillion), and the Greater London region ($1.2 trillion). Each of them would place among the top ten national economies in the world; they are all bigger than Italy, Canada, India, South Korea, Russia, or Brazil. There are forty that produce more than $100 billion in economic output each. Not only are mega-regions becoming the economic powerhouses behind national economies; they're behind the global economy as well.

Although they do not yet rival those of the United States, Europe, or Japan, the economies of both India and China are also considerably spiky. In China, according to Gulden's light emission calculations, 68 percent of economic output is produced in places that house just 25 percent of its people. In India, places with 26 percent of the population produce more than half (54 percent) of the nation's total output. Compare that to the United States, where regions produce economic output roughly in proportion to their population. The population and productive capacity of the United States, as spiky as it is, is spread over a relatively large number of places. China and India, which industrialized much later, have seen their resources and productive capability concentrate to a much greater degree. Our current round of globalization is making the world even spikier than before.

Smart Spots

Population and economic activity are both spiky. But it is innovation—the engine of economic growth—that is most concentrated. It's here that the playing field is least level. Our third
map shows the world's innovation centers, as measured by
patents granted worldwide (see Figure 2.3). Gulden developed
these maps through another ingenious method. Using light
emissions to define economic regions, he applied U.S. Patent
and Trademark Office data that traces the geographic location
of every single inventor who files a patent in the United States.
But because U.S. patent data is biased to U.S. inventors and inventors from firms and countries that patent in the United
States, he then used data from the World Intellectual Property
Organization to create more accurate estimates for every location in the world.[8]

Our map of global innovation clearly shows a world composed
of innovative peaks and valleys. The leaders—the tallest spikes—
are the metropolitan regions around Tokyo, Seoul, New York, and
San Francisco. Boston, Seattle, Austin, Toronto, Vancouver,
Berlin, Paris, Stockholm, Helsinki, Osaka, Seoul, Taipei, and Sydney also stand out. Innovation is also cropping up in certain locations in China and India, as their economies develop. Though
they are not nearly as tall as the biggest spikes, a number of cities
in these countries are developing significant innovation capability.
In India, Bangalore produces about as many patents as Syracuse,
while Hyderabad is comparable to Nashville. In China, Beijing
produces about as many patents as Seattle or Phoenix, while
Shanghai produces about as many as Toronto or Salt Lake City.
Our own estimates show that innovation in these cities has increased fourfold between 1996 and 2001 and has likely grown at
an even greater rate in recent years. Beijing and Shanghai appear
poised to join the ranks of global innovators.

FIGURE 2.3 INNOVATION IN A SPIKY WORLD

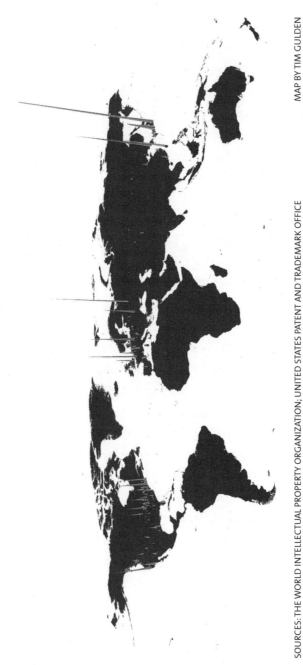

SOURCES: THE WORLD INTELLECTUAL PROPERTY ORGANIZATION; UNITED STATES PATENT AND TRADEMARK OFFICE

MAP BY TIM GULDEN

This trend may come at the expense of the United States, which has long depended on the innovative and entrepreneurial capabilities of Indian and Chinese immigrants. The detailed research of AnnaLee Saxenian, of the University of California, Berkeley, has shown that Indian and Chinese entrepreneurs ran roughly 25 percent of all Silicon Valley startups from 1980 to 1999, which generated $17 billion in annual revenue and about 58,000 jobs.[9] By 2005, that percentage had increased to 30 percent.

But as the map shows, there are still at most two dozen places worldwide that generate significant innovation. These regions have ecosystems of leading-edge universities, high-powered companies, flexible labor markets, and venture capital that are attuned to the demands of commercial innovation—and there aren't many of them.

This spiky pattern for commercial innovation can also be seen in its financing. Venture capital—funds invested in high-tech companies—is also geographically concentrated. The United States boasts a major center in Silicon Valley, and smaller ones in Boston, New York, and a few other cities. Outside the United States, several locations in Europe, as well as in India, China, and Israel, are considered up-and-coming, according to the research of University of California, Davis, technology expert Martin Kenney.[10] But despite the relatively limited number of venture capital (VC) hot spots, VC firms often invoke the "twenty-minute rule." Only companies within a twenty-minute commute of the VC firm's office are considered worthy of a high-risk investment. Not even high-tech companies whose very products and services are based in long-distance communication are considered worth the risk if their physical location is too far away. That isn't to say firms don't make exceptions—but given the hands-on demands of venture capitalism, being close to clients, investors, and colleagues is highly prioritized. The twenty-minute rule in part explains why so many start-up companies eventually find themselves moving to Silicon Valley, even if they were founded elsewhere. And just three cities worldwide dominated the global market in initial public offerings (IPOs) as of summer 2007: London ($51 billion), New York ($46 billion), and Hong Kong ($41 billion).[11]

Star Scientists

Scientific discovery—the source of much technological innovation—is also concentrated and spiky. Most significant discoveries occur not just in a handful of locations—primarily in the United States and Europe.

The fourth map (see Figure 2.4) shows the residence of the 1,200 most heavily cited scientists in leading fields. It is based on data originally compiled by geographer and urban planner Michael Batty of University College London.[12] A 2006 National Bureau of Economic Research study by Lynne Zucker and Michael Darby identifies a similar pattern. Tracking the location of more than 5,000 star scientists and engineers between 1981 and 2004, across 179 U.S. regions and twenty-five countries, Zucker and Darby find major concentrations on the East (Boston, New York, Washington-Baltimore) and West coasts (San Francisco, Los Angeles, and Seattle), Chicago, and several other U.S. regions, as well as major European (London, Amsterdam, Paris) and Japanese cities, as well as in several other locations.[13]

Note the similarities between the third and fourth maps. Commercial innovation and scientific advance are both highly concentrated—and there are places that enjoy both and do very well in the global economy. But not all regions do both really well. Several cities in East Asia—particularly in Japan—are home to significant commercial innovation but still heavily depend on scientific breakthroughs made elsewhere. Similarly, other locations excel in scientific research but not in commercial adaptation.

FIGURE 2.4 STAR SCIENTISTS IN A SPIKY WORLD

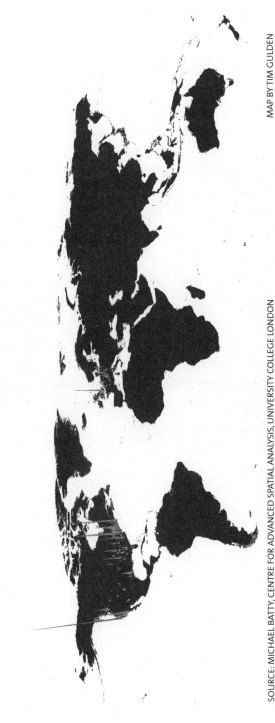

MAP BY TIM GULDEN

SOURCE: MICHAEL BATTY, CENTRE FOR ADVANCED SPATIAL ANALYSIS, UNIVERSITY COLLEGE LONDON

When you look at the four maps together, an intriguing pattern appears. With each layer that is added—population density, economic activity, and innovation—the map becomes increasingly concentrated. At the base, population is already highly concentrated: most of the world's people live in a relatively small number of big cities. The distribution of economic activity is even more skewed: Many locations, despite large populations, barely register. Innovation and star scientists come from fewer places still.

The world gets spikier and spikier the farther you climb up the ladder of economic development, from producing basic goods to undertaking significant new innovations.

Geographic concentration is particularly important for innovation, as we'll examine further in Chapter 4. Ideas flow more freely, are honed more sharply, and can be put into practice more quickly when innovators, implementers, and financial backers are in constant contact with one another, in and outside of work. Creative people cluster not simply because they like to be around each other, or because they all happen to prefer cosmopolitan centers with lots of amenities, though both of those things tend to be true. Creative people and companies cluster because of the powerful productivity advantages, economies of scale, and knowledge spillovers such density brings.

So although one might not *have* to emigrate to innovate, geographic concentration remains a prerequisite for cutting-edge innovation. Innovation, economic growth, and prosperity continue to occur in places that attract a critical mass of top creative talent. Because globalization increases the returns on innovation—by allowing for fast rollouts of innovative products and services to consumers worldwide—it increases the lure of innovation centers for our planet's best and brightest. All this only reinforces the spikiness of economic activity across the globe.

Peaks and Valleys

In the past, cities of one country or region competed for investment and for talent with other cities in that same country or region. Now locations across the globe compete with one another. Increasingly, the most competitive global contests are for bright, innovative, and entrepreneurial people.

The landscape of the spiky world can be characterized by four kinds of places.

- The first group comprises the relatively small number of locations that generate innovations. Those are the tallest spikes. They have the capacity to attract global talent, generate new knowledge, and produce the lion's share of global innovation. Thanks to the ever-increasing efficiency of long-distance communication and transportation, ideas circulate among these places easily and constantly.

- The second group includes regions that use established innovation and creativity—often imported from other places—to produce goods and services. Those are the world's emerging peaks. Some of them, such as Dublin, Seoul, and perhaps Singapore and Taipei, are transitioning into places that not only use knowledge but generate it. Most of them, though, function primarily as the manufacturing and service centers of the twenty-first-century global economy. From Guadalajara and Tijuana to Shanghai and the Philippines, they produce the world's goods, take its calls, and support its innovation engines.

- The third group is composed of the mega-cities of the developing world—with large population concentrations

but insufficient economic activity to support their
people. Many of these mega-cities are ravaged by large-
scale "global slums" with dense concentrations of
homelessness, poverty, and deprivation, high levels of
social and political unrest, and little meaningful
economic activity.[14] These places, increasingly
disconnected from the global economy, make it difficult
to celebrate what appears to be a level world for only a
fortunate few.

- Finally, there are the huge valleys of the spiky world—
rural areas and far-flung places that have little
concentration of population or economic activity, and
little connection to the global economy.

The main difference between now and even a couple of decades ago is not that the whole world has become flatter but that
the world's spikes have become more dispersed, and that the
world's hills or emerging peaks—the industrial and service centers—have proliferated and shifted. For the better part of the
twentieth century, the United States claimed the lion's share of
the world's economic and innovative peaks, with a few outposts
in Europe and Japan. But the United States has since lost many
of those peaks, as industrial-age powerhouses such as Pittsburgh, St. Louis, and Cleveland have fallen back from the global
front lines. At the same time, a number of regions in Europe,
Scandinavia, Canada, and the Pacific Rim have stepped up.

For some, the world today looks flat because the economic and
social distances between the peaks have gotten smaller. People
in spiky places are often more connected to each other, even
from half a world away, than they are to people and places in
their own backyards. This peak-to-peak connectivity is accelerated by the highly mobile creative class, of about 150 million

people worldwide. They participate in a global technology system and a global labor market, both of which allow them to migrate more freely among the world's leading cities. While the world itself is far from flat, the dense network of interconnections among its peaks can make it appear that way to a privileged minority.

A Brookings Institution study by demographer Robert Lang and world-cities researcher Peter Taylor documents the connective fiber linking the world's peaks—as well as the growing economic and social distance separating them from the world's valleys.[15] Lang and Taylor identify a relatively small group of leading interconnected locations—places like London, New York, Paris, Tokyo, Hong Kong, Singapore, Chicago, Los Angeles, and Milan. They also identify a much larger group of city-regions that enjoy far less connectivity to the world economy.

A 2007 *Economist* report on global finance markets reached similar conclusions. While technology has made cross-border financial dealings a snap, the world's major financial centers are spikier and more clustered than ever. "Why would financiers want to live and work in pricey, jam-packed urban jungles?" the article asks. "Armed with broadband, mobile phones and Black-Berries, they could work from almost anywhere." But London, New York, and Tokyo, as well as rising hubs like Hong Kong and Singapore, are consolidating their hold on global finance. The article adds, "Unlike the walled medieval city-states, today's financial centers are increasingly dependent on their connections to one another. Technology, the mobility of capital and the spread of deregulation around the globe have created a vibrant and growing network. When one city is asleep, another is wide awake, so trading goes on round the clock. The number of transactions between financial centers has surged recently as investors have diversified across regions and asset types."[16] It's just more evidence of peak-to-peak connectivity among the world's

spikiest places, the flip side being the growing economic and social distance between them and the rest of the globe.

Conceiving of the world as spiky has very different geopoliti-
cal and economic implications than seeing it as essentially flat.
The flat world theory says that emerging areas can easily plug in
to the rest of the world. Emerging economies like India and
China certainly combine cost advantages, high-tech skills, and
entrepreneurial energy, which allow them to compete effectively for manufacturing and standardized service industries. In
the flat world view, the tensions set in motion by the increasingly leveled playing field afflict mainly the advanced countries,
which see not only manufacturing work but also higher-end
jobs, in fields like software development and financial services,
moving off-shore.

That theory blinds us to far more insidious problems building
in the world economy and, worse yet, leaves policymakers with
little leverage over them. It's no longer sufficient to think of the
world in traditional binaries: rich and poor, advanced and developing. For the foreseeable future, global politics will hinge on
the growing tensions among the world's growing peaks, sinking
valleys, and shifting hills. Through that lens, we can see growing divides and tensions on several overlapping fronts: between
the innovative, talent-attracting "have" regions and the talent-
exporting "have-not" regions; in the escalating and potentially
devastating competition among second-tier cities from Detroit
to Nagoya to Bangalore for jobs, people, and investment; and in
rapidly worsening inequality across the world and even within
its most successful and innovative regional centers.

This is a noxious brew—far more harrowing than the flat
world Freidman describes and a good deal more treacherous
than the old rich-poor divide. Contrary to Samuel Huntington's
famous thesis, which pits so-called modern Judeo-Christian values against "backward" Muslim ones, what we face is not a clash

of civilizations but a deepening economic divide among the world's spikes and valleys. Most of the world's conflicts—even those seemingly unrelated to economics—stem from the underlying forces of a spiky world.

More than a decade ago, the political theorist Benjamin Barber presciently wrote that the rise of the global economy, which he called "McWorld," was so powerful and all-encompassing that it was reinforcing an enormous backlash.[17] That tendency— what he dubbed "Jihad"—has its roots in the anxiety and fear felt by millions upon millions of people in regions whose factions or "tribes" are being threatened by the impersonal force of globalization. Lacking the education, skill, or mobility to connect to the global economy, these people are stuck in places that are falling further and further behind.

Not surprisingly, spiky globalization is wreaking havoc on the transitional and emerging economies. China's rapid growth in the past decade has brought it to the front lines of the global economy. It is increasingly seen as the "world's factory," *the* manufacturing center and outsourcing destination for the world's leading companies. Experts note that China is quickly moving up the creative ladder by expanding its science workforce, improving its universities, and attracting the world's top technological workers.

But China's remarkable growth is a result of only a handful of propulsive regions, which are attracting the majority of its talented people, generating the great bulk of its innovations, and producing most of its impressive wealth. Talent is concentrated in a few spiky centers such as Shanghai, Shenzhen, and Beijing, each of which is a virtual world apart from its vast impoverished rural areas. The top ten Chinese regions account for just 16 percent of the nation's population, yet they house nearly 45 percent of its talent-producing universities and 60 percent of its technological innovations.[18]

China exemplifies the growing class divide affecting rapidly developing economies. Its major cities are home to some 560 million people who reside in increasingly innovative, energetic, and cosmopolitan places. Left in their wake are their country-men—750 million Chinese who inhabit the rest of the mostly rural country. According to detailed polling by the Gallup Orga-nization in 2006, average household incomes in urban China were two and a half times those in rural areas, and have nearly doubled since 1999. According to our own calculations, resi-dents of China's leading mega-regions are three and half times wealthier than those in the rest of the country. A Chinese stu-dent of mine summed it up succinctly: "In Shanghai, regular middle-class people live better than those in the United States, while in the countryside, just outside the city, people live in what can only be described as precivilized conditions." His im-pressions are borne out in statistics: 17 percent of China's popu-lation lives on less than a dollar a day, almost half lives on less than 2 dollars a day, and 800 million farmers cannot afford to see a doctor.

This spiky and uneven nature of China's economy is rearing its head in the country's politics. In 2005, the Chinese country-side was the scene of an estimated 87,000 riots and demonstra-tions, up 50 percent from 2003.[19] In response, the national government began implementing new mechanisms—such as rural development projects in business, education, and health care—to cope with the widening socio-economic rift.[20] Still, the prospects for bridging the gap are bleak. As China's internation-ally connected peaks grow closer to their global counterparts, rural areas and their populations are sure to be left behind.

But all that pales in comparison with the growing pains felt by India's poor. India's growing economic spikes—city-regions such as Bangalore, Hyderabad, Mumbai, and parts of New Delhi—are also pulling away from the rest of that crowded country. As

Stanford University's Rafiq Dossani has noted, India's technology and business services—industries that are quickly growing—lack the broad employment base enjoyed by China's manufacturing industry.[21] Until India figures out how to provide jobs to its low-skill workers, globalization will only deepen the country's internal economic, political, and social divisions.

The backlash to the spiky world extends beyond emerging economies. At the heart of the rejection of the European Union constitution by the populations of France and The Netherlands in 2005 were lower-skilled suburban and rural workers who understandably fear globalization and integration. They may live in the advanced world, but they are also being left behind.

Spiky globalization is also behind political and cultural polarization in the United States, where economic and social rifts between innovative and globally connected metropolitan regions and the rest of the country are ever increasing. As my own calculations show, the spikiest, most innovative centers in the United States—Silicon Valley, Boston, and North Carolina's Research Triangle, for example—also boast the nation's highest levels of inequality.

This spikiness also plays a key role in the divergence of the two ends of an increasingly split housing market (more on this in Chapter 8). As homes in cities like London, New York, San Francisco, and Hong Kong have appreciated over the past two decades, home values in the hinterlands of those countries stagnate or decline.

Left unaddressed, the festering anxiety caused by spiky globalization has already spurred a potentially devastating political backlash against the global engines of innovation. Across the world, there is fear, insecurity, anger, and resentment emanating from those falling farther and farther below the world's peaks. On top of that, countries are witnessing the departure (or intended departure) of their best and brightest. And there is no shortage of narcissistic political zealots out there—whether in rural Pennsylvania, the French countryside, Eastern Europe, or the Middle East—willing to stoke these mounting fears simply for political gain.

If this resembles a Hobbesian world, it's because globalization, poverty, and affluence have all given rise to a new sorting process that geographically separates economic and social classes both domestically and globally. In today's spiky world, social cohesion is eroding within countries and across them. Little wonder we find ourselves living in an increasingly fractured global society, in which growing numbers are ready to vote—or tear—down what they perceive to be the economic elite of the world.

The flat-world theory is not completely misguided. The world is clearly becoming more interconnected. More goods are being produced than ever before, and wealth is growing in the aggregate. Overall, people around the world have more opportunity to participate in the global economy. But most people don't care about aggregate effects; justifiably, they care about their own well-being. While emerging economies do stand to gain the most from spiky globalization, they will not be immune to its negative effects. And because modern communication makes the world smaller at the same time that globalization makes it spikier, those trapped in the valleys are looking directly up at the peaks, the growing disparities in wealth, opportunity, and lifestyle staring them right in the face.

We are thus confronted with the greatest dilemma of our time. Economic progress requires that the peaks grow stronger and taller. But such growth simply exacerbates economic and social disparity, fomenting political reactions that further threaten innovation and economic progress. By maintaining that the world is flat, that the playing field is level, and that anyone and everyone has a shot, we make it impossible to confront the problems of globalization that afflict so much of the world. Only by understanding that the spiky nature of our world's economy is one beset by growing disparities and tensions can we begin to address them. Managing the disparities between peaks and valleys worldwide—raising the valleys without sacrificing the peaks—is surely the greatest political challenge of our time.

3
RISE OF THE MEGA-REGION

T HE ROLLING STONES ARE WORLD FAMOUS. THEY'VE
traveled the globe countless times. But their 2006 World
Tour included a new, first-ever stop—Shanghai. "We all know
that Shanghai is a big important city," Mick Jagger told the
press, "so we wanted to make sure it's on our itinerary." The
Stones recognized what international investors, global manufacturing firms, and investment bankers have known for years:
Shanghai looks and feels nothing like the rest of China. Not only
is it attracting talent and investment, it is determined to transform itself into a global creative center by supporting the arts,
fostering a bustling nightclub district, and forging connections
with cosmopolitan centers around the world.

The growing divergence between Shanghai and the rest of
China is not an isolated case. It reflects a much broader and
powerful process—the rise of the *mega-region* as the fundamental economic unit of our time. Today, mega-regions range in
size from 5 to more than 100 million people, and they produce

hundreds of billions—sometimes trillions—in economic output. They harness human creativity on a massive scale and are responsible for most of the world's scientific achievement and technological innovations.

Cities have always been the natural economic units of the world. But over the past several decades, what we once thought of as cities, with central cores surrounded by rural villages and later by suburbs, have grown into mega-regions composed of two or more city-regions, such as the Boston–New York–Washington corridor. Mega-regions are more than just a bigger version of a city. In the way that a city is composed of separate neighborhoods, and like a metropolitan region is made up of a central city and its suburbs, a mega-region is a new, natural economic unit that results from city-regions growing upward, becoming denser, and growing outward and into one another.

The mega-regions of today perform functions that are somewhat similar to those performed by great cities of the past—massing together talent, productive capability, innovation, and markets. But mega-regions do so on a far larger scale. While cities in the past were part of national systems, globalization has exposed today's cities to worldwide competition. As the distribution of economic activity has gone global, the city-system has also gone global—meaning that cities now compete on a global terrain. That means that bigger and more competitive economic units—mega-regions—have superceded cities as the real engines of the global economy.

The Only Economic Unit that Matters

When we think about economic growth and development, we usually think in terms of nation-states. The classical economists Adam Smith and David Ricardo both argued that nation-states were the geographic engines behind economic growth. As Ricardo famously theorized, discretely defined countries have incentive to specialize in different kinds of industries, which would allow them to gain and maintain "comparative advantage" over others.[1]

Most students of economic history see a progression from rural villages to cities to nation-states. The reality is that economic activity—such as trade, commerce, and innovation—has always originated in cities. Cities, and now mega-regions, have always been the central engines of economic growth and development.

The first person to see this was the great urbanist Jane Jacobs, who is best known for her scathing critique of urban planning, *The Death and Life of Great American Cities*, and less famous for two other important volumes, *The Economy of Cities* and *Cities and the Wealth of Nations*.[2] In *The Economy of Cities*, published in 1969, Jacobs refutes the longstanding theory that cities emerged only after agriculture had become sufficiently productive to create a surplus beyond what was needed to survive. In fact, the earliest cities, according to Jacobs, formed around rudimentary trade in wild animals and grains, which led their inhabitants to discover agriculture and the economic benefits of product exportation. Even activities typically considered "rural" originated in cities before proliferating into outlying regions. Productivity improvements in agriculture, Jacobs points out, always originated in cities before they were adopted in farming areas. The mechanical reaper, for instance, was originally invented, perfected, and used in cities before the technology reached and revolutionized rural agricultural areas. To illustrate her point, Jacobs describes how the suppression of cities in a post-famine Ireland made it impossible for the country to recover during the 1840s:

> There were no ports to receive relief food. . . . There were
> no mills for grinding relief grain. There were no mechanics
> or tools and equipment to build mills. There were no ovens

for baking bread. There were no ways to spread information about how to grow crops other than potatoes. There was no way to distribute the seeds of other crops, nor to supply the farm tools that were indispensable for a change of crops.

Jacobs goes on to say that it was the iron fist of British rule that put the Irish in this dreadful situation:

> But the very core of that subjection—and the reason why it was so effective and had rendered them so helpless—was the systematic suppression of city industry, the same suppression in principle that the English had unsuccessfully tried to enforce upon industry in the little cities of the American colonies.

A dynamic city, according to Jacobs, integrates its hinterland and becomes a full-blown "city-region." As nearby farmland is revolutionized by city-created technology and innovation, rural dwellers move closer to town to assume jobs in urban industry. As the city generates more output, more money becomes available for civic and infrastructure improvement as well as for new technology and innovation to aid the city's outlying areas.

The comparative advantage Ricardo identified still matters today, but national borders no longer define economies. Instead, the mega-region has emerged as the new *natural* economic unit. It is not an artifact of artificial political boundaries, like the nation-state or its provinces, but the product of concentrations of centers of innovation, production, and consumer markets. Today's mega-regions, which are essentially agglomerations of contiguous cities and their suburbs, extend far beyond individual cities and their hinterlands.

In 1957, the economic geographer Jean Gottman first used the term "megalopolis" to describe the emerging economic hub that was the Boston-to-Washington corridor.[3] Derived from the Greek and meaning "very large city," the term was later applied to a number of other regions: the great swath of California stretching from San Francisco to San Diego; the vast Midwestern megalopolis running from Chicago through Detroit and Cleveland and down to Pittsburgh; and the bustling Tokyo-Osaka region of Japan.

In 1993, the Japanese management expert Kenichi Ohmae wrote an influential *Foreign Affairs* article which argued that the globe's natural economic zones, or "region states," had replaced nation-states as the organizing economic units of what he famously dubbed the "borderless world."[4]

> Region states may lie entirely within or across the borders of a nation-state. This does not matter. It is the irrelevant result of historical accident. What defines them is not the location of their political borders but the fact that they are the right size and scale to be the true, natural business units in today's global economy. Theirs are the borders— and connections—that matter in a borderless world.

But not all large cities function successfully as mega-regions. Cities like Calcutta or Delhi are immense but poor. As Ohmae writes, they "either do not or cannot look to the global economy for solutions to their problems or for the resources to make those solutions work."

Ohmae's point is important. Population is not tantamount to economic growth. These mega-cities differ substantially from true mega-regions that have large markets, significant economic capacity, substantial innovative activity, and highly skilled talent, on top of large populations.

Looking at economic growth and the creation of wealth solely through nation-state data is hugely misleading because national borders are less relevant to where economic activity is located. Money and capital flow to where the returns are greatest, and people move where opportunity lies. To be sure, this results in a more fully integrated global economy. But it also means that both capital and talent concentrate where opportunities for productivity and returns are highest.

National borders also have less to do with defining cultural identity. We all know how different two cities can be despite being in the same state or province, much less the same country. Those valley-bound places are experiencing more than just lagging economies: they're becoming culturally distinct from their mega-region neighbors as well. These growing pains, on top of glaring economic disparities, are exacerbating the divide between the haves and the have-nots—the urban "sophisticates" and rural people—of the world.

At the same time that cities within national borders are diverging, mega-regions whose geographic locations could not be farther apart are growing closer. The more that two mega-regions—regardless of their physical distance or historical relationship—have in common financially, the more likely they are to develop similar social mores, cultural tastes, and even political leanings. That isn't true just for New York and London, dubbed the twin city-states of "NyLon" by some; even New York and Shanghai arguably have more in common than, say, New York and Louisville.[5]

Mega Mapping

So let's dig beneath the surface of the nations of the world and look at a more realistic portrait of the global economy.

A number of experts have updated Gottman's and Ohmae's work with empirical data, charting the scope and extent of mega-regions in the United States and elsewhere. In a 2005

study, Robert Lang and Dawn Dhavale of the Metropolitan Institute at Virginia Tech found that the ten mega-regions that
power the U.S. economy are home to nearly 200 million
Americans, more than two-thirds of the national population,
and are growing at considerably faster rates than the nation as
a whole.[6]

Yet to this day, we still compare the size and growth of the
U.S. economy with those of established competitors such as
Germany and Japan, or those of emerging ones such as India
and China. National borders dictate how we measure economic
output and productivity, count population, tally innovation, and
account for growth. All parties—from international organizations and media outlets to global financial firms—are limited to
the same data.

Fortunately, Tim Gulden came up with a clever solution. He
used the satellite images of the world at night (described in the
last chapter) to identify mega-regions as contiguous lighted areas. Based on that, he was able to distinguish those large areas
of economic activity from smaller centers. And by combining
the light data with other economic measures and finely calibrat-
ing against existing estimates of national and regional output, he
was able to derive estimates of economic activity—the light-
based regional product—for every mega-region in the world.[7]
Gulden likes to say a mega-region is somewhere you can walk all
the way across, from one side to the other, carrying nothing but
some money without ever getting thirsty or hungry.

I realized the power of these world-at-night images on a
plane trip from Columbia, South Carolina, to Toronto late one
evening in fall 2007. When we left Columbia in the heart of the
great Char-Lanta mega, one could see brilliant lights for at least
forty-five minutes. Then the sky went dark for about an hour,
until we approached Buffalo at the outskirts of the Tor-Buff-
Chester mega. The light in the clouds on the horizon ahead

looked as if day were breaking, even though we were traveling in the dead of night.

Technically, a mega-region must meet two key criteria. First, it must be a contiguous lighted area with more than one major city or metropolitan region. Second, it must produce more than $100 billion in LRP. By that definition, there are exactly forty mega-regions in the world (see Appendix A). Here are some key statistics—

If we take the largest megas in terms of population:

- The ten biggest are home to 666 million people, or 10 percent of world population;
- The top twenty comprise 1.1 billion people, 17 percent of the world total; and
- The top forty are home to 1.5 billion people, 23 percent of global population.

When we look at economic activity, the figures are even more striking:

- The world's ten largest mega-regions in terms of economic activity (or LRP), which house approximately 416 million people or 6.5 percent of the world's population, account for 43 percent of economic activity ($13.4 trillion), 57 percent of patented innovations, and 53 percent of the most-cited scientists.
- The top twenty mega-regions in terms of economic activity account for 10 percent of population, 57 percent of economic activity, 76 percent of patented innovations, and 76 percent of the most-cited scientists.
- The top forty mega-regions in economic activity, which make up about 18 percent of the world's population,

produce 66 percent of economic activity, 86 percent of patented innovations, and house 83 percent of the most-cited scientists.

Let's now take a look at some detailed maps of the world's most important mega-regions.

The United Megas of America

The first map shows the mega-regions that compose the North American economy, showing, among other things, what a mistake it is to conceive of the U.S. economy as composed of fifty states (see Figure 3.1). In reality, the core of the U.S. and North American economies is made up of roughly a dozen mega-regions that stretch into Canada and in some cases Mexico, and generate the great bulk of the country's economic output.

As the map shows, the largest mega-regions are concentrated on the coasts. The Bos-Wash corridor stretching some 500 miles down the East Coast from Boston through New York to Washington is the world's second largest in terms of economic output—only Greater Tokyo is bigger. When originally identified by Gottman in 1957, it was home to about 32 million people. Today it is home to some 54 million, more than 18 percent of all Americans. Generating $2.2 trillion in output, it would rank among the biggest national economies in the world. Though broadly based, its economy has considerable specialization and strengths. New York is highly specialized in finance and business services, as well as arts and culture. Boston is known for its biotech industries and educational resources. Media, strategic intelligence, and biotech cluster in and around Washington, D.C.

Farther south, the Char-Lanta mega-region is home to 22 million people and produces $730 billion in LRP. Included in this mega is the regional headquarters center and talent magnet of

FIGURE 3.1 MEGA-REGIONS OF NORTH AMERICA

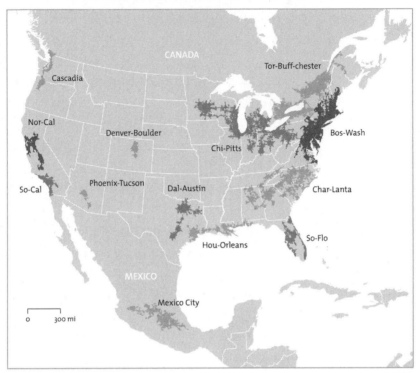

MAP BY TIM GULDEN AND RYAN MORRIS

Atlanta, a regional financial center in Charlotte, and a regional tech-center in the North Carolina Research Triangle.

Even farther south is a substantial mega-region covering southern Florida that includes Miami, Orlando, and Tampa—housing 15 million people and producing $430 billion. Its strengths include Miami's role as a center for Latin American banking and investments as well as entertainment and design; there is also considerable capability in arts and entertainment technology in Orlando, which is home, of course, to Disney World—a major incubator for pop culture.

On the west coast, we also have three substantial mega-regions. The largest, home to 21 million people and the source of $710 billion in cross-national LRP, runs from Los Angeles through San Diego and into Tijuana, Mexico. LA boasts preeminence in film, entertainment, and popular culture. It is also a major port and a key destination for finance, banking, and technology firms. San Diego adds world-class information technology, telecommunications, and biotechnology. And Tijuana brings one of the world's largest manufacturing centers—specializing in television, electronics, and high-tech production. This is a powerful combination. The region is one of very few in the world that combines cutting-edge creativity and innovation with the ability to manufacture products in a relatively low-cost environment.

A second mega-region surrounds the San Francisco Bay area. Claiming 13 million people and more than $470 billion in output, it is a leading center of technology industry and venture capital and is home to a cluster of world-class universities, each boasting its own specialty: Stanford and UC-Berkeley in science and engineering; UC-San Francisco in biotechnology; and UC-Davis in agriculture and wine-making. The region has established substantial capabilities in entertainment technology, housing companies such as Pixar, Electronic Arts, and Industrial Light & Magic. Of course, its core is Silicon Valley with its remarkable concentration of technology producers and innovators.

The West Coast also claims the Cascadia mega-region, which stretches up from Medford and Portland, Oregon, through Seattle and into Vancouver, Canada, and is home to nearly 9 million people generating $260 billion in LRP. On top of its historical strength in aerospace manufacturing, it is also a global center of software and Internet-based industries home to companies like as Microsoft, Amazon, and Real Networks, as well as leading lifestyle and consumer companies such as Starbucks, Nike, REI, and Costco. Two additional mega-regions, Denver-Boulder and Phoenix-Tucson, each generate about $140 billion in LRP.

The southern coast of the United States does its part, too. The great energy-producing belt that runs from Houston to New Orleans is home to nearly 10 million people and the source of $330 billion in LRP. Also in Texas is the region encompassing Dallas, San Antonio, and Austin, also housing nearly 10 million people while producing $370 billion in regional output. These megas may well combine to form a gargantuan "Texas Triangle," according to a 2004 report by the Federal Reserve Bank of Dallas. The successful discount carrier Southwest Airlines got its start shuttling passengers across these Texas cities. "Combining Houston's port, Dallas's inland distribution function, San Antonio's reach into deep South Texas and northern Mexico, and even the state's political capital into one place could have produced a Third Coast megalopolis to rival New York, Los Angeles and Chicago," the study finds.[8]

But the so-called fly-over states need not worry: a series of mega-regions dot North America's heartland as well. Running from Pittsburgh and Cleveland through Detroit, Chicago, and Minneapolis, the great Chi-Pitts mega-region covers more than 100,000 square miles and is home to 46 million people. Churning out $1.6 trillion in LRP, it is the third largest mega-region in the world.

Nearby is another great bi-national mega-region. I actually named this mega-region myself when speaking at a conference on the future of Buffalo in 2002. When asked about the economic future of the Buffalo region and what recommendations I had for revitalizing the region, I blurted out, "Tor-Buff-Chester" in an effort to promote the integration of Toronto, Buffalo, and Rochester. But now with the benefit of our mega-region maps, I can see that it stretches much farther than that—from Waterloo and London, Ontario, through Toronto eastward to Ottawa, Montreal, and Quebec City and down to Syracuse, Ithaca, and Utica in the United States. Given that geography, perhaps a more appropriate name might be "Tor-Buff-Loo-Mon-Tawa." Whatever it's called, this bi-national mega is home to a population of more than 22 million people and an economy of more than $530 billion, making it the fifth largest mega-region in North America and the twelfth largest in the world. Toronto is a significant economic center with superb universities, leading arts, entertainment, design, and culture industries; it also has what is arguably the most diverse population in the world. Like London, but unlike most major U.S. cities, Toronto offers schools that work, low crime, and safe streets. Unlike London, New York, Los Angeles, or San Francisco, it also remains reasonably affordable, which allows it to retain a wide mix of social and economic classes. Nearby, Waterloo in Ontario provides a major technology center, housing Research In Motion, the BlackBerry company. Montreal is home to Cirque du Soleil and a world-class music scene that produced the Arcade Fire, one of the leading and most successful bands of the early 2000s.[9] On the U.S. side of the border, Rochester, though losing residents, remains one of the world's leading centers for optoelectronic and research-intensive companies such as Xerox, Kodak, and many of their key suppliers.

Euro-Megas

Like the fifty states of America, the countries of Europe are also historical artifacts defined by political boundaries. The real economies of Europe are a dozen or so mega-regions that house the bulk of the continent's innovation and production (see Figure 3.2).

Europe's largest mega-region is the enormous economic composite I call Am-Brus-Twerp. Housing nearly 60 million people and producing nearly $1.5 trillion in economic output, it is the fourth largest mega-region in the world.

FIGURE 3.2 MEGA-REGIONS OF EUROPE

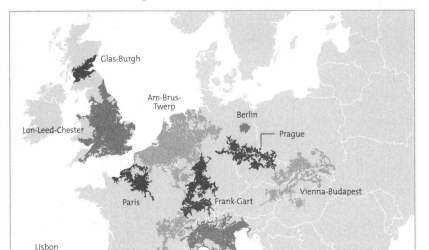

MAP BY TIM GULDEN AND RYAN MORRIS

Next in size is the British mega-region stretching from London through Leeds, Manchester, Liverpool, and into Birmingham. Home to a huge global creative class, including a significant number of U.S. expatriates, London is emerging as the world's leading financial and creative center, rivaled only by New York City. Specializing in cultural creativity that includes film, theater, and music—some of the world's best bands originated in this area, including the Beatles, Rolling Stones, Led Zeppelin, and the Sex Pistols—this mega is home to 50 million people and responsible for $1.2 trillion in economic output, making it the sixth largest regional economy in the world.

The great Italian mega-region stretching from Milan through Rome to Turin is a leading center for fashion and industrial design. Some 48 million people produce roughly $1 trillion in output, making it the third largest economic conglomerate in Europe and the seventh largest in the world.

In Germany, the mega-region encompassing Stuttgart, Frankfurt, and Mannheim is home to 23 million people, many of whom work in finance and manufacturing, producing $630 billion in LRP.

To the west is Greater Paris, a mega-region of nearly 15 million people accountable for $380 billion in output and the leading authority in fashion and haute-culture.

The binational mega-region Barce-Lyon claims some 25 million people who churn out $610 billion in LRP. While Northern Europeans have long vacationed in this region, job seekers are increasingly relocating there as well. A high-ranking minister of trade from The Netherlands confided privately to me that she is nervous about losing Northern European companies to the sunbelt's climate, physical beauty, and talent pools.

Vienna-Budapest ($180 billion in LRP), Prague ($150 billion LRP), Lisbon ($110 billion LRP), Scotland's Glas-burgh ($110 billion LRP), Madrid ($100 billion LRP), and Berlin ($100 billion LRP) complete the list of Europe's mega-regions.

Mega-Tigers

Asia's economy, too, is defined by its mega-regions (see Figure 3.3). Japan is home to four of them, including two of the world's largest. Greater Tokyo, home to more than 55 million people and responsible for nearly $2.5 trillion in economic output, is the world's biggest mega, with world-class strengths in finance, design, and high technology.

FIGURE 3.3 MEGA-REGIONS OF ASIA

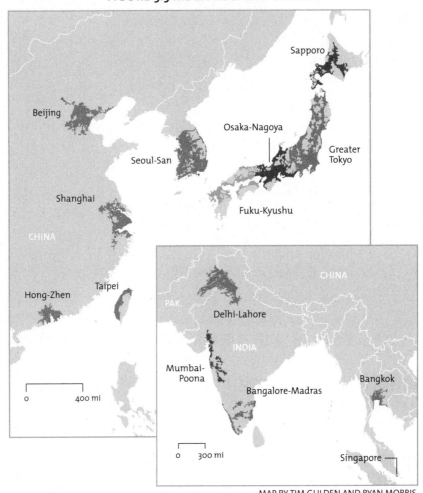

MAP BY TIM GULDEN AND RYAN MORRIS

A second Japanese mega-region, stretching from Osaka to Na-gasaki, is home to 36 million people who generate $1.4 trillion in output. Its niche specialties include high-tech innovation and manufacturing—from automobiles to cutting-edge electronics. Fuku-Kyushu houses 18 million people and produces $430 billion in LRP, while Greater Sapporo is home to more than 4 million people, producing $200 billion in LRP. The boundaries of Japan's great mega-regions are already blurring. Much of Japan may be well on its way to becoming the world's first integrated super-mega-region—a single, gargantuan, and geographically overlapping economic entity of more than 100 million people producing $4.5 trillion in LRP.

The mega-region that runs from Seoul to Busan houses 46 million people and produced $500 billion in LRP, housing a growing number of highly innovative companies whose portfolios include everything from electronics and telecommunications to semiconductors and flat panel displays.

Taipei is the nucleus of a mega-region of more than 20 million people whose $130 billion LRP includes products similar to those of its northern neighbor, housing some of the world's leading semiconductor production facilities.

Greater Singapore is a classic city-state, whose population of 6 million generates LRP of $100 billion. It has "willingly and explicitly given up the trappings of nation states," Ohmae writes, "in return for the relatively unfettered ability to tap into . . . the global economy." A major center for global disk drive production, Singapore boasts strong niche industries in science and technology and, as a result, has succeeded in luring top Western universities to establish branches there. Its long-term strategy to be a creative center has paid off: considerable investments in the arts—both high-culture and street-culture—have made Singapore a top destination for innovative people of all lifestyles and interests. In Thailand, the Bangkok mega-region is home to 19 million people, producing $100 billion in economic output.

Megas on the Move

Mega-regions play an even larger role in the economic development of the so-called emerging economies. Some years ago, Goldman Sachs's researchers coined the term "the BRICs" to identify the rapidly growing emerging economies of Brazil, Russia, India, and China.[10] But growth and development in the BRIC nations and other emerging economies from Mexico to Malaysia are far from uniform, geographically speaking.

Powering the growth of these emerging economies are large mega-regions. In some cases, these megas are experiencing rapid economic growth, while others are growing more slowly if at all, attracting large population influxes from rural areas, and giving rise to large global slums in which people live in destitution. Most of these emerging economy megas are sources of significant economic and geographic inequality, both because their economies are doing much better than surrounding rural areas and because of the significant economic divide separating the haves and have-nots inside their borders.

China's economy, for example, is dominated by just three mega-regions along its eastern coast. The largest in terms of population is the Shanghai-Nanking-Hangzhou Triangle, home to more than 66 million people and $130 billion in LRP. To the north, Greater Beijing houses 43 million people, generating $110 billion in LRP. To the south, the Hong-Zhen corridor encompasses about 45 million people and produces $220 billion in LRP. Just these three megas account for $460 billion in LRP, 43 percent of the country's total economic activity measured as LRP. And when we add up all of China's mega-regions, they produce $735 billion in LRP, 68 percent of the country's total.

Boasting massive investment in new universities, increasing flows of global research and development, and a seemingly unlimited talent pool, these three mega-regions are likely to transform quickly from their current status as the world's factory into an emerging center for innovation and creativity. What remains to be seen is whether China's mega-regions can generate the necessary openness, tolerance, and independence required of such a world center.

India's economy, too, is defined by mega-regions. The mega-region of Delhi-Lahore is home to more than 120 million people, generating $110 billion in LRP.

There are two other great population centers in India that are on track to become full-fledged mega-regions. To the north, 62 million people inhabit a mega-region stretching from Mumbai to Poona that generates $60 billion in LRP. This region is home to the Bollywood film industry, the largest single producer of films in the world, responsible for releasing more than 900 each year.

The technology corridor of Bangalore through Madras in southern India, is home to 72 million people producing $50 billion in LRP. Both of these regions are growing explosively, about 10 percent per year or more. Since our estimates are from 2000, it is reasonable to think that both have already crossed the $100 billion threshold to become full-fledged mega-regions. Possessing both Bollywood film and Bangalore technology, India is not just a low-cost offshore production center. Its prestigious Indian Institutes of Technology is one of the preeminent engineering and technology schools in the world; its fashion and product designers are on the rise; and the music scenes of London, Toronto, and New York are infused with Bhangra beats. Little known to most, its video game industry is projected to grow tenfold by the end of the decade, and its animation industry is expected to nearly triple its current size.

Mega-regions play an increasingly significant role in other emerging economies around the world. In Latin America, Greater Mexico City is home to more than 45 million people and generates $290 billion in LRP, more than half of Mexico's total.

In Brazil, the mega-region of Rio-Paolo generates $230 billion, more than 40 percent of the country's total, and is home to 43 million people.

Greater Buenos Aires is home to roughly 14 million and generates $150 billion in LRP, more than half of that country's total.

In the Middle East, the giant mega-region stretching across Tel Aviv to Amman, Damascus, and Beirut is home to more than 30 million people and pumps out $160 billion in LRP.

It is important to emphasize that many of these emerging economy mega-regions, while home to huge populations and a significant level of economic activity, also suffer from tremendous economic and social inequality, and in some cases are home to millions upon millions of people living destitute lives in the world's worst slums and shantytowns.

The last two chapters have provided empirical and visual proof that the world is not flat but spiky, powered by mega-regions— substantial conurbations of multiple cities and suburbs—which at times span national borders and form vast swaths of trade, transport, innovation, and talent.

So far I've demonstrated the *what* but not the *why*. What explains such concentration of economic activity and growth? Why is place still such a critical factor in the global economy? How can it be that economic activity is not pulled apart by the powerful forces of global-stretching trade and world-shrinking technology? How do cities and regions stay physically connected in the face of such forces? And what exactly enables them to beat the odds stacked so considerably against them?

4

THE CLUSTERING FORCE

"I F WE POSTULATE ONLY THE USUAL LIST OF ECONOMIC forces," the Nobel Prize–winning economist Robert Lucas wrote in 1988, "cities should fly apart."[1] After all, Lucas reminds us, land "is always far cheaper outside cities than inside." Why, then, didn't businesses and people move en masse out to where costs are substantially lower? Lucas answered his question with another, equally simple observation: "What can people be paying Manhattan or downtown Chicago rents for, if not to be around other people?"

With that one sentence, Lucas brought *place* front and center into the debate over the forces behind economic growth. He identified the underlying economic power of the *clustering force*—the clustering of people and productivity, creative skills and talents that powers economic growth.

That's why cities and mega-regions are the true economic units that drive the world forward. These organized geographic production systems and markets, where human beings and talents cluster, Lucas argued, offer social and economic advantages that other places simply can't. Their benefits in terms of innovation and productivity far outweigh the higher costs of living and doing business there.

The study of economic growth is an arcane field. And until recently, it paid little attention to the importance of location. In 1776, Adam Smith published *The Wealth of Nations,* which argued that the main cause of prosperity is increasing division of labor, also know as specialization. With his classic pin factory example, in which he illustrated how ten workers each specializing in his own task can produce a far greater number of pins than could ten workers working independently, Smith captured how firms need specialization to become more efficient.[2]

Some twenty-five years later, David Ricardo began formulating his own theories about economic wealth. Before he died an early death in 1823, Ricardo outlined the idea of comparative costs, reconciling a fundamental economic conundrum of how countries benefit from trade that had puzzled Smith until his death.

His theory of comparative advantage describes the relative edge one country has over another in terms of resources and production capability, which positions them both to gain from trade. In its simplest terms, this idea makes intuitive sense: let's say that Country A excels at producing cloth, while Country B is skilled at producing buttons. In order for each country to make shirts with relative ease (and little cost), they should engage in trade. But what happens if Country A enjoys an absolute advantage, meaning that it can make cloth *and* buttons, while Country B can make only buttons? The trade still makes sense, Ricardo argued, because Country A is still better off focusing its resources and labor on producing the goods that Country B cannot. In that way, Country A can profit more by making cloth (which it can trade to obtain buttons from Country B) than it ever could by diverting a portion of its capital and labor to making buttons.[3]

Still for Ricardo as for Smith, nations were the fundamental economic unit. But by the late nineteenth century, the early location theorists were beginning to formulate new ideas on why manufacturing industry was clustering in industrial centers such as Manchester and Pittsburgh. A little later the great economist Alfred Marshall developed his basic theory of why firms and industries agglomerate or cluster: to capture the economic benefits of colocation. (See Chapter 7 for a more detailed discussion on this topic.)

Even as economists and geographers were developing new insights into the nature of clustering and cities, the study of economic growth still revolved around firms and nations. For most economists, cities had little bearing on economic growth—they were simply contributing parts of their national economies. When it came to determining the forces behind economic growth—what caused economies to get bigger in size—economists continued to ignore the relevance of location.

Up until the mid-twentieth century, prevailing theory held that more labor and capital equaled bigger economies. In other words, the more giant factories or machine tools applied, the more money would be made.

That changed after the Great Depression and World War II, when a growing number of economists, business leaders, and policymakers became captivated with Joseph Schumpeter's theory that it is innovation and entrepreneurship—not simply economies of scale and specialization—that power economic growth and give rise to what he called the great gales of "creative destruction" that destroyed established systems and replaced them with new firms and industries.[4] Yes, he conceded, improvements are important, but let's not underestimate the value in creating something entirely new. In his later years, Schumpeter would bemoan the growing bureaucracy afflicting so many corporate research and development laboratories and predict that the impulses toward invention and entrepreneurship—so vital to the enterprising spirit of capitalism—would soon be stamped out.[5]

In 1957, Robert Solow expanded on Schumpeter's theory, using the formal tools of econometrics to rigorously measure and identify the effect of technology on economic growth.[6] In his model, Solow calculated that about four-fifths of the U.S. economy's growth per worker was attributable to technical progress, which helps to make capital and labor more efficient. In Solow's framework, no particular place has a permanent advantage in technology, though some can have short-term advantages. The fruits of technology, Solow's thesis implies, flow freely across space.

The new growth theory pioneered by Stanford University economist Paul Romer in the 1980s and 1990s builds on Solow's ideas but makes an important tweak. Growth doesn't happen exogenously through innovations that occur "outside" the system. Rather, economic wealth is created when new discoveries are fashioned from existing resources.[7] Technical knowledge is not produced outside the system and then applied to it; it is generated from within, through processes that create new ideas and knowledge, which in turn lead to new technologies and useful information—the wellsprings of growth. In Romer's words:

> Economic growth occurs whenever people take resources and rearrange them in ways that are more valuable. A useful metaphor for production in an economy comes from

the kitchen. To create valuable final products, we mix inexpensive ingredients together according to a recipe. The cooking one can do is limited by the supply of ingredients, and most cooking in the economy produces undesirable side effects. If economic growth could be achieved only by doing more and more of the same kind of cooking, we would eventually run out of raw materials and suffer from unacceptable levels of pollution and nuisance. History teaches us, however, that economic growth springs from better recipes, not just from more cooking. New recipes generally produce fewer unpleasant side effects and generate more economic value per unit of raw material.

These are certainly important ideas. But with the exception of some recent commentary on the growth of Silicon Valley, the new growth theory has remained conspicuously unconcerned with the importance of location. It, too, sees knowledge as something that flows easily from place to place. In theory, economic growth was an abstract process in which place was irrelevant.

Jane Said

That is, until Lucas brought cities and place squarely back into the picture. To do so, he went back to the earlier writings of Jane Jacobs. He realized the enormous debt that he, along with the entire field of economic growth, owed Jacobs and predicted that her insights would ultimately become the focus of future study of growth economics: "I will be following very closely the lead of Jane Jacobs, whose remarkable book, *The Economy of Cities*, seems to me mainly and convincingly concerned (although she does not use this terminology) with the external effects of human capital." He later added in a widely circulated e-mail that these insights were so fundamental that Jacobs—who was neither a trained economist nor a college graduate—deserved the Nobel Prize.

Building on Jacobs's fundamental contribution, Lucas declared the multiplier effects that stem from such talent clustering to be the *primary* determinant of economic growth. Labor, capital, and technical knowledge are all well and good, he conceded, but none of those would amount to anything significant if people could not combine their talents, ideas, and energy in real places.

When people—especially talented and creative ones—come together, ideas flow more freely, and as a result individual and aggregate talents increase exponentially: the end result amounts to much more than the sum of the parts. This clustering makes each of us more productive, which in turn makes the place we inhabit even more so—and our collective creativity and economic wealth grow accordingly. This in a nutshell *is* the clustering force. One consequence of the clustering force is a sorting of regions into an economic hierarchy. As Chapters 6 and 7 will show, as talented and highly educated people cluster together in certain regions, the location of work becomes more concentrated and specialized as well. According to the theory, when people cluster together in cities, they will produce more and thus the cost of living in those places will inexorably rise, generating those "Chicago rents" Lucas mentions. Eventually, communities and people will sort themselves into an economic pecking order.

Lucas picked up on what I consider to be Jacobs's most fundamental contribution to the field—the central role played by the clustering of people and their creativity on economic growth. Actually, Jacobs herself saw it that way, too. When asked in 2001 what she hoped to be remembered for, she responded:

If I were to be remembered as a really important thinker of
the century, the most important thing I've contributed is,
"What makes economic expansion happen?" This is something that has puzzled people always. I think I've figured
out what it is, and expansion and development are two different things. Development is differentiation—new differentiation of what already existed. Practically every new
thing that happens is a differentiation of a previous thing.
Just about everything—from a new shoe sole to changes in
legal codes—all of those things are differentiations. Expansion is an actual growth in size or volume of activity. That is
a different thing.[8]

By expansion, Jacobs is talking about the more ordinary side
of economic growth. Expansion simply means increasing the
volume of economic output—for example, revving up the production of an assembly line. Looked at this way, a city is just a
bigger version of a town, a mega-region just a bigger version of a
city.

But there is a second, more explosive kind of economic
growth. For Jacobs as for Schumpeter, this kind of economic development turns on innovation—the ability not just to do more
of something but to do something new. It is not specialization
that drives economic growth. Rather, it is the innovation that
stems from a diverse pool of resources. And diversity, Jacobs argues, is most likely to happen in certain kinds of places. In *The
Economy of Cities*, she argued:

The diversity, of whatever kind, that is generated by cities
rests on the fact that in cities so many people are so close
together, and among them contain so many different tastes,
skills, needs, supplies, and bees in their bonnets.

While companies tend to specialize, places give rise to a wide variety of talents and specialties, the broad diversity of which is a vital spur to innovation. This is an epigenetic process. Cities don't just get bigger in size; they become multifaceted and differentiated. And in doing so, they—and not firms—are the wellspring of new innovations that generate new work and new branches of industry. The city, Jacobs argued, is a complex, self-organizing ecology whose form cannot be predetermined or controlled from the outside. Its diversity is the true source of innovation and economic growth.[9]

Faster, Faster

Jacobs's insights illustrate how place affects productivity and innovation. But what about the inevitable drawbacks and obstacles to city growth? Traffic congestion, rising crime rates, and unaffordable housing are all predictable by-products of city life. Eventually, they are likely to pose significant barriers to a city's future development.

It would seem that such diseconomies could kill a city. However, there is compelling research that suggests otherwise. According to a multidisciplinary team of researchers led by Geoffrey West of the Santa Fe Institute, large cities and mega-regions possess a basic mechanism by which they can transcend such limitations.[10]

Any scientist will tell you that the metabolic rate of biological organisms—the rate at which living things convert food into energy—slows as organisms increase in size.[11] The Santa Fe team wondered whether cities and mega-regions, though not literally living things, might function in a similar way. Do their "metabolisms" increase as their populations and, therefore, their productivity and innovation grow? To test this idea, the researchers collected data from the United States, Europe, and China at a variety of times, and looked at a wide range of characteristics— things such as crime rates, disease transmission, demographics, infrastructure energy consumption, economic activity, and innovation. Sure enough, they found that

> Social organizations, like biological organisms, consume energy and resources, depend on networks for the flow of information and materials, and produce artifacts and waste. . . . Cities manifest power-law scaling similar to the economy-of-scale relationships observed in biology: a doubling of population requires less than a doubling of certain resources. The material infrastructure that is analogous to biological transport networks—gas stations, lengths of electrical cable, miles of road surface—consistently exhibits sublinear [less than one] scaling with population.

This might all have been expected. But what the researchers had not expected to see was that the correlation between population growth and characteristics with little analogue to biology—such as innovation, patent activity, number of supercreative people, wages, and GDP—was *greater* than one. In other words, a doubling of population resulted in more than two times the creative and economic output. Unlike biological organisms, all of which slow down as they grow larger, cities become wealthier and more creative the bigger they get. They called this phenomenon "superlinear" scaling: "By almost any measure, the larger a city's population, the greater the innovation and wealth per person." This increased speed is itself a product of the clustering force, a key component of the productivity improvements generated by the concentration of talented people.

How Big Will They Grow?

Thanks to thinkers like Lucas and Jacobs, those at the Santa Fe Institute, and others, we now have a handle on how cities and regions stimulate innovation and drive economic development. We know that the clustering of human talent and labor leads to increased productivity and creativity, and we have seen that city development is spurred from within. And know that the world is composed of many cities and mega-regions of various sizes— large ones like Tokyo, New York, and London, fast-growing ones like Shanghai and Bangalore, highly innovative ones like Silicon Valley, smaller and medium-sized ones, and declining ones. How does this broader system of cities form and evolve?

To get at this, I partnered with Robert Axtell, a brilliant computer modeler at George Mason University, whose research includes everything from how societies evolve to how firms form to how economies grow.[12] Together, we endeavored to build a basic model that could simulate the growth and development of the cities and regions that compose the world economy. We wanted our model to address how these cities initially emerged, why some grew while others failed, and how they ultimately evolved into a global system.

We structured our model around three basic assumptions:

1. People can choose how hard they want to work. People are different. Some work hard, others less so. We prefer to spend our time in different ways. Not everyone chooses to accumulate the same skills or work at the same intensity.
2. As in the real world, we established that the hardest working and ablest people would cluster together, at least initially. These firms would be most likely to grow,

      while those that employed less productive people would languish and ultimately fail.

3.   We presumed that productive firms would be drawn to similarly productive locations. Places that housed dynamic firms would grow, while places that didn't would decline.

Economic growth in our model takes place through a basic law of "preferential attachment," in which skilled and productive people attract the presence of other skilled and productive people. As they team up to form firms, these creative organizational units begin to develop new ideas and products. And as those units grow, they attract other hard-working and productive agents.

It's a dynamic model built to emulate the real world. Hard-working, adventurous, and creative people come together to form new firms that migrate to certain places. Some of these destinations, so long as they can retain their talent, grow and prosper. Others dissolve when their residents decide to migrate elsewhere. Places in the former group experience their first wave of economic growth during the early phases of firm formation, when relatively high skilled individuals populate small to mid-size companies. Over time, these cities attract more like-minded people and more business, and eventually they grow into regions. These regions attract an even more diverse range of people who begin to cluster around the original population. As new firms continue to form and old ones dissolve, the newcomers are absorbed into the mix. Certain cities expand and grow.

Then something very interesting starts to happen. Rather than simply growing upward, these city-regions expand outward until they are forced to combine with other city-regions.

Through this process of nucleation, these city-regions merge together as a mega-region. The largest mega-regions have the longest staying power. Smaller mega-regions, or individual large cities, rise and fall at a much faster clip. But no city or regional formation is invincible. While they tend to last longer, even the largest mega-regions can and do decline at various times.

This model proves to be a near perfect simulation of our world today. Creative people and their firms cluster tightly to form the top of a hierarchy of city-regions that strikingly reflects George Zipf's famous *power law*. In the middle of the distribution, individual cities and regions constantly vie for prime spots, while at the top, there is far less moving around. This is more than a hierarchy of places. It is a hierarchy of productivity rates, metabolic rates, and costs. Places at the top are more productive, operate at faster speed, and are more expensive that those further down the hierarchy. The people that can afford to be in the top places are increasingly required to work in a highly productive way in specialized industries (think investment funds in London or New York, or movie production in Los Angeles). Consequently, there is less and less economic space for, say, the struggling artist or even the average person at the top of the hierarchy. The sorting of places due to the clustering force is inevitably a sorting of people.

Our model also forecasts a world increasingly dominated by massive mega-regions. By 2025, our world will be considerably more concentrated around mega-regions than it is today. By then, something as sci-fi sounding as a mega-region with several hundred million people may exist. It may sound far-fetched, but given historical precedents and current rates, such a world may well be far from fantasy. Think of it this way: just two hundred years ago, the largest cities held fewer than 100,000 people; back then, a city of 1 million people was unimaginable. By 1900, the population of New York—the largest city in the United States—had reached roughly 3.5 million. Do you think a city of 10 million was unfathomable then? It didn't take long: just fifty years later, the populations of metropolitan areas like New York and London hovered just under 10 million. Today, there are already mega-regions of 25, 50, 100 million people and more.

Given these growth patterns, is a mega-region of several hundred million beyond the pale? I'd say hardly so. When Axtell calculated how big the largest mega-region would be in a world with mega-regions that were perfectly Zipf-distributed, with the smallest one housing 10 million people, he came up with a super-mega-region of 400 million people. What kind of place could hold that many people? This is how Axtell explains it:

> Assume every person needs 5000 square feet of space for living, parking, offices space, schools, roads and green space. So that's 25,000 square feet for a family of five. People in Tokyo use 1,900 square feet each, so Tokyo is two and a half times denser than my assumption. Then, 400 million people need 2 trillion square feet of space which equals 45 million acres or 72,000 square miles—a square 270 miles on a side, or alternatively 100 miles wide by 700 miles long. That could be Gottman's BosWash from the New Hampshire border to Norfolk, Virginia 100 miles wide from the Atlantic coast, or Sacramento to Tijuana, 100 miles from the Pacific inland.

As our models show, it's less likely that an existing mega-region will simply grow upward by adding taller buildings or more people. More likely, such expansion will occur as two or more come together to form a super-mega-region. Already, the light-emission patterns that span Japan suggest that a super-mega-region running from north of Tokyo all the way to Fukuoka could emerge. For the foreseeable future, mega-regions will be the economic units that structure and orient the world economy.

Of course, super-mega-regions will bring all sorts of new and exacerbating challenges. As rates of innovation and migration accelerate, we can expect more key functions to concentrate in the world's leading mega-regions. And the social and economic distance between leading mega-regions and lagging cities and regions will grow larger. Mega-regions will become more congested and pricier, causing greater social and economic segregation. Major new advances in transportation and environmental technology will surely be required. For the leading mega-regions, retaining rates of innovation will be their primary challenge. Without it, as West and his colleagues caution, they "will stop growing and may even contract, leading to either stagnation or ultimate collapse."

The challenges facing second- and third-tier regions worldwide will be even greater. While some will thrive and grow, many more will struggle under the weight of ferocious global competition. The global system of cities and regions is going through the same kind of consolidation and restructuring that reshaped global industries like steel and autos and electronics around a smaller number of larger and more efficient players worldwide. The many second- and third-tier city-regions of the United States may be hit particularly hard, as both global and domestic mega-regions up the ante, accelerating their rates of innovation while drawing in more top talent. The Clevelands and Pittsburghs of the world will find themselves increasingly squeezed between twin pincers as top business functions gravitate to larger regions like Chicago, while production shifts to centers like Shanghai. The Austins and Research Triangles of the world will face increasing competition not only from Silicon Valley but also from up-and-comers like Bangalore, Dublin, and

Tel Aviv. The world economy of the future is likely to take shape around an even smaller number of mega-regions and specialized centers, while a much larger number of places will see their fates worsen as they find themselves struggling just to stay in the game.

PART II

THE WEALTH OF PLACE

5

THE MOBILE AND THE ROOTED

E VER SINCE MARX, CLASS HAS BEEN SEEN AS A DIVISIVE force in all societies. Much has been written on the widening gulf between the highest paid and the average worker and the growing share of economic output pocketed by society's top 1 percent.[1]

But there is another angle to our diverging economic fortunes that few have looked into—the role of location.

I have come to think of this additional geographic dimension of socioeconomic class in terms of two groups that I refer to simply as the *mobile* and the *rooted*. The mobile possess the means, resources, and inclination to seek out and move to locations where they can leverage their talents. They are not necessarily born mobile, nor are they inevitably rich. What the mobile understand is that the pursuit of economic opportunity often requires them to move.

The Hungarian-born investor George Soros has said many times that had he stayed in his home country he would have amounted to little—there was simply no infrastructure there through which he could leverage his talents. But once he moved to the United States—well, the rest, as they say, is history.

Today it is estimated that approximately 200 million people— one in every thirty-five people worldwide—live outside the country in which they were born. And many, many more are the first- and second-generation descendents of those international migrants. The late *New York Times* writer Herbert Muschamp dubbed the growing ranks of the internationally mobile as a new class of "global nomads."[2] Regardless of what they are called, in some city-regions in the United States, Canada, and Australia, the ranks of the foreign born run upward of 40 percent. My own classroom is a perfect microcosm of our highly mobile society: I have students who hail from Europe, Japan, China, India, South America, and Africa—not to mention Canada and, of course, the United States.

A far greater number constitute the rooted—people who are tied to place. Some, of course, have the good fortune to be rooted in places with thriving economies and optimistic futures. But many others are essentially trapped in areas with limited resources, moribund economies, and declining financial opportunities. Of course, many are born poor and do not possess the resources to move.

But not all of those who are rooted are stuck because of economic circumstance. Many people with the means to move choose to stay rooted. Sometimes they are satisfied with the lives they lead, even if they know they could potentially do better elsewhere. This isn't always a bad thing; research indicates that being near to family and friends and seeing them regularly can increase our well-being and happiness.

Should I Stay or Should I Go Now?

When social scientists talk about mobility, they are typically referring to socioeconomic mobility—the ease with which people move up or down the ladder of social and economic status. But my research and personal experience have convinced me that socioeconomic mobility and geographic mobility are interdependent and far from mutually exclusive.

A 2007 study by researchers at Sheffield University shows just how powerful a role location plays in our class position, health status, education options, and economic mobility. The study found that people born in disadvantaged locations tended to carry that initial disadvantage across subsequent life stages. "Every step of the way your chances are much more constrained," said Bethan Thomas, one of the study's authors. "This is not deterministic; obviously there are people from disadvantaged areas who do make the leap and people from the most advantaged who can't be bothered, but those cases are much less common." The researchers found that while the number of neighborhoods that ranked above and below average once resembled a bell curve (with rich and poor areas at each end but most in between), today our locational topography is split into just two distinct categories, with one set of locations for the disadvantaged and another for the advantaged. The researchers conclude that this new geography of class reveals "ever more clearly that where you live can limit or assist your life chances from cradle to grave."[3] Today, location constitutes an additional divisive line that separates the haves from the have-nots, alongside race, education, occupation, and income. In the past, a person's status was largely determined by where they were born. In today's highly mobile and interconnected society, one's life chances are significantly affected by the ability to move and relocate as well.

Economists and demographers have shed some light on the mobile and the rooted. Those who move tend to be highly educated people whose careers require them to do so. They also include young people, who, as attached as they may be to family and friends, have much bigger gain to be made from relocating.

Still, even most of us who meet the criteria for the mobile give little thought to moving. Who has the time or ability to assess all the options and calculate all the costs and benefits of every possible location? When push comes to shove, most of us, to steal a line from Nike, "just do it." Something eventually tips the scale—a significant other in another city, the prospect of a better home, a more exciting job, the promise of a clean slate and a new start—so we make a decision. We tell ourselves that the grass is likely always greener on the other side. I'm not just saying this; psychologists and behavioral economists who have studied the subject have also found this to be true. Most of us overestimate the benefits of moving. Then we take the plunge.

There's a funny episode of the popular TV show *30 Rock* that gets at this. A producer of a *Saturday Night Live*–like show, Tina Fey's character Liz Lemon is all about New York. But her brand-new boyfriend is from Cleveland, so they decide to go check it out for a weekend, after he's denied a promotion at his job in New York. They stay downtown and walk the Flats, Cleveland's riverfront entertainment district. They visit the Rock and Roll Hall of Fame. People are nice. They say hello. They ask the average looking Liz if she's a model. He considers taking a job with a law firm in Cleveland. At dinner, a local TV executive offers Lemon a slot hosting a morning cooking show. The neighborhoods are great; housing is affordable. When they return to New York, all they can do is think about how great life would be in Cleveland. Their vivid memories are a sharp contrast to the crudities they suffer back home in the Big Apple: armed police guard subway entrances; people shove each other on the sidewalk; a strange man spits on Lemon. When her boyfriend accepts the job offer from the law firm in Cleveland, he can't contain his excitement and presses Lemon to join him. But after a long, angst-filled contemplation over what such a move would mean for her career and social life, Lemon decides she would be foolish to leave her high-powered job and all the things—good and bad—New York has to offer.

Whether Lemon made a mistake or not, I can't judge. For Lemon's boyfriend, the choice was seemingly easier. Why wouldn't he trade a dead-end job and high rent for a higher-paying position and lower housing costs?

For most of human history migration has been involuntary. People moved out of necessity—to avoid war, escape political or religious persecution, or find work. Even as recently as the 1950s and 1960s most people—white-collar and blue-collar workers alike—moved to find jobs. Nobody had much choice, actually. Blue-collar work was heavily concentrated in cites that had grown up around natural resources and transportation hubs. As for white-collar workers, they were company men who went where their superiors told them to go. In the 1970s, IBM workers joked that their company name stood for "I've Been Moved." There was much truth to that joke, and it applied to companies other than the computer giant.

Today, however, more moves are voluntary. And in the advanced nations only a minority are tied to work. According to data from the U.S. Census Bureau on who moves and why, only a small minority of today's movers cite a "new job or job transfer" as their primary reason for relocating.[4]

The leading reason people in the United States move is for housing. According to the census, over half (51.6 percent) of all people who move do so for that reason. They are renters wanting to own, young couples wanting to upgrade, and retirees looking to downsize. Another quarter (26.3 percent) of people say that they move for family-related reasons—getting married, getting divorced, having children, combining families, because of the death of a spouse, and that sort of thing.

Moving on account of work actually comes in third. Fewer than one in six Americans says that the main reason for moving is work related. Not surprisingly, highly educated people are most likely to move because of work. But even among those with bachelor's degrees, only one in four moves for work-related reasons.

Still the notion that we move for jobs persists, despite evidence to the contrary. Ever since I became interested in the question of how people choose where they live and work, I've routinely asked my students where they plan to go after graduation.

"I'll go wherever the best job is," is a common reply.

"OK," I ask, "would you move to Fargo, North Dakota?"

"Probably not."

"How about Lafayette, Louisiana?"

"I don't think so."

This continues for a while until at some point I ask: "So where *would* you go?"

"Well," they inevitably respond, "I'd go to Chicago, Boston, Seattle, maybe Austin, the New York area, Atlanta, or greater Washington, D.C."

"And why is that?"

"They're all great job markets," they say. "There's a lot of opportunity there. They're great places to live, and I have lots of friends there."

This common pattern suggests three important things. First, people tend to orient their job searches around particular places. Second, where one's friends reside also matters. Third, and arguably most telling, we wouldn't move just anywhere for a job.

Various studies confirm this trend. A 2002 survey by Next Generation Consulting found that three-quarters of recent college graduates first choose where to live, *then* look for a job in that market. A more comprehensive June 2006 survey conducted by a division of Yankelovich for the group CEOs for Cities found that nearly two-thirds (64 percent) of young people between the ages of twenty-five and thirty-four follow the same pattern.[5]

The reasons people move are many and varied, but why do so many stay put?

For many, economic circumstance plays the key role: the decision is seemingly not much of a choice. Many of the rooted have relatively little education or money and relatively low professional aspirations or personal expectations.

My own family history reflects the tension between the rooted and the mobile. My grandparents, who hail from the Campania region of southern Italy, immigrated to the United States in the early part of the twentieth century. Knowing not a word of English, they made the nearly 5,000-mile trip from their peasant village in southern Italy to New York—then the largest and most dynamic city in the world. In the span of one generation, they made their way from Ellis Island to New York's Little Italy and then to Newark to take up simple factory work and raise families. And in doing so, they improved their economic position from rural peasant class to urban working class, creating even greater potential for upward economic mobility for their children and grandchildren.

But upon settling in Newark, my family became rooted. Only one of my dozens of aunts or uncles ever moved more than twenty miles from where they grew up. That made it possible for my mother and her five sisters, her brothers, and all their children to gather routinely on Sundays for supper at my grandmother's home in Newark.

Fortunately, my parents constantly stressed the importance of going to college. For them, a college degree was tantamount to social mobility—a way to a better life. Unfortunately, their preference was that we stay close by—attend a local college, live at home, and commute by car. But I wanted desperately to go away to school. To be sure, I was enticed by the freedom that being away promised—the ability to come and go as I pleased, to stay out late and have fun with my friends without parents and relatives looking over my shoulder. But my intuition also told me that I would benefit even more from leaving the working-class, tough-guy peer group of my youth. Many of my friends were already well into drugs and petty crime. Few who stayed behind had ambitions to go to college, let alone pursue careers. I knew on some level even then that going off to college would do more than help me achieve my dreams—it would be my way out.

A Garden State scholarship allowed me to do just that. With financial aid that covered not only tuition but room and board as well, I was able to convince my parents to let me enroll at Rutgers College, just thirty or so miles south of home on the New Jersey Turnpike in New Brunswick. It was hard for me to believe that Rutgers—which felt so far away growing—had been so close by all along. Still, my family behaved as if I were moving a world away. From the looks of their Chevy Impala, in which they made a monthly pilgrimage to bring me food, beer, and other necessities—you'd think I had.

College was just the first of many moves, and with each one my parents treated me as if I were embarking on a great journey. Even when I was a graduate student at Columbia in New York City, just a commuter train ride away, they made the trek to the Big Apple a total of two times over a period of five or so years. By the time they passed away, they had visited maybe three states—and not once did they fly on a plane or take a proper vacation. Travel was expensive; taking trips would have required taking funds away from more important things. But it also meant leaving home and family, which is the primary place my parents wanted to be.

My parents may have been happy, but they were rooted. I was mobile. Through hard work and by purchasing a small home in a suburb of Newark, they were able to improve their economic position from urban working class to lower middle class. But had it not been for my geographic mobility, I would never have been able to attend graduate school, and ultimately become a professor and author. Still, without ever taking a course in economics, my parents were quite aware of the respective tradeoffs involved in staying rooted or going mobile.

A 2007 study by economist Nattavudh Powdthavee of the University of London used survey data to estimate the monetary value of frequently seeing friends and relatives.[6] The study found that seeing friends or relatives in person almost every day is worth more than six figures in additional income. For example, Powdthavee found that if you relocate from a city where you regularly see your family and friends to one where you would not, you would need to earn $133,000 just to make up for the lack of happiness you feel from being far from those people. Powdthavee drives home the importance of making a conscious choice about your time when he writes, "Since it normally requires both time and effort to achieve either higher income or a stable social relationship with someone, the weight attached to each individual's investment decision thus depends upon the type of possession—money or friendship—that he or she believes will yield a larger impact on happiness than the other."

I'm not sure it's possible to put an accurate price tag on our personal relationships. Still, by Powdthavee's accounting I owe my wife, Rana—who left behind five siblings, two parents, a host of nieces and nephews, and countless close relatives and friends when we got married—a very big pile of money.

Many people elect to stay rooted even when it's economically feasible to move elsewhere. Perhaps they are intuitively aware of the economic value of close social relationships. And many who have moved ultimately decide to return home someday. The draw of home is incredibly powerful—the pull of family ties, the need to take care of aging parents or to help with children, the desire to be close to lifelong friends. It was striking to see that, out of the roughly 200 detailed locational histories I collected for this book, many of those who had moved around quite a bit actually chose to return home later in life.

Take, for example, Linda Maguire, a talented opera singer who left her hugely successful career in Toronto to return to her home state of Virginia. "I have had the unbelievable luxury of living an artistic, creative, and academic life, thanks to a government-supported career and via having sung as a top-level professional singer," she wrote. "I just got to the point where I could not deny who I really was—an American from Virginia soil. It is unbelievable and most wonderful to be home again."

Or Verónica Escobar, a young and dynamic political leader from Texas, who left her hometown in search of graduate school and an eventual career. I met Escobar when she participated in our Creative Cities Leadership Project there. My team was so impressed, we asked her to work with us as a facilitator in other cities. "My desire [to leave] stemmed from knowing that there was nothing for me in El Paso: I didn't believe I would find a job, a profession or a future there. I knew other cities were more alluring and interesting, more glamorous and exciting." Graduate school took her to New York City, which she loved as a student. "Who would live anywhere else?" she wrote. "I figured once I had my master's degree, I'd move to San Francisco because of the PhD programs available in the Bay Area, as well as more of the same great amenities and qualities in New York City." But she made a pit-stop in El Paso on her way out West and was overwhelmed by the stark contrasts. Even so, she added, "local writers were flourishing, and politics were heating up." She was surprised to find herself reconnecting with her hometown in a way previously unimaginable. "El Paso suddenly seemed like a whole new place to me. I became involved in political campaigns, with literary groups, and my world opened up. I realized how exciting it was to be in a border town where anything was possible. I hooked up with people like me—twenty-somethings back then, now thirty-somethings—who decided to come back, to stay, to work, to fight the good fight because we loved our town." Even the most mobile, it seems, cannot always resist the pull of home.

The brilliant social scientist Albert O. Hirschman provides a framework that can help us think about our own choice of whether to go mobile or stay rooted. Born in Berlin in 1915, Hirschman immigrated to the United States from Germany during the Nazi years and later served in the U.S. Army during World War II, before taking up professorships at Yale, Columbia, Harvard, and the Institute for Advanced Study at Princeton. In his 1970 classic *Exit, Voice and Loyalty*, Hirschman argued that when faced with an unsatisfactory situation we can either "exit" the situation or "voice" our discontent. The more "loyalty" we feel, the more likely we are to use the latter option. As far as location is concerned, our decision to move turns on our loyalty to the place we live in and our social relationships there.[7]

But today's economy may be tipping the ever-sensitive balance between these two poles. As the benefits to clustering increase and the world becomes spikier, more people may feel compelled to join the ranks of the mobile in order to prosper economically. This does not mean that we are all doomed to be global nomads forever. It does mean that to reach our potential and find happiness, we must recognize the importance of place, know how best to weigh our options, and be willing to move when necessary.

6

WHERE THE BRAINS ARE

H UMAN BEINGS HAVE ALWAYS MIGRATED—TO FIND
food, to escape military conflict, to avoid religious or political persecution, or to gain economic opportunity. For most of
history, however, human settlements remained relatively small.
A 2007 story in *The Economist* summed up the long sweep of
human migration this way:

> Whether you think the human story begins in a garden in
> Mesopotamia known as Eden, or more prosaically on the
> savannahs of present-day east Africa, it is clear that Homo
> sapiens did not start life as an urban creature. Man's habitat
> at the outset was dominated by the need to find food, and
> hunting and foraging were rural pursuits. Not until the end
> of the last ice age, around 11,000 years ago, did he start
> building anything that might be called a village, and by that
> time man had been around for about 120,000 years. It took
> another six millennia, to the days of classical antiquity, for

cities of more than 100,000 people to develop. Even in
1800 only 3% of the world's population lived in cities.
Sometime in the next few months, though, that proportion
will pass the 50% mark, if it has not done so already. Wisely
or not, Homo sapiens has become Homo urbanus.[1]

And this trend is far from finished. According to UN predictions, by the year 2030, more than two-thirds of the world's population (4.4 *billion* people) will be urbanites.[2]

Some contend that since the 1960s, migration patterns have
shifted away from cities and urban centers and toward the suburbs. This outward movement of millions to the suburbs, they
argue, has reversed the great rural-to-urban trend. Indeed, tens
of millions of people have moved from urban centers to suburbs
that offer newer housing, newer infrastructure, and a perceived
better quality of life.[3] That has undoubtedly given rise to new divisions of class and race, a heightened dependence on the automobile, ever growing mass consumption, and wholly new living
patterns.

There is also the much cited shifts of population from the
older, colder, urban centers of the Northeast and Midwest—the
Frostbelt, so to speak—to the Sunbelt regions. Indeed, states
like Texas, Arizona, Florida, and Nevada have posted phenome-
nal rates of growth in recent years, as the regions surrounding
Phoenix and Las Vegas have attracted new residents at an incredible clip. And finally, there is the continued outward movement of many Americans to the exurbs and edge cities,
originally identified by Joel Garreau—places, such as California's Silicon Valley or Tyson's Corner in Northern Virginia,
which are organized around highway interchanges, business
parks, and shopping malls.[4]

But confounding this trend is the worldwide urban shift as
well as a significant back-to-the-city movement in the United

States. A powerful wave of gentrification has swept urban areas, bringing loft housing, condo-conversions, historic preservation, new restaurants, retail, and nightlife back to city neighborhoods. Some predict that even this trend might soon recede, as housing becomes less affordable for the very groups that powered the gentrification in the first place.

One of the many upshots of these two competing movements, according to leading demographers and political sociologists, is a new "sorting" of population by values, culture, and politics. This tension is perhaps best captured by David Brooks's two iconic American characters, the cappuccino-drinking urban "bourgeois-bohemian" ("bobo" for short) and suburbia's "patio man."[5]

The Means Migration

In 2006, I argued in *The Atlantic* that an even more significant demographic realignment is currently at work: the mass relocation of highly skilled, highly educated, and highly paid people to a relatively small number of metropolitan regions, and a corresponding exodus of traditional lower and middle classes from those same places. Such geographic sorting of people by economic potential, on this scale, is unprecedented. I call it the *means migration,* and refer to the regions capturing this demographic group as *means metros.*

The means migration can be seen most clearly in the increasing geographic concentration of college graduates (see Figure 6.1). According to research by Harvard University's Edward Glaeser and Christopher Berry of the University of Chicago, in 1970 human capital was distributed relatively evenly across the United States.[6] Nationally, 11 percent of the population over twenty-five years of age had a college degree, and that figure ranged between 9 percent and 13 percent in fully half of

America's 318 metropolitan regions. At the low end of the spectrum, only 4 percent of adults in Cleveland had a college degree; Detroit and St. Louis did only slightly better—their figure was 6 percent each. At the high end of the spectrum, 17 percent of adults in San Francisco had college degrees, though Washington, D.C., claimed first place with 18 percent.

Over the past three decades, the percentage of Americans holding a college degree has more than doubled, reaching 27 percent by 2004. But as the map shows, those gains have not been evenly spread. For instance, more than half of all residents in the San Francisco region now have college degrees. And there are five regions nationwide where more than 45 percent of adults have graduated from college. In Washington, D.C., nearly every other person has a college degree. Even as the national share of adults with college educations has doubled, regions like Detroit and Cleveland perform only slightly better than they did three decades ago—11 percent and 4 percent, respectively. In 2004, there remained twelve metropolitan regions nationwide where less than 20 percent of the adult population had graduated from college, and in several of those, fewer than one in ten residents had a bachelor's degree.

The trends for those with graduate degrees show a similar pattern. In 2004, more than 20 percent of the adult populations in Washington, D.C., and Seattle held advanced degrees, compared with 5 percent in Cleveland, 4 percent in Detroit, and just 2 percent in Newark. In the downtown neighborhoods of high-powered cities, the concentration of well-educated people is even greater. In 2000, more than two-thirds of the residents of downtown Chicago and midtown Manhattan held college degrees—levels that are more typically seen in advantaged suburbs.[7] Many older industrial cities, suburbs, and outlying rural areas are being left behind. Significantly, as Chapter 13 will show, young, single populations are flocking in ever-greater

FIGURE 6.1 THE HUMAN CAPITAL MAP

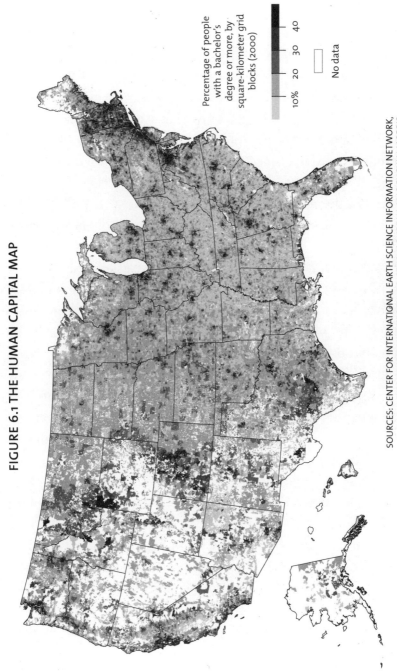

Percentage of people
with a bachelor's
degree or more, by
square-kilometer grid
blocks (2000)

10%   20   30   40

No data

SOURCES: CENTER FOR INTERNATIONAL EARTH SCIENCE INFORMATION NETWORK,
COLUMBIA UNIVERSITY; U.S. CENSUS BUREAU; MAP BY RYAN MORRIS

numbers to these means metros (those with high concentrations of highly educated and higher-income people) where they nonetheless often live in penury until either making it or being forced out by the high cost of living.

The means migration can also be seen in regional differences in income. The past decade or two has seen a dramatic concentration of high-income households in the means metros. In 2006, the median household income in San Jose, California, was $80,638, and $78,978 in Washington, D.C. By comparison, New Orleans and Oklahoma City claimed under $50,000. The discrepancies grow even larger when one includes metropolitan regions with fewer than a million people. Median household income was $28,660 in McAllen and $27,672 in Brownsville, Texas.

What's behind this phenomenon? It's not just that people prefer to live in means metros. To be sure, many of them are aesthetically pleasing—beautiful, energizing, and fun to live in—but others are cramped, dense, and expensive.

But there is a deeper, more fundamental reason, rooted in economics. Increasingly, the most talented and ambitious people *need* to live in the means metros in order to realize their full economic potential. The proximity of talented, highly educated people has a powerful effect on innovation and economic growth, as Chapter 4 has shown. Places that bring together diverse talent accelerate the local rate of economic evolution. When large numbers of entrepreneurs, financiers, engineers, designers, and other smart, creative people are constantly bumping into one another inside and outside of work, business ideas are formed, sharpened, executed, and—if successful—expanded. The more smart people, and the denser the connections among them, the faster it all goes. It is the multiplier effect of the clustering force at work.

In addition to the benefits of living near smart people and their creative ideas, the means metros have a larger and simpler

FIGURE 6.2 THE INCOME MAP

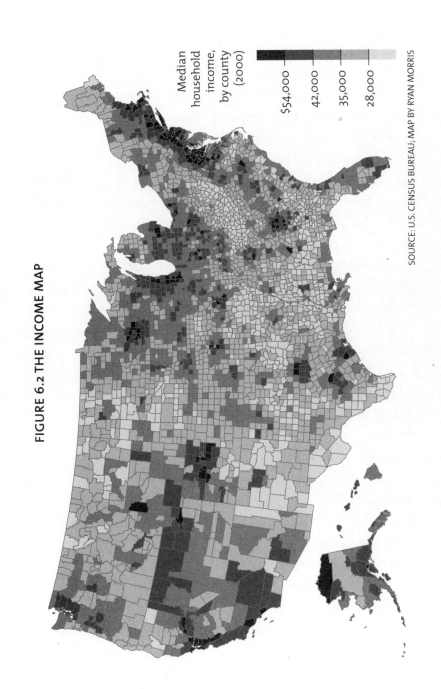

Median
household
income,
by county
(2000)

$54,000

42,000

35,000

28,000

SOURCE: U.S. CENSUS BUREAU; MAP BY RYAN MORRIS

advantage over other regions: a head start. For a variety of historical reasons—the presence of great universities is usually one—the means metros started off with a relatively high concentration of relatively talented people. And as more and more of such people are added, the multiplier effect on growth keeps increasing. That's not true just for growth in the aggregate but for individual incomes and opportunities as well.

Of course, opportunities do not exist equally for everyone. For most of human history, population growth has meant economic growth. That was certainly the case in agricultural economies in which population growth meant more people to work the farms. In industrial economies, too, population growth meant more people to man the factories. In both cases, overall population growth was key to economic growth, and economic growth meant more opportunities across the board.

The means migration severs the long-held connection between population growth and economic development. Changing technology, increased trade, and the ability to outsource routine functions have made highly skilled people less reliant on colocation of the unskilled and moderately skilled.

What matters most today isn't where most people settle, but where the *greatest number of the most skilled* people locate. Because the returns from colocation among the ablest is so high, and because high-end incomes are rising so fast, it makes sense for these workers to continue to bid up the price of real estate (as I'll discuss in Chapter 8) and accept other costs that traditional middle-class workers and families cannot afford. As traditional middle-class families are displaced by smaller, higher-income households, population can decline even as economic growth continues. The most successful cities and regions in the United States and around the world may increasingly be inhabited by a core of wealthy and highly mobile workers leading highly privileged lives, catered to by an underclass of service workers living farther and farther away.

The consequence is this: the means migration is dividing the world into two kinds of regions with very different economic prospects. A small number of means metros attract the lion's share of the mobile and the skilled, who see their incomes and real estate values climb, while the great majority witness the exact opposite. Some of today's means metros could eventually fall back as housing prices and living costs rise. But there are powerful reasons to believe that the economic disparity between some city-regions and others will continue to grow, and perhaps even accelerate, thanks to the snowball effect of talent attraction.

"This spatial sorting," says Wharton economist Joseph Gyourko, "will affect the nature of America as much as the rural-urban migration of the late nineteenth century did."[8] He asks us to imagine a future society in which people interact only with others who share the same educational, financial, and psychological backgrounds. "We already have fairly intense segregation by income within metropolitan areas," he writes. "But how different will things be if almost every community within the metro region is roughly as rich and skilled as mine?"

To Gyourko's question, I add my own: how will the growing division between the mobile and the rooted affect the very fabric of society? How are we to maintain diversity if wealthy city-regions remain inaccessible to people of different backgrounds? As the United States becomes more and more polarized, with those who move on one end and those who stay on the other, what will ensure that we remain the land of opportunity we have so long promised our children and ourselves?

7
JOB-SHIFT

———

L ET'S LOOK AT THINGS ON A FINER SCALE. JUST AS THE clustering force concentrates talent within regions, it also sorts us by our work and careers. What we earn is influenced by where we are; so is what we do and how well we are able to do it.

Regions are becoming more distinct in the kinds of jobs they offer. The work we do is growing more and more specialized, not just by field but also by location. The concentrations of high-end finance in London and New York, technology in Silicon Valley, filmmaking in Los Angeles, and the music industry in Nashville are a few of the most obvious examples. While this is not happening in every career—doctors, lawyers, nurses, and teachers are in demand just about everywhere, and their pay is fairly consistent around the country—its effects can be seen in a growing number of jobs and careers.

Most of us put a lot of thought into what we do for a living. We study hard, go to college, and in many cases continue on to graduate school. After we graduate, we spend a great deal of time identifying companies we'd like to work for. We conduct job searches, send out resumes, and go on interviews. Once employed, we try to impress our boss. We work our way up and earn raises and promotions. We spend time and money to upgrade our talents and acquire new skills. We network with others in our field to broaden our prospects. Some of us decide to be our own bosses and become free agents, which requires finding work and clients.[1] We do all of this to make a living and support our families.

Few people appreciate how much it matters *where* we work. I'm not talking about people who decide where to live before they search for work. I'm talking about the job market itself: how employment opportunities and salaries differ by location. Software jobs are not only more plentiful in Silicon Valley; high-tech employees there are paid 75 percent more than the national average for the same work, and many of them participate in stock option plans that allow them to get rich.

"I actually think it's important to know this in order to realize how important it might be for ambitious people to move someplace they *wouldn't* otherwise find satisfying," *Cato Unbound* editor Will Wilkinson wrote to me. "You love acting but you hate LA, New York, D.C., and Chicago? Tough luck: Suck it up or resign yourself to dinner theater in Biloxi."

Geeks and Grunts

The advanced economies today are going through an epochal transformation. It is bigger in scale and magnitude than the shift from farms to factories a century or two ago. As a consequence, they are shedding manufacturing jobs and generating jobs in two other economic sectors—low-paid service work in everything from retail sales to personal service and high-paid professional, innovative, and design work in what I call the creative

sector of the economy. This transformation is painful and dis-
ruptive for many. It is especially tragic for the scores of people
who have lost good, high-paying jobs in manufacturing over the
past several decades.

I know firsthand how much those jobs mean to the families
that depend on them. My father worked for more than fifty
years at Victory Optical in Newark's Ironbound neighborhood.
That job provided the means by which my parents bought our
small house outside Newark, sent my brother and me to private
Catholic school, and ultimately put us through college.

My years in Pittsburgh, at a time when the region was losing
more than 150,000 blue-collar jobs and steel mills were being
shuttered and torn down, afforded me a close view of how
painful economic dislocation is for people and entire regions.

More recently, I have seen what the decline of automotive
manufacturing has meant to Detroit, my wife's hometown.

In the United States, for example, manufacturing jobs, which
made up 49 percent of all employment in 1950, declined to 27
percent in 1990 and 24 percent in 2005, and they continue to
decline. Over the coming decade, the United States is projected
to lose another half-million such jobs.

Meanwhile, the United States and other advanced nations are
generating new kinds of jobs. The workforce is splitting into two
distinct labor groups, which UCLA economist Edward Leamer
has dubbed the "geeks" and the "grunts." The geeks enjoy
higher-paying, higher-skill work in the creative sector; the
grunts are laborers in the service sector, who have fewer skills
and receive less pay.

We've effectively become the "postindustrial society" that the
Harvard sociologist Daniel Bell predicted in the 1970s, hinging
our prosperity on the growth of a knowledge class, reliant on
science to bring forth innovation and social change, and more
dependent on services than goods. Some 59 million Americans,

more than 45 percent of the U.S. workforce, are employed as
retail salespeople, physical therapists, dental hygienists, home
health aides, food service workers, haircutters, manicurists,
landscapers, and the like. Many of these jobs are growing at incredible rates. By 2014, the Bureau of Labor Statistics projects
that the U.S. economy will add millions more new service jobs,
including 735,000 in retail sales, 550,000 in food services,
470,000 in customer service, 440,000 in janitorial work, 375,000
in restaurants, and 230,000 in landscaping. But these jobs are
mainly low paying, at least for now. The average worker in the
service sector makes less than $27,000 annually.

The future of the service sector matters a great deal to both
the U.S. and global economies. Not everyone can or wants to be
a doctor, lawyer, engineer, or professional. Given that the bulk
of manufacturing jobs have been lost forever, it seems crucial to
elevate the millions of new service sector work opportunities
our economy is generating into secure, respectable, high-paying
jobs. When I asked a group of my students whether they would
prefer to work in a reliable, high-paying job in a factory or a
lower paying, temporary job as a hair stylist, they overwhelm-
ingly chose the latter—it was more creative and therefore seemed
more rewarding. The market appears to reflect this psychology.
Vocational training programs for machinists are in dire need of
students, while cosmetology classes are routinely over-enrolled.

This hit home for me in the spring of 2005, when I visited a
local health spa. I tend to feel awkward at such places, so I decided to make small talk with the attendant. I asked her where
she was from.

"Connecticut," she replied.

"How did you end up in D.C.?"

"For college."

"Where did you go to school?"

"The University of Maryland."

That's a very good school, I thought. What had she studied there?

"Economics."

Hold on, how had economics led her to taking a job in a spa?

"Well, after college I went to work for the Bureau of Labor Statistics."

My jaw dropped.

"The BLS?" I asked. *The government source of nearly all my best data? The basis for the arguments of my previous books?*

"Yep."

So I asked her why she'd switched jobs. I told her that, quite frankly, moving from the BLS to a spa didn't sound like a shrewd career move for someone in her twenties with her educational background. She didn't care about that, she said.

"I was bored. I sat in a cubicle all day and looked at spreadsheets. It was tolerable only because I could go out with my friends every night, since I didn't have to think too hard during the day. But after a while I just couldn't take it. It was just so boring."

A career change was in order. "I wanted a purpose."

She enrolled in cosmetology school. She took a job in a plastic surgeon's office and got to know the work better. Now she works in the Four Seasons in Georgetown and another spa in the Virginia suburbs.

I asked her whether her salary was steady, did she get good benefits, things that we're all supposed to want. "None of that matters," she said, without a moment's hesitation.

She makes great money—based on commission—and can work as much or as little as she wants. She loves her job. She's excited every day. She likes the freedom; she's mobile. She wasn't looking for job security—at least not yet. Still, I had to imagine that at some point she would want—and need—the assurance that she could continue to do what she loved without risking her financial well-being.

In her old life, this woman had been what the late Peter Drucker called a "knowledge worker." She'd gotten a good education and scored a job in high-level information with a reputable agency of the federal government.[2] And she ended up hating it. The key to her professional happiness, she realized, was not in applying the knowledge she had learned in school but in using her innate creative abilities. My point is not that her current line of work is objectively better than her old one—or the factory job my father held for so many years, for that matter—but that it is in our society's best interests to make sure that these creative service jobs are stable and well paying because, among other things, they are the ones least likely to be outsourced.

Why these jobs don't already pay well is a controversial question. Some contend that market forces conspire to keep wages for this kind of work low. Others say the sector needs vast improvement before higher pay could possibly be granted. But while economists and politicians bicker, companies around the world—from Starbucks and Whole Foods to Target and the Container Store—are devising strategies aimed at upgrading service work. They are bumping up pay and benefits, and enabling employees to use their creative talents to serve customers better, all on the assumption that such efforts will add to their bottom lines.

Best Buy is a good example. The world's largest specialty retailer of consumer electronics, it employs some 140,000 people and boasts annual sales of $36 billion. Taking a page from Toyota's much-lauded management system, Best Buy CEO Brad Anderson has made it his company's stated mission to provide an "inclusive, innovative work environment designed to unleash the power of *all* of our people as they have fun while being the best." In its effort to increase sales and profits while making the workplace more productive and enjoyable, Best Buy encourages its employees to improve upon the company's work processes and techniques and to design new ways to better serve customers. In many cases, small ideas devised on the salesroom floor—a teenage sales rep redesigning a Vonage display, or an immigrant salesperson acting on an idea to increase outreach and service to non-English-speaking communities—have been implemented in stores nationwide, generating hundreds of millions in added revenue. Anderson understands that succeeding in a service industry like retail means more than implementing new technology and designing attractive new products. He likes to say that the great promise of the creative era is that, for the first time in our history, our nation's economic competitiveness hinges on the development of human creative capabilities.

Or as I would put it, our future economic success is increasingly dependent on our ability to harness the creative talents of each and every member of the workforce—regardless of sex, age, race, ethnicity, or sexual orientation.

Working Smarter

A second group of jobs, those held by the creative class, is growing even more quickly and is even more important to our nation's economic growth. This sector includes jobs in science and technology, arts and design, entertainment and media, law, finance, management, health-care, and education.

While hardly new, the creative sector has experienced tremendous growth over the last century. Constituting just 5 percent of all employment in 1900, the creative class rose to roughly 10 percent in 1950, 15 percent in 1980, and more than 30 percent by 2005 (see Figure 7.1). Today, nearly 40 million Americans hold jobs in the creative sector. At $2.1 trillion, they generate *half* of all wages and salaries and enjoy nearly 70 percent ($474 billion) of all discretionary income.[3] These figures dwarf those of the service sector, which accounts for only 31 percent of all wages and salaries and only 17 percent of discretionary income. By 2014, according to our estimates, the U.S. will add another 10 million creative sector jobs to the nation's economy. The same pattern holds for virtually all of the advanced nations, where the creative class makes up 35 to 45 percent of the workforce, depending on the country.

Some might assume that the creative class is essentially just a group of highly educated people. Not really. When economists measure human capital—the total knowledge and skill of the workforce—they typically focus on formal education—that is, the percentage of the population with at least a bachelor's degree. But education is only one indicator of a person's creative potential.

Our society is rife with examples of remarkably creative and successful people who never graduated from college. Bill Gates, Steve Jobs, and Michael Dell are three of the most important entrepreneurs of our time, and all three dropped out of college. In fact, of the twenty-six self-made people on the *Forbes* 2007 list of the world's fifty richest people, eleven did not graduate from college.[4]

This is not to say that anyone can drop out of college and become a wildly successful entrepreneur like Steve Jobs. For most people a college education pays significant economic dividends. But it is to say that skill is made up of more than a college degree. On-the-job experience, wisdom and savvy, creativity, ambition, and entrepreneurial talent are among the many qualities that can't be formally taught but are requisite for success in the creative economy.

While education and creative occupations are correlated—most people who work in creative occupations have college degrees—the two play very different roles in economic growth. Through research I undertook with Charlotta Mellander and

FIGURE 7.1 RISE OF THE CREATIVE ECONOMY

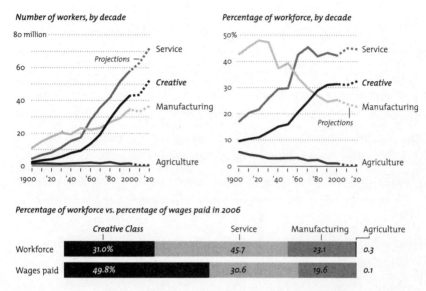

Number of workers, by decade

Percentage of workforce, by decade

Percentage of workforce vs. percentage of wages paid in 2006

	Creative Class	Service	Manufacturing	Agriculture
Workforce	31.0%	45.7	23.1	0.3
Wages paid	49.8%	30.6	19.6	0.1

SOURCE: KEVIN STOLARICK; GRAPHIC BY RYAN MORRIS

Kevin Stolarick, we found that the creative sector and the general college-educated populace affect regional economic development through different channels.[5] Compared with members of the creative class, people with college degrees did enjoy higher incomes—defined as money from all sources, including work earnings, investments, capital gains, benefits, and so on. But members of the creative class earned higher wages—money paid for a specified quantity of labor. Because wages reflect work that is done in a particular place, they are much better indicators of a region's productivity. Naples, Florida, and Silicon Valley are two of the country's wealthiest metropolitan regions. But the origins of that wealth are strikingly different. While wages make up less than a third (32 percent) of income in Naples, they are more than 90 percent of all income in San Jose.

Our research uncovered another important way in which occupations affect regional growth. When we looked at the correlations between occupations and regional income, we found that
certain kinds of jobs mean more to regional economies than
others. Business and financial operations and computer and
mathematical occupations had the largest correlation to regional
income, followed by sales occupations and then arts, design,
media, and entertainment. Next in line were management and
engineering occupations, followed by lawyers and scientists.[6]
The finding for artistic and entertainment occupations is particularly interesting. Many people presume that wealth generates
and sustains arts and entertainment, not the other way around.
But what if arts and entertainment occupations actually contribute to regional wealth as well?

Many regions that have lost manufacturing jobs have rebuilt
their economies around education and health-care. In former
manufacturing hubs like Detroit, Cleveland, St. Louis, and
Pittsburgh, the largest employers are colleges, universities, and
hospitals. This is seemingly good news—it means, at least, that
residents of these cities can find work. But according to my
team's analysis, high concentrations of these sectors ultimately
do not bode well for cities' economies. Although they may employ many people and provide great services, education and
health-care add relatively little to regional income.[7] That is even
truer when we look at education and health-care jobs as a share
of a region's creative economy. As the share of education and
health-care jobs rises, regional earnings fall. The more creative
class members take jobs in education and health-care, the lower
their region's wages tend to be.

Why might this be? For one, education and health-care sectors tend to monopolize a region's workforce—because the demand for employees is so great, it leaves other sectors with

smaller hiring pools. Education and health-care —like police and fire departments—are basic necessities. Every region must devote some of its workforce to them. They also bring in relatively little money from outside the region. Aside from out-of-state tuitions and government research grants, most of their income comes from within the region. Contrast that with an innovative and creative company, or cluster of companies, that brings in money from clients worldwide. Growing regions tend to have relatively higher concentrations of other key occupational groups—and it's those other jobs that are concentrating geographically.

Come Together

Jobs and industries have always clustered to some extent. The great concentration of steel factories in and around Pittsburgh and the huge automobile-manufacturing complex of Detroit are just two historical examples of the clustering force.

The classical theorists on location, Johann-Heinrich von Thünen and Alfred Weber (brother of the famous sociologist, Max), wrote extensively on processes of industrial location as a trade-off between raw materials and transportation costs.[8] Firms in heavy industries would seek out locations in which raw materials were abundant and where major waterways and transportation routes could minimize transportation costs.

The regions of the industrial era were organized around a single core industry or, in some cases, several core industries. They grew upward and then outward, in concentric zones around the center.[9] Particular sections for manufacturing developed around ports, and, over time, these cities saw the rise of specialized downtown business districts that offered a mix of business and financial services. Houses and apartments, which originally surrounded ports and factory complexes, gradually developed along streetcar lines, giving rise to the early suburbs. Most of these regions were served by farms and agricultural producers located relatively close by.

The rise of the creative economy changed this calculus by dramatically reducing dependence on natural resources. The expectation was that jobs and industries would decentralize. Many in fact did, as jobs in basic manufacturing industries relocated from the advanced nations to developing ones. But not all industries decentralized. A good example is Italy in the 1980s, where economists and sociologists were struck by the resilience of the nation's garment and fashion industries. How were these traditional sectors continuing to thrive in Italy when they were being driven out of business elsewhere (or at least to off-shore locations) by lower cost competitors in India or China?

The answer can be found in the great economist Alfred Marshall's concept of "agglomeration."[10] Some firms take advantage of economies of scale by integrating their activities and growing larger. But companies can also benefit by the agglomeration economies that come from locating close to one another. More recently, social scientists have dubbed this the power of the "industrial district." Whatever it is called, companies like Armani, Prada, and Gucci benefited from high levels of productivity and innovation, but even more so from being part of a tight cluster of suppliers, users, and customers. The economic power and efficiency of these clusters was more than enough to offset mounting pressures to relocate abroad.

By the early 1990s, such resilience of certain industrial clusters had captured the attention of leading economists and social scientists, like Harvard Business School professor Michael Porter.[11] Considered one of the most important management thinkers in the world, by the mid–1990s Porter was devoting almost all of his research and resources to the study of the world's leading industrial clusters.

Porter's research generated a new economic map of the United States—and of the world—that took shape around clusters: the insurance industry in Hartford, Connecticut; amusements and casinos in Las Vegas; furniture in High Point, North Carolina; office furniture in Grand Rapids, Michigan; golf equipment in Carlsbad, California; advanced imaging in Rochester, New York, and so on. According to Porter, these clusters managed to survive because of their proximity to sophisticated users and customers, their ability to draw employment from highly skilled pools of local talent, and their access to supportive regional institutions such as universities and vocational training programs. Many believed that offshoring and globalization would undercut these clusters, but Porter argued the opposite: "Now that globalization continues to power forward," he said in a 2006 online interview with *Business Week*, "what has happened is that clusters must become more specialized in individual locations. The global economy is speeding up the process by which clusters get more focused."

What's even more interesting is that high-tech industries like software and biotechnology—which have few if any industrial inputs—exhibit even greater clustering. In a detailed study of the biotech industry published in 2001, Joseph Cortright and Heike Mayer found that three-fourths of all biotech firms founded in the 1990s were located in just nine regions.[12] Compared with others, those nine regions boasted eight times as much biotech research, ten times as many biotech companies, and thirty times more biotech venture capital.

Venture capital is another useful indicator of how high-tech industries cluster. As of the second quarter of 2007, three regions—Silicon Valley, San Diego, and greater Boston—accounted for more than half of all venture capital investment, and more than two-thirds of that went to Silicon Valley, which commands between a fifth and two-thirds of all venture investments in a wide range of high-tech fields.[13]

And Silicon Valley shows no signs of slowing down. Despite the costs of doing business in the Valley, high-tech firms and jobs continue to flock there. A 2006 *Wall Street Journal* story entitled "New Hot Spot for High Tech Firms Is the Old One" noted the relocations of six companies to Silicon Valley: Mobius Microsystems, a maker of technology that regulates timing pulses in microchips, moved from Detroit; VideoEgg, a web-video company, and LicketyShip, an Internet firm that facilitates local deliveries, both moved from New Haven, Connecticut; Meetro, a maker of mobile social-networking software, shifted from Chicago; and Box.net, an online file-storage-and-sharing site, relocated from Seattle.[14] The Internet video company moved all the way from Tel Aviv, Israel.

These economies relocated even though the average annual wage for high-tech workers in the Silicon Valley that year was some $50,000 higher than the national average. But the resources offered by the cluster more than offset these costs. "There's a unique set of resources in Silicon Valley that don't exist in other places," VideoEgg founder, Matt Sanchez, told the *Journal.* "So if you're going to build a tech company, this is the place to do it."

It's not just high-tech industries that cluster. Many other industries also benefit from colocating. To start, let's look at the trends in the two main sectors of the economy: the service sector and the creative sector.

Many places that top standard lists of those with the fastest growing job markets—places like Las Vegas, Nevada, and smaller regions in Texas and Florida—do so because they generate large numbers of service jobs. On the other hand, regions such as Silicon Valley; Washington, D.C.; North Carolina's Research Triangle; Boulder, Colorado; Seattle; and Austin, Texas, are far more popular when it comes to creative-sector jobs. Roughly 40 percent of the workforce in those areas is employed in creative-sector work—four times as many as the national average (see Figure 7.2).

A number of urban economists and regional scientists have charted the increasing geographic specialization of work. Ann Markusen, a regional economist and pioneer in the field of occupational analysis, calls this the rise of the "distinctive city," where much of work and economic life has become more specialized.[15]

Roger Martin, my dean and colleague at the Rotman School of Management, says that while firms can do a lot internally to bolster their competitive advantage, location plays an additional role in business success. He calls it *jurisdictional advantage*, the fact that every location has unique assets which are not easily replicated.[16] Or, as he explains:

> . . . the means by which a jurisdiction—whether a city, a region, a province or a country—gains advantage over other jurisdictions in attracting certain types of human capital and certain types of business enterprises by being the optimal place for them to locate to carry on their appointed tasks. We refer only to certain types of people and businesses because we believe that no jurisdiction on the planet is or will be the optimal jurisdiction for all types of people and businesses. Some varieties of highly skilled people and some great businesses may think Boston, Massachusetts, is the best place on the planet, while others may think that Grand Rapids, Michigan, is—and for each, they are undoubtedly right. For this reason, numerous jurisdictions in

FIGURE 7.2 THE CREATIVE CLASS MAP

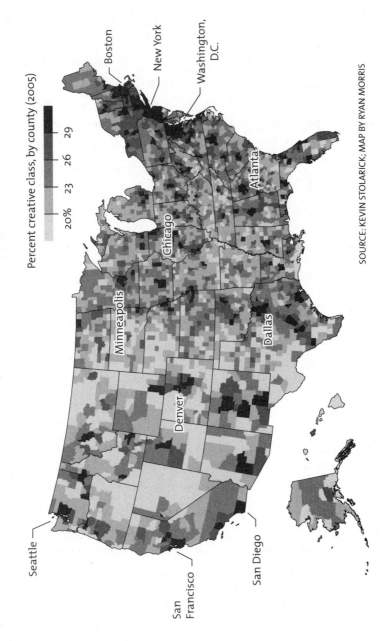

Percent creative class, by county (2005)

20%   23   26   29

Seattle

San Francisco

San Diego

Minneapolis

Denver

Dallas

Chicago

Atlanta

Boston

New York

Washington, D.C.

SOURCE: KEVIN STOLARICK; MAP BY RYAN MORRIS

the modern economy will enjoy jurisdictional advantage in their areas of specialization.

My team and I used detailed occupational data from the U.S. Bureau of Labor Statistics to estimate the clustering of jobs and work by region. We estimated employment "location quotients" (or LQ)—a statistical ratio that compares a region's share of a particular activity with that of the nation—for all major occupations and all major regions across the United States. An LQ of 1.25 is considered reasonably high by most experts, indicating a regional cluster of work.

There are nine regions across the country with LQs over 100—places like Dalton, Georgia, a center for textile jobs, or Thibodaux, Louisiana, the place to be if you're a "water vessel pilot." Thirty-seven regions have LQs over 50; and there are more than 500 with LQs over 10, still a very high concentration.

That is neither surprising nor terribly important when we're talking about relatively rare jobs like river piloting, unless, of course, that's your profession. But it becomes very interesting when we look at fields that employ economically significant numbers of people. Have a look at the map of the key job clusters across the United States (see Figure 7.3).

- Three-quarters of the nation's entertainers and performers work in Los Angeles, as do 25 percent of agents.
- Washington, D.C., is home to 78 percent of all political scientists, as well as a huge share of economists, mathematicians, and astronomers.
- More than half of all fashion designers work in New York. The New York region is also home to a quarter of all jobs for brokerage clerks. My editor Bill Frucht

118

FIGURE 7.3 THE NEW GEOGRAPHY OF WORK

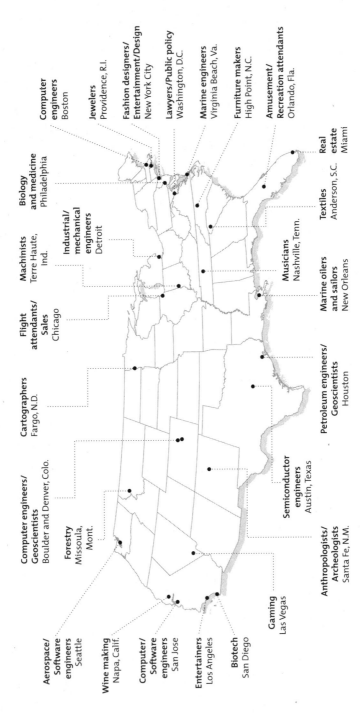

SOURCE: BUREAU OF LABOR STATISTICS; MAP BY RYAN MORRIS

points out that there's a corner in Manhattan, 23rd
Street and Fifth Avenue, with six or seven major
publishing companies within a five-minute walk: Basic,
Holt, FSG, St. Martin's, Abrams, Sterling, and a few
others. Not only can you change jobs without changing
parking lots, you can spend an entire career within one
or two subway stops.

- More than a third of petroleum engineering jobs are in
  Houston.
- And nearly a third of all gaming supervisors work in Las
  Vegas, along with 20 percent of the nation's booth
  cashiers and 16 percent of all slot key and costume
  attendants.

Some people would endure super long-distance commutes
rather than leave these clusters. An August 2005 article in the
Post-Gazette caused quite the brouhaha when it reported that several top executives were making commutes from New York and
Charlotte to Pittsburgh because they did not want to damage their
long-run careers by leaving those leading financial centers.[17] They
felt they had to be part of the core cluster—to keep their contacts
and networks up—to move ahead in their professions.

This regional concentration and specialization of jobs is a direct consequence of the clustering force we covered back in
Chapter 4. Recall Lucas's answer to his now infamous question
"What would people be paying sky-high rents for?"—to leverage the productivity of others. What makes it advantageous for
people who do the same type of work to live near each other—
software engineers in Silicon Valley, investment bankers and
fashion designers in New York, entertainment moguls, actors,
and directors in LA—is not just that the industries and the
companies are there. The companies are there in the first place
because people can plug into the existing cluster, increase their

overall productivity, and make good money. Or as the Santa Fe Institute researchers have found, these larger cities and larger clusters have to generate faster and faster rates of urban metabolism to keep up. The productivity gains brought on by clustering of work is creating a new and more specialized geography of work in the United States and around the world, as jobs and employment opportunities sort into a regional hierarchy by city and location.

Making the Scene

The physical proximity inherent in clustering provides ample face-to-face communication, information-sharing, and teaming required to innovate and improve productivity. In contrast to highly standardized work of the industrial age, in which knowledge could be codified in and taught through standardized procedures and engineering diagrams, creative work relies heavily on innate knowledge—the kind that can be found only in—and, as I like to say, *"in between"*—people's heads.

Networks are the human connections that make it possible for people and firms to share this vital information, described in detail by Harvard political scientist Robert Putnam in his best-selling book *Bowling Alone*. Putnam's ideas on the decline of tightly formed networks (the sort represented by 1950s bowling leagues) and the rise of a less caring society, more isolated individuals, and the decline of civic life have become incredibly popular.[18] These networks are formed by two kinds of social capital: bonding and bridging. Bonding represents the close ties that exist within extended families or ethnic communities and is the phenomenon whose decline Putnam lamented.

Bridging reflects looser ties that extend across and connect different groups. For clustering, this second type is what matters. It "puts people in the flow of the many different thoughts

and actions that reside in any one world," writes Andrew Hargadon, director of Technology Management programs at the
University of California, Davis.[19] At its heart, bridging, he continues, "changes the way people look at not just those different
ideas they find in other worlds, it also changes the way they look
at thoughts and actions that dominate their own. Bridging activities provide the conditions for creativity, for the Eureka moment when new possibilities suddenly become apparent."

In her study of the high-tech industry in Silicon Valley and on
Route 128 outside Boston, Berkeley's AnnaLee Saxenian found
that the resilience and superior performance of Silicon Valley
companies during the 1990s turned on the adaptive capabilities
of the region's decentralized but cooperative networks of entrepreneurs, venture capitalists, technologists, and newly minted
university talent.[20]

No matter what form it takes, networking reflects what Stanford University sociologist Mark Granovetter calls "the strength
of weak ties," a remarkable phrase that captures the very
essence of what's going on.[21] In a widely influential study that examined how people actually find jobs, Granovetter concluded
that it is our numerous weak ties, rather than our fewer strong
ones, that really matter. The idea that proximity to total
strangers is more important than connections to lifelong friends
may seem strange, until you think about how networks function.
The beauty of weak ties is that they bring us new information.
Chances are, you and your friends travel in mostly the same circles. You know the same people, frequent the same places, and
hear about the same opportunities. Weak ties are more numerous and take less effort to maintain. They introduce a bit of
chaos into the equation, which more often than not is the key to
identifying new opportunities and ideas.

While the venues in which we network undoubtedly differ
depending on our occupation, the role and function of these

activities are the same. In traditional office jobs, they may take the form of conversations around the water cooler or weekend games of golf. For investment bankers, it's power lunches and company retreats in the Hamptons. In high-tech fields, it's breakfast meetings, beer-bashes, or bicycle rides. One Silicon Valley venture capitalist drove this last point home when he said, "If you're not part of the *peloton* [the main pack of bicycles in a road race], you're not part of the deal." He wasn't being metaphorical.

Or consider the scenes that grow up around artistically creative work like music, writing, and art. These provide a useful lens through which to better understand why jobs and work cluster. Creative work requires little, if anything, in the way of physical inputs (like iron ore or coal) to succeed, and they don't generate economies of scale. Artistic endeavors are textbook cases of individual production. They require little more than small groups to make their final products, which are themselves unique and different.

What's behind a scene? When most people think of an art or music scene, they think of a concentration of people who make art or music—what economists call producers. This is certainly important. Since the artist colonies of long ago, scenes have enabled talented people to collaborate and compete with one another—to seek inspiration, look over and learn from each other's work. In the world of music, the term "scene" was used in relation to a distinct style of an area's musical taste—such as New Orleans jazz, Nashville country, or Chicago blues. But scenes cannot survive without social and economic infrastructure.

As Harvard economist Richard Caves explains in his book *Creative Industries*, the success of the music industry is contingent on a system in which artists, writers, and musicians do the work, and agents and managers sell that work. And as Elizabether Currid's book, *The Warhol Economy*, shows, these scenes also draw from a social environment of clubs, restaurants, and performance venues where networking takes place.[22]

Scenes are vehicles for producing, consuming, and improving products—and they're responsible for creating experiences, too. They represent "modes of organizing cultural production and consumption," according to Daniel Silver, Terry Clark, and Lawrence Rothfield, leading students of the subject at the University of Chicago.[23] Scenes are many and varied. There's the music scene in Nashville, the theater scene in New York, the nightlife scene in Miami, and LA's film scene. But, the authors ask, "What makes these scenes 'scenes'?" What makes a collection of theaters on Broadway in New York City different from theaters anywhere else?

A scene is defined, the authors note, by the opportunities it gives you to "look at other people and be looked at by them." It is "total entertainment culture that pushes work out of mind." The key, they argue, lies in the way "collections of amenities and people serve to foster certain shared values and tastes, certain ways of relating to one another and legitimating what one is doing or not doing." Scenes provide a key lens into why work continues to cluster today.

Jack White Goes to Nashville

One would think that as individual artists, musicians should be able to live anywhere they want. The arts are needed everywhere—these places have every reason to "fly apart." But they don't, and the numbers prove it.

A George Mason University graduate student, Scott Jackson, tracked the locations of musicians and musical groups between 1970 and 2004 using data from a wide range of sources.[24] Since the definitions for metropolitan regions have changed several times since 1970, Jackson took great care to ensure that all regional boundaries and all data would match up. This left him with detailed information on musicians in thirty-one metropolitan regions.

His analysis documents the clear trend toward increasing concentration and specialization in the music industry. The proportion of musicians across the thirty-one metro regions increased from 52 percent in 1970 to 63 percent in 2004. But one region rose head and shoulders above the rest. In 1970, Nashville was only a minor center for country music. By 2004, only New York and LA, both huge cities, housed a greater number of musicians.

Nashville's rise is even more impressive when you look at its location quotient. In 1970, Nashville was not even among the top five regions as ranked by their music industry location quotient. By 2004, it was the national leader, with a location quotient nearly four times the national average. The extent of its growth was so significant, Jackson found, that when he charted the growth in location quotients between 1970 and 2004, Nashville was the *only one* that registered positive growth. It had, in effect, sucked up all the growth in the industry by expanding its reach from country to all musical genres, particularly rock and pop. Today it is home to much of the world's best studio talent and has eclipsed even New York and LA as *the* place for music writing, recording, and publishing.

Just as high-tech companies trek to Silicon Valley, a great deal of top musical talent eventually ends up in Nashville's orbit. In 2005, one of the most significant rock musicians of the past decade, Jack White, founder of the legendary White Stripes, relocated his newest band and recording project, The Raconteurs, from Detroit's legendary music scene (the home of innovative and highly influential rock bands the MC5 and Iggy Pop and the Stooges as well as Motown and other musical styles) to Nashville.[25] Earlier, White had produced and performed on

Loretta Lynn's highly regarded album *Van Lear Rose*, which was recorded in Nashville. Impressed by what he saw, he left Detroit and bought a house in Nashville. None of the musicians in The Raconteurs is originally from Nashville. White and Brendan Benson are from Detroit; the drummer, Patrick Keeler, and bass player, Jack Lawrence, had been members of a Cincinnati band, The Greenhornes. When asked why he relocated, White said that Detroit's scene had become too negative and confining. People who were once his friends and associates reportedly got jealous of The White Stripes' success. Nashville was different, he said: more professional, less confrontational, less melodramatic. Like Silicon Valley, it was a place the best and the brightest in their field could collaborate with other top talent and draw from a world-class economic infrastructure.

The kind of work we do is a critical part of our economic wealth and well-being. But how we use the money we make is a different matter. For most of us, the biggest investment we will make is in our home. And if the place we choose to live has a big effect on how much we pay for our house, it has an even bigger impact on how fast and how much our biggest investment will grow over time.

8
SUPERSTAR CITIES

'M NOT A BIG FAN OF TV, BUT THERE'S A SHOW I'VE BEEN watching more and more often. It's called *What You Get for the Money*. Each episode features four or five places around the country and shows viewers the real estate available there—starting around $300,000 and going to over $1,000,000. About $300,000, for instance, buys you a late-fifties fixer-upper in Flagstaff, Arizona; a 2,300-square-foot four-bedroom colonial outside Rochester, New York; or an 1,800-square-foot modern townhouse in Louisville, Kentucky. For a million bucks, the options include a modernized log cabin in Denver; a contemporary house in Nashville; or a penthouse condo in downtown Boston.

Why such wide divergence in what you can buy for the same amount of money? It all boils down to that old real estate adage: "location, location, location." Many people say they want to stretch their money in order to get a big house at an affordable price. In my travels around the globe, I've often heard people boast, "You can buy a mansion here for less than the price of a studio apartment in Manhattan." Nobody ever questions why those mansions are less valuable than 400 square feet overlooking an airshaft on 83rd Street.

Buying real estate is not a single purchase. The cost of the structure is usually the less valuable part. It's the cost of the land—the value of location—that really matters. That's where that old real estate adage originates. Where demand is high, and especially where it exceeds supply, the location itself can cost a fortune.

Location matters not only in determining what you pay to begin with, but how much your investment will grow over time. In real estate, as with any other investment, the test is not how much it costs to get in but how much your purchase will gain in value. Buying a house is the largest investment most of us make. It's crucial to realize how big an effect the rate of appreciation can have on our personal wealth in the long run.

As this chapter will show, location is becoming a bigger and bigger factor in real estate. Housing prices are growing more varied by location. Leading real estate economists have charted the rise of so-called superstar cities, where prices have appreciated far greater than the national average. The most dynamic of these real estate superstars are located in this nation's and the world's leading mega-regions.

Everything Has Its Price

Economists say that the price of real estate is the best reflection of the effective demand for a location. There is a large gap between the most affordable and the most expensive communities, according to data from the American Community Survey of the U.S. Census Bureau[1] (see Figure 8.1). The most expensive

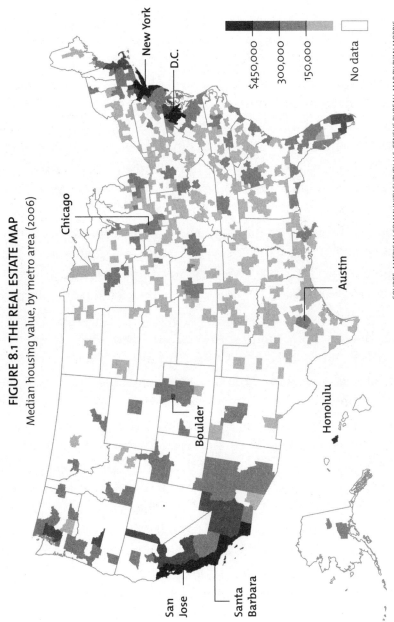

FIGURE 8.1 THE REAL ESTATE MAP
Median housing value, by metro area (2006)

New York

D.C.

Chicago

Austin

Boulder

Honolulu

San
Jose

Santa
Barbara

$450,000
300,000
150,000
No data

SOURCE: AMERICAN COMMUNITY SURVEY, U.S. CENSUS BUREAU; MAP BY RYAN MORRIS

metro area in 2006 was San Jose, where the median housing value was more than $740,000; the least expensive was Odessa, Texas, where the median house was valued at a mere fraction of that, $54,000. Housing was also notably expensive in San Francisco, LA, New York, Boston, and Washington, D.C.

The discrepancies are even greater when you look at finer geographic detail—zip codes, for example. According to a 2007 *Business Week* report, there were five zip codes in the United States in which the median price of a home was more than $2 million. There were twenty-four in which the median price was between $1.5 and $2 million. In another sixty-six zip codes, the median price was between $1 and $1.5 million.[2] And these are *median* prices. Fully half the homes in these areas were more expensive.

On the flip side, there are a great number of metro areas—including Tulsa, El Paso, Wichita, and Buffalo—where the median value of a house in 2006 was less than $120,000, according to the American Community Survey. In El Paso, the median monthly cost for owning your own home was $936. It was less than $1,300 in Tulsa, St. Louis, Buffalo, Tucson, Cleveland, Toledo, Wichita, and Memphis. These are fantastic deals, especially considering how many people pay $2,000 or more a month to rent a studio apartment in Manhattan.

All are great places. I've lived in some and worked in or visited virtually all of them. As a visiting professor in Buffalo in the early 1980s, I rented a great little apartment near Elmwood, the city's upscale shopping, restaurant, and nightlife district. My team and I have worked extensively in El Paso. It's a great border town offering incredible cross-cultural excitement and energy.

I know Memphis well—we hosted the Memphis Manifesto Summit there, a major national conference devoted to rebuilding cities along creative lines. I've worked with community leaders in Cincinnati, Cleveland, Louisville, Lexington, Tulsa, and Oklahoma City, and am impressed with all of those cities, too.

But despite their affordable housing, virtually every one of those places is losing talented people.

Several years ago, *New York Times* economic columnist David Leonhardt called me with some questions on this very subject. Why weren't firms and people moving to Buffalo or Cleveland? Basic economics would suggest that at least some cost-sensitive businesses and people would want to take advantage of inexpensive real estate. But most don't, and for a very basic reason. Housing costs reflect what people are willing to pay to live in a particular location. Prices rise in places that are hotly desired, and stagnate or fall where demand is lower.

Star Struck

Using long-run trends in housing prices as their gauge, Wharton real estate expert Joseph Gyourko and his colleagues Todd Sinai and Chris Mayer of Columbia University identified the rise of what they call "superstar cities" (made up of central cities and their suburbs) across the United States.[3] After examining changes in housing prices across fifty American metro regions from 1950 to 2000, Gyourko, Mayer, and Sinai identified a handful of such superstar cities where growth in housing has consistently and rapidly outpaced the national average increase, and where growth in housing supply is limited. The top ten included San Francisco, Oakland, Seattle, San Diego, Los Angeles, Portland (Oregon), Boston, Bergen-Passaic (New Jersey), Charlotte, and New Haven.

Talk about outpacing the national average. From 1954 to 2000, housing prices in Silicon Valley grew more than eleven-fold. In San Francisco, they increased by a factor of nine. In 1940, the average house in Cincinnati cost $65,000—more than the average house in San Francisco. By 2004, the median house in San Francisco was worth $661,900, more than five times the

median value of a house in Cincinnati ($118,350) and ten times
the median house in Buffalo ($59,370), the lowest price of the
fifty cities in Gyourko et al.'s sample.

According to Gyourko and his collaborators, the dramatic real
estate appreciation in superstar cities is a long-run trend. In the
short term, real estate prices in superstar cities experience significant ups and downs, but over time they will consistently appreciate in value. But some may ask, What about a place like
Las Vegas, which has witnessed dramatic population growth—at
or near 50 percent—in four of the past five decades? Most
people would think that makes Las Vegas a major growth center.
It's a mistake to equate population growth with superstar status,
Gyourko says, unless it's accompanied by a significant rise in
housing prices. As for Las Vegas, he adds, given its relatively low
price appreciation and falling housing prices, most anyone who
would like to live there can.

The amounts that many people are willing to pay to live in
this small set of superstar cities says something powerful about
their economic importance. Of course, housing markets fluctuate and bubbles burst, but superstar cities possess a remarkable
staying power that dates back at least half a century. They are,
Gyourko says, "by their nature exclusionary—and due to the
prices they command, residents have to pay a significant financial premium to live there." They maintain their status by consistently attracting more of the same—increasingly skilled and
wealthy households. In Darwinian fashion, richer households
move in over time, and lower-income households are forced
out. Because demand for space in superstar cities is so great,
and because there is only a limited supply of it, Gyourko and his
collaborators argue, all it takes is an increase in national income
for these cities to appreciate faster than the rest of the nation.

Adding fuel to the fire is the globalization of real estate markets in the United States and around the world. This dawned on

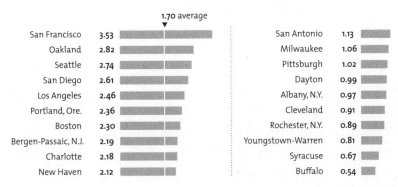

FIGURE 8.2 SUPERSTAR CITIES

Real annualized house price growth, 1950–2000
(Top and bottom 10 metro areas with 1950 population of greater than 500,000)

		1.70 average			
San Francisco	3.53		San Antonio	1.13	
Oakland	2.82		Milwaukee	1.06	
Seattle	2.74		Pittsburgh	1.02	
San Diego	2.61		Dayton	0.99	
Los Angeles	2.46		Albany, N.Y.	0.97	
Portland, Ore.	2.36		Cleveland	0.91	
Boston	2.30		Rochester, N.Y.	0.89	
Bergen-Passaic, N.J.	2.19		Youngstown-Warren	0.81	
Charlotte	2.18		Syracuse	0.67	
New Haven	2.12		Buffalo	0.54	

SOURCE: JOSEPH GYOURKO, CHRISTOPHER MAYER, TODD SINAI

me when my wife and I were looking for a house in Toronto last spring. Noting the high prices in Toronto's inner-ring residential neighborhoods (significantly higher than northwest Washington, D.C., where we were coming from), I asked our real estate agent what was driving this. She replied without missing a beat: "Foreign buyers, not Americans, mainly Russians, are taking virtually all the properties at the high end of the market."

With globalizing markets and a weak dollar, real estate in Manhattan or Beverly Hills can look like a bargain compared to London, Tokyo, Hong Kong, Moscow, or other global centers. This causes quite an affordability dilemma in these superstar markets. In the past buyers competed for real estate with others in a relatively local market; now demand extends literally across the world.

With the rise of a spiky world organized around a relatively small number of global mega-regions, we may be entering a new phase in real estate in which the housing market splits into globally oriented centers where prices rise considerably over time and local ones where prices are stable or, in some cases, decline.

However, not all economists think that high real estate prices in superstar cities are here to stay. Among those who see this trend ending is Yale economist Robert Shiller, author of the best-selling *Irrational Exuberance*, which predicted the collapse of tech stocks in the early 2000s. In a May 2007 op-ed,[4] Shiller asked: "Why should home values in glamour cities increase forever?" To be sure, there is no way to increase the size of superstar cities like New York or London. But "in every case," Shiller writes, "there are vast amounts of land where a new city could be started," as has been done time and time again in the past. Private developers, Shiller points out, "tend to be ingenious at developing glamorous new areas from little towns within an hour's commute from major cities. It happens in so many places and so regularly that we take it for granted and rarely even notice it."

Shiller's analysis suggests that during the housing boom of the early 2000s, overall housing values appreciated to such a degree that by 2007 they had become completely misaligned with incomes.[5] He predicted that housing prices would fall anywhere from 30 to 50 percent by the end of the decade.

Maybe. But, housing is different from other investments, and for a very simple reason. The primary purpose of investing in a home is not to make money but to have a roof over one's head.

"This is the problem I have with the real-estate-equals-dotcom argument," Roger Lowenstein, former reporter for the *Wall Street Journal*, writes. "Most homeowners buy to have a place to live. If prices fall, they react precisely unlike stock traders; rather than bail out, they stay put longer. Every share of Cisco may be for sale every day, but every house is not."[6]

When times are bad, many homeowners simply sit tight. Housing markets seldom adjust through an instantaneous pop. Rather, they stagnate for many years until incomes catch up and demand grows so great that the cycle of rapid price appreciation starts over.

Karl Case, an economist at Wellesley College and Shiller's research partner, tracked more than 600 real estate listings in Boston during 2006 as prices began to decline. After four months, most of the houses had not sold, yet the sellers would still only lower their prices by 4 percent at most. Case's conclusion was that real estate is "stickier" than other financial assets. Shiller disagreed and called owners naive for thinking that real estate only goes up.

Cities are not interchangeable, as Washington, D.C.–based urbanist Ryan Avent points out.[7] Living and working in New York is nothing like living and working in a smaller place where only a few thousand people reside. Cities—especially well-established superstars like New York, or San Francisco, or London—have advantages in production and consumption other cities can't replicate. Moreover, newcomers to these places are likely to increase those advantages, not reduce them.

Additionally, Avent reminds us, it makes sense that a superstar citiy would act as a natural filter for residents who expect to see high returns to their education and skills. After all, individuals who expect to achieve smaller returns to their skill sets will not find it advantageous to locate in New York, especially if housing costs are high. They'll go elsewhere, and the gap between New York's advantages and those in other cities will continue to widen. The clustering force and the superstar city work together to sort people geographically.

Why Colbert Got So Worked Up

As with any investment, the key to getting a great return on real estate is figuring out how to identify the hotspots in advance. Real estate developers and investors have been interested in my indices of city and regional performance—like the bohemian index and the gay index—for years. Albert Ratner, cochairman of the board at Forest City Enterprises, one of the biggest real estate companies in the world, likes to remind me that he alone has promoted *The Rise of the Creative Class* enough to secure its spot on the bestseller list. Another real estate investor once said of my work, "You have provided a map of where to invest." That was hardly what I had intended, but it is nonetheless true: by their very nature, my regional indicators identified real estate hotspots.

Intrigued by the correlation, I decided to take a closer look. In winter 2007, Charlotta Mellander and I examined how various regional factors—amenities and population, among others—might shape housing prices.[8] According to economic theory, these prices are set at the intersection of supply (the availability of housing units) and demand (determined by wages and income). In places where new homes can be built relatively easily, supply will increase to meet demand, and prices will stay more or less stable. But if highly desirable areas or places with complex or strict zoning rules experience a rise in resident incomes, prices will increase and values will appreciate.

Superstar cities command a premium because of their extremely limited supply of housing. There is no single national real estate market, and there are many reasons why certain places are more expensive than others. Regions that attract highly educated and high-earning households tend to experience high demand for housing, especially from people willing to pay extra to live there. Regions with concentrations of high-tech, high-growth industries are also likely to see housing prices exceed income gains, as a 2002 study of Silicon Valley reveals.[9]

Areas with more amenities and attractions, such as coastal locations, typically command higher real estate prices—a correlation pinpointed in 1982 by economist Jennifer Roback Morse, who found that amenities carried as much weight in determining housing prices as did land costs and wages.[10]

Other studies confirm this. In their research on the "Consumer City," Edward Glaeser and his colleagues found that in cities, housing prices tend to rise faster than wages, suggesting that urban amenities, not high incomes, explain higher housing values.[11] Glaeser and his collaborators stated this in a simple formula: Urban Productivity Premium + Urban Amenity Premium = Urban Rent Premium.

But beautiful beaches, sidewalk cafes, and bicycle trails aren't the only indicators of a real estate hotspot.

"Want to know where a great place to invest in real estate will be five or ten years from now?" asked a 2007 *Business Week* article provocatively entitled "Bohemian Today, High-Rent Tomorrow."[12] "Look at where artists are living now." The article notes that sociologists and policymakers have long thought of artists, designers, musicians, and writers as urban pioneers— economic cure-alls who stimulate local economies and drive up neighborhood real estate values with their presence.

Regional economist Ann Markusen and her colleague call this phenomenon the artistic dividend.[13] Similarly, sociologists have shown how gentrification, frequently set in motion by artists, creatives, and gays, pushes up urban housing prices.

Yet artistic and gay populations are relatively small, and evidence of their relation to housing prices is limited. As of 2000, there were approximately 1.3 million bohemians in the United States, including everyone who works in arts, design, entertainment, and media occupations. That was only 1.3 percent of the entire U.S. workforce. There are 8.8 million self-identified gay and lesbian people in the United States, totaling roughly 4 percent of the country's adult population.

Can groups this small really be so highly associated with housing prices?

Mellander and I probed all of these factors and more in our study. We looked closely at the effects of high-tech industry, human capital, high-paid workers and occupations, wages and incomes, and artist, bohemian, and gay populations. We used statistical techniques to isolate the correlations between each of these factors on housing values as well as on each other across more than 300 U.S. metropolitan regions. The results are striking.

We found that two factors combine to shape housing values. The first is pretty obvious: income—the wealthier the residents, the pricier the housing. But the correlation was to wealth, not salaries. Wages alone, in the absence of capital gains and other earnings, had little relation to housing values. For that matter, neither did levels of education, human capital, the presence of a creative class, or the mix of occupations.

The second and much larger factor is reflected by our Bohemian-Gay Index, which combines the concentration of artists, musicians, and designers with the concentration of gays and lesbians in a region. Regardless of which variables we applied, what version of the model we used, or which regions we looked at, the concentration of bohemians and gays consistently had a substantial correlation with housing values.

Many people believe that gays and lesbians do not cause growth but are merely drawn to certain types of places. By using path models (advanced statistical tools that relate independent, intermediary, and dependent variables), we were able to isolate the relationships between the bohemian and gay populations and other factors on housing values and on each other.

Our initial findings were on target. We found that the presence of these populations had a direct relation to housing values as well as other locational variables (such as income and human capital), making these places more attractive to other populations and demographics. In other words, the presence of these groups was not only related to higher housing values, *but higher incomes* as well.

Why would this be? Our theory is that bohemian and gay populations capitalize on two distinct factors of high-value housing.

The first is an aesthetic-amenity premium. Artists and bohemians not only produce amenities but are attracted to places that have them. As selective buyers with eyes for amenity, authenticity, and aesthetics, they tend to concentrate in places in which those things abound.

The second is a tolerance or open culture premium. Regions with large bohemian and gay populations possess low cultural barriers to entry, allowing them to attract talent and human capital across racial, ethnic, and other lines. Artistic and gay populations also cluster in communities that value open-mindedness and self-expression.

And, their status as historically marginalized groups means that artistic and gay populations tend to be highly self-reliant and receptive to newcomers. They've had to build networks from scratch, mobilize resources independently, and create their own organizations and firms.

For all of these reasons, regions in which artists and gays have migrated and settled are more likely than others to place high premiums on innovation, entrepreneurship, and new firm formation. It's not that gays and bohemians drive up housing simply by paying more; their effect on housing prices is far less direct. Bohemian and gay residents drive up housing value because they make areas that were already ripe for growth even more desirable, and to a greater number of people.

When a Place Gets Boring . . .

As usual, not everyone benefits from this kind of growth. Housing in certain U.S. superstar cities has become prohibitively expensive for all but the truly wealthy. The least affordable places in the country include coastal cities, such as New York, San Francisco, San Diego, and Los Angeles, a host of high-tech university towns, and elite resort destinations, according to measures developed by Kevin Stolarick. Experts and financial advisers have long recommended that housing consume 25 to 30 percent of a person's total income, but in these places, some people devote half or more of their earnings to paying for their homes.

My research with Mellander highlights what's behind the affordability problem. Housing has become disconnected from local wealth-building, local productivity, and local economic development. According to our findings, the key determinants of housing prices are income, human capital, and concentrations of bohemian or gay populations, rather than local wages or local occupations. Income, unlike wages, follows the person who owns it. For example, there are a lot of rich people in regions like southern Florida, but chances are they made their money elsewhere. The problem is not the local labor market generating too much demand. Rather, it's the combination of desirability and increased mobility that drive housing prices out of reach.

Escalating real estate prices can inhibit innovation. Many forms of innovative and creative activity—whether they are new high-tech businesses, art galleries, or musical groups—require the same thing: cheap space. That's what Jane Jacobs was getting at when she famously wrote: "New ideas require old buildings." These spaces, formerly abundant in places like Silicon Valley, San Diego, Cambridge, Massachusetts, and downtown New York City, are where everyone from Steve Jobs to Bob Dylan got their start. Cheap space in these towns is now hard to come by. Several Silicon Valley garages that witnessed high-tech start-ups in the 1990s have been turned into museums. When housing prices rise and buildings are converted into expensive condos or high-end retail shops, venues for fostering creativity disappear.

Extreme real estate prices also hinder the ability of places to attract and amass new talent. Thirty years ago, a young researcher at MIT, Stanford University, or the University of California at San Diego could find affordable housing near campus. Today, it is hard to imagine how a young scientist could afford to buy a house within a ten-mile radius of any of those schools. I know *professors*—midcareer people in their forties with families—who cannot buy in. They're forced to move from apartment to apartment as their rentals turn into condos. When creative, productive regions become the province of affluent people who have already made their money (usually elsewhere), the cycle of local wealth building falls apart. At that point, Jacobs once presciently told me, "When a place gets boring, even the rich people leave."

And yet, somehow, these places survive. That is partly due to the efforts some universities have made to provide housing for their own. Other people are simply willing to devote disproportionate shares of their income to live where they want or to double and triple up with roommates in order to cut costs. There are the regional productivity gains that come from the colocation of talented and creative people. And of course certain industries, such as finance and high-tech, promise compensation so great that their workers can afford to live in places like New York City and Silicon Valley.

When I asked a high-ranking official at a leading investment bank if rising Manhattan real estate prices were affecting his firm's ability to attract talent, he said simply: "We're the cause, not the effect, of the real estate market." This doesn't mean that such places aren't paying a price. While Manhattan remains a place where creative markets are located, the actual production of creative and innovative work is moving beyond city limits to the outer boroughs, nearby cities in New Jersey, and even downtown Philadelphia.

An even bigger danger lies in the ways housing markets can thwart mobility. Tim Hartford, author of *The Undercover Economist*, recently asked in his regular *Slate* column: Why do some people "still live in Detroit, which has suffered so much? Why not move to Chicago or New York?"[14] He cites a study by British economist Andrew Oswald which found that home ownership can essentially trap people, especially those who are not well off.[15] Across both the United States and Europe, Oswald found, high levels of home ownership are correlated with high levels of unemployment, and more so than with other factors such as unionization or welfare benefits. Other research, Hartford points out, indicates that while homeowners and nonhomeowners are able to find work in the same amount of time, non-homeowners are far less resistant to commuting longer distances for that work.

Real estate limits mobility. "Houses do not walk"—that's the way one economist put it. The availability of housing simply does not correlate with economic opportunity. "No matter how bad things get in Detroit or Treorchy [Wales], the houses will still be there, and if they are cheap enough, people will want to live in them," Hartford writes. "The likely result is a gloomy sort of segregation: those who feel that they can find a good job in the boom cities will move there and pay the higher rents. Those who are less confident of that would rather have no job in a cheap house than no job in an expensive house." This simple fact ensures that declining cities "will have residents for a long time to come."

In this respect, the way we house people today seems a bit out of sync with other demands of our highly mobile and flexible economy. The United States has long prided itself on being a nation of homeowners. We boast that more than 60 percent of Americans own their homes. We encourage young people to save enough to buy one of their own. We provide all sorts of public in-

centives—from tax write-offs on mortgage interest to public investments in infrastructure—to encourage home ownership. It
is, after all, the centerpiece of the American dream.

I can't help but wonder whether this dream doesn't belong to
a bygone industrial era. A central element of the creative economy is its flexibility. People change jobs often. Companies outsource tasks. Technology enables us to work from places we
never could before. An increasing number of individuals and
businesses find their mobility a necessity for taking advantage of
new opportunities. Strangely, our system of home ownership
dramatically limits mobility, and in a country where nearly two-
thirds of residents are tied to their houses, this means that the
economy will suffer.

The creative age may well require alternative forms of housing—something between ownership and renting. In many markets today, it makes more financial sense to rent rather than
own. But rental options can be limited, and renovating a rental
apartment to suit your taste can be pricey. One option might be
to follow the lead of commercial real estate developers and
managers who often build out office space to owner specifica-
tions in exchange for a long-term commitment. As we've seen,
there are many reasons to live in a superstar or hotspot city, but
wanting to own a home should not necessarily be among them.

PART III

THE GEOGRAPHY
OF HAPPINESS

9
SHINY HAPPY PLACES

WE HAVE ALWAYS MEASURED HUMAN PROGRESS IN material terms. Success is registered in wealth. A family's social status is defined by its house and cars; a country's development is gauged by its gross domestic product; a city's by the economic opportunities it provides for its residents. This doesn't make us shallow people. Material wealth has been crucial to our survival and growth as a species since time immemorial.

But as Aristotle observed, human beings seek happiness above all else. A growing interest in the psychology of happiness—or, as psychologist Martin Seligman put it in a 2005 *Time* magazine cover story, the "enabling conditions that make human beings flourish"—has brought an abundance of new research and coverage to the subject.[1] Some might call this new concern a by-product of our narcissistic age. From the confluence of Internet sites like "MySpace" and "YouTube" to *Time*'s 2006 "Person of the Year" cover, which featured a mirror with the word *YOU* underneath it, we as a society have become preoccupied with ourselves and our happiness. For better or worse, that is unlikely to change.

Those who study happiness argue that while money and material progress remain important, those things alone cannot guarantee true satisfaction. "Measures of wealth or health do not tell the whole story of how society as a whole, or particular populations within it are doing," says Princeton University's Daniel Kahneman, who won a Nobel Prize in 2002 for his pioneering studies in behavioral economics.[2] Most who study happiness say that true well-being comes from social relationships—close and loving relationships with family and friends, and from doing work that has purpose and that you are passionate about.

In his captivating bestseller *Stumbling on Happiness*, Harvard psychologist Daniel Gilbert writes that "most of us make at least three important decisions in our lives: where to live, what to do, and with whom to do it."[3] He happens to list the "where" question first. But like most who study happiness, his book mostly focuses on the "what" and the "who."

Gilbert and other happiness researchers have mainly ignored the "where." But it's clear that many elements of a happy life—how much we make, how much we learn, how healthy we are, how stressful we feel, the job opportunities we have, and the people we meet—are in large part determined by where we live. Place plays a fundamental role in our endeavors to be happy. In many ways, it is the precursor to everything else.

This chapter and the next show how where we live affects our ability to lead happy and fulfilled lives. Drawing from a large-scale Place and Happiness Survey I conducted with the Gallup Organization, this chapter shows how much the place we live matters to our overall happiness, while the next one outlines the things we truly value—and that make us truly happy—in the places we live.

Finding Happiness

There's one thing happiness researchers agree on: money alone does not buy happiness. In wealthier countries, where many citizens already enjoy a relatively high quality of life, individuals tend to seek satisfaction through less tangible things such as personal fulfillment, self-actualization, pleasure, and positive emotion. Seligman and Edward Diener explain this in their comprehensive review of hundreds of studies in the field. "Because goods and services are plentiful and because simple needs are largely satisfied in modern societies," they write, "people today have the luxury of refocusing their attention on the 'good life'—a life that is enjoyable, meaningful, engaging and fulfilling."[4] They note that "people rank happiness and satisfaction ahead of money as a life goal" and go on to suggest that advanced countries should account for well-being in the way that they account for income and economic output. If there is GDP for gross domestic product, why not a GNH for "gross national happiness"?

Happiness is surely associated with income—but only up to a point. People in wealthier countries are generally happier than those in the poorest ones. But after a certain threshold of income is crossed, the effect of money and material goods on happiness levels out. Higher levels of income or economic growth do not necessarily translate into higher levels of happiness. Proof of this is in the United States, where GNP has risen substantially since the 1940s and 1950s while the national level of happiness has remained virtually constant.

According to careful studies of the subject, happiness seems to level off, or at least increase much more slowly, once yearly incomes reach about $10,000 per person. That's not a lot of money. Also surprisingly, when researchers look at individuals rather than nations, they find that when happiness does increase with income, the correlation is relatively small.

Other studies suggest that while the correlation between money and happiness is real, conventional wisdom has it backward. It is not that people with more money are happier; it's that happier people may be better earners: "Part of the typical correlation between income and well-being," write Diener and Seligman, "is due to well-being causing higher incomes, rather than the other way around. Happy people go on to earn higher incomes than unhappy people." Unhappy people tend to channel their time and effort into the pursuit of material goods. They become materialistic, missing out on the relationships and experiences that researchers believe have the greatest effect on personal fulfillment. A new car, a new set of golf clubs, a new handbag, or even a new house makes its owner only temporarily happy. The car gets scratched, the handbag goes out of style, the basement develops a leak. Experiences and relationships, even with their ups and downs, tend to bring longer lasting returns than any one material thing.

If not money, what are the things that genuinely make us happy?

According to research, a vibrant social life is one. People who do things they enjoy with people they like are happier than others.

Good physical and mental health is another. Not surprisingly, people who suffer from depression and other mental illness report far lower levels of well-being.

A large part of happiness hinges on the quality of one's personal bonds. Loving relationships with a spouse or significant other, with children, and a high frequency of meaningful interactions with family members and friends, are essential to one's happiness. Studies find that on balance, married people are happier than single people. Religion and faith can also have a highly positive effect.

Happiness is related to one's job, though again, it's the substance of the work not the pay that appears to matter.

The Place Connection

Place is the missing link in happiness studies. That is surprising, since so many people take a great deal of joy and fulfillment from where they live. The closest most studies get to the "where" factor is to examine the negative effects of commuting. Generally speaking, commuting is one of the things in life that makes us most unhappy.

But even researchers who look at commuting often miss a key connection: in spite of its negative effects, people do it anyway. According to a 2007 article in the *New Yorker*, about one in every six American workers commutes more than forty-five minutes to and from work; and "extreme commuters"—those who travel at least ninety minutes each way—are the fastest growing category.[5] Why would people do this to themselves? The obvious answer is that they aren't able or willing to move their home closer to work, and at the same time they aren't able or willing to work where they live. Either way, it's clear that the choice or the need to commute is grounded in place. Something—keeping a good job, sleeping somewhere (or close to someone) you love, working in a stimulating environment, staying close to aging parents—makes all that driving worth it. But no studies I'm aware of have systematically probed why place remains a decisive factor in our subjective well-being.

In partnership with the Gallup Organization, I undertook a major study of the subject, which I refer to as the Place and Happiness Survey. We divided happiness into four basic categories. Three of them we took from leading happiness studies—happiness in personal life, happiness on the job, and financial happiness. To these three categories we added a fourth: *happiness with one's place.* The survey asked people direct questions about their level of satisfaction with their communities; about their experiences and expectations in those communities; about their intentions to move or stay; and whether they would recommend their community to a friend or relative.

Then we zeroed in on the elements of place that might affect community satisfaction and overall well-being, asking questions about the job market, schools, health-care, arts and culture, parks and open space, and many other factors. (More on this in the next chapter.) We ended up posing more than 100 questions on every aspect of happiness and community satisfaction we could imagine. We pretested the survey and did a detailed statistical analysis to ensure that we would elicit answers that accurately reflected the concepts and theories we wanted to examine. The first survey, conducted in the summer of 2005, raked in 2,300 responses from people in twenty-two U.S. cities. A follow-up survey done a year later covered a much larger group—more than 27,000 people across some 8,000 communities nationwide. That diverse sample reflected a full range of incomes, occupations, ages, races and ethnicities, household types, sexual orientations, and educational levels.

Our findings show the overwhelming importance of place to our happiness. Place forms the third leg in the triangle of our well-being, alongside our personal relationships and our work. When asked to rate happiness in relation to things like work, finances, personal life, and place on a 1-to-5 scale, place scored 3.63, behind personal life (4.08) and work (3.98) but ahead of finances (3.46).

To more accurately gauge how these factors interact, Irene Tinagli of Carnegie Mellon and I conducted a multivariate statistical analysis that included measures of place satisfaction, job satisfaction, financial satisfaction, and a sense of safety and stress, as well as control variables for demographic factors such as age, race, gender, and income.

Together, according to Tinagli's analysis, place, financial, and job satisfaction accounted for a quarter of the total variance in overall life satisfaction—a substantial amount statistically speaking. This becomes even clearer when we realize that all of the demographic factors taken together, including income, account for only 1.2 percent of the variance in overall life-satisfaction.[6] The place we live in is more important to our happiness than education or even how much we earn.

All of this was further confirmed when we examined happiness from the other end of the telescope. High levels of depression or stress reflect low levels of well-being or satisfaction. By all accounts, stress is a significant issue in the United States and around the world. More than two-thirds (67 percent) of survey respondents reported at least moderate stress. Eleven percent described their stress as "extreme." But place barely registers as a source of stress. When asked to name what stressed them out, more than 30 percent of respondents said their jobs; 20 percent said finances; 13 percent said family; 10 percent said health; and 8 percent said crime. Only 3 percent identified their location alone as a source of stress in their lives. Out of all the possible factors, place ranked dead last.

Tinagli and I also looked at how factors such as income, education, age, and gender affect how happy we are with where we live. A close parsing of the survey data shows several clear trends.

- *Income:* Income in general has only a relatively small effect on how happy we are with our community.[7] But when we looked at specific income groups, it became clear that community satisfaction rises with income at least to a point. Only 43 percent of those making less

than $20,000 reported to be either satisfied or very
satisfied with their community. This rose to 56 percent
for those making $20–40,000; 65 percent for those in
the $40–60,000 range; 72 percent for those making
$60–100,000; and peaking at 77 percent for those
making $100–150,000 before falling off for the bracket
higher than that.

- *Homeownership:* Interestingly, while most people
  believe that homeownership is the core of the so-called
  American dream, renters, according to the survey
  results, are actually slightly more satisfied with their
  communities than homeowners.

- *Education:* Most studies find that education is closely
  correlated with professional and financial satisfaction.
  The more education people have, the more likely they
  are to feel professionally and financially satisfied. Tinagli
  also found a significant positive correlation between
  education and place satisfaction. Seventy-three percent of
  respondents with a graduate-level education and 68
  percent of college graduates reported being satisfied or
  very satisfied with their communities, compared with 57
  percent of those without a high-school degree and 63
  percent of those who had completed only high school.
  Conversely, those who lack high school education were
  more than twice as likely than those with graduate
  degrees to report being very unsatisfied or not satisfied
  with where they live (7 percent and 16 percent,
  respectively). People with higher levels of education have
  greater levels of mobility and choice in where they live.

- *Marital Status:* Married people are happier with the
  place they live. Sixty-nine percent of married people
  reported being either satisfied or very satisfied with the
  place in which they live, compared to 53 percent of

those who are separated and 60 percent of those who are divorced.

- *Age:* Older people on balance are happier with their communities: 71 percent of those over sixty-five years of age reporting being satisfied or very satisfied with their communities, compared to 65 percent of those twenty-five to forty-five and 56 percent of those under twenty-five.

- *Race:* Race has a significant effect on community satisfaction. Of all racial groups, Hispanics report the highest level of community satisfaction, followed by whites; African Americans report much lower levels of satisfaction with place.

Town and Country

With the correlation between place and happiness firmly under our belts, my team and I then looked into how various types of communities affect our well-being.

What we found is that different cities—and different kinds of communities—affect our happiness in different ways. Part of the reason is that our communities are not just physical places but homes to job markets and personal relationships. A couple of cities showed high rankings in all categories: Denver and Austin, for example. People in those communities report high levels of satisfaction with their personal lives, jobs, financial security, and the communities themselves.

Other communities were less well rounded, showing particular strength in one dimension over others. Respondents from such places as Washington, D.C.—where the first question at a cocktail party is more often "What do you do?" than "Where do you live?"—cited job satisfaction as the highest contributor to their overall happiness.

Other places house residents who derive an especially great proportion of their happiness from their personal lives. The place that stands out here, according to the Place and Happiness Survey, is New Orleans. Despite talk of its fraying social fabric, the people of New Orleans reported the highest level of satisfaction with their personal lives of any city in the original survey, completed just weeks before Hurricane Katrina hit.

But regions like these are big places. They are composed of various downtown, suburban, and ex-urban neighborhoods. Many people assume that people in suburbs or rural areas are happier than those in dense city centers, and a 2006 survey by the Pew Center found that, over all, this is in fact only slightly true.

But people can find happiness in all kinds of places. Some of us may find peace in the quiet pace of small town life, but plenty of others need the hustle and bustle of the big city to feel at home.

According to the Place and Happiness Survey, urban dwellers derive satisfaction from features that rural people may not value. While people who live in rural communities derive great satisfaction from clean air and natural beauty, urbanites tend to put a premium on schools, job opportunities, and safety. They value their ability to meet new colleagues and make new friends; they prize their access to diverse cultural resources such as theaters, museums, art galleries, live music, and vibrant nightlife filled with bars, clubs, and restaurants. They appreciate the availability of public transit; many city residents tell me that they would rather not use, or even own, cars. They also derive satisfaction from living in communities that are open to a wide range of groups—racial and ethnic minorities, immigrants, young people, and gays and lesbians. And, of course, there are other incentives for living in cities: Some people trade their big suburban house for an urban condo when the kids move away, or they decide to live closer to the city center. Or maybe their lifelong dream was always to live near all the action.

But here's the really interesting point: the Place and Happiness Survey shows that the majority of us are quite happy with where we have chosen to live.

On the question of whether they were merely "satisfied" or "very satisfied" with their communities overall, 68 percent of suburbanites, 67 percent of rural dwellers, and 64 percent of city residents responded affirmatively. More than half of all city residents (56 percent) and 57 percent of both suburbanites and rural residents ranked their communities as the "best" or "near-best" places to live.

When asked whether they would recommend their communities to their friends, 61 percent of suburbanites and 57 percent of city residents and rural residents, respectively, said they would.

Most respondents reported that they would be likely to stay put: 71 percent of city dwellers, 73 percent of suburbanites, and 78 percent of rural residents—the group most traditionally tied to their land. And even here, New Yorkers managed to blow all other respndents out of the water. Despite its reputation as a cold and anonymous place, it appears that New York pride—so evident to the entire world in the wake of the 9/11 tragedies—remains stronger than ever. Most of us—though not all of us—are finding the kinds of communities that seem to fit us.

In her analysis of the Place and Happiness Survey, Tinagli discovered that what we value about our communities is remarkably similar across the board, whether we reside in a city center, a suburb, or a rural area. To be sure, city residents and country dwellers experience their communities differently, but the psychological mechanisms that influence place happiness are pretty much the same. There seem to be three basic reasons for this.

First, place is a major source of excitement and creative stimulation, an essential component of our psychological well-being. The leading psychologist of creativity, Mihaly Csikszentmihalyi, has long argued that creative activities such as writing, playing music, computer programming, mountain climbing, and chess playing are major sources of enjoyment and productivity. Such activities, he says, put us in a state of "flow," or intense, unfettered focus and concentration.[8] The beauty of this state is that we can have fun and be productive. The most creative people tend to fluctuate between intense interaction and intense concentration. They also tend to be the happiest when engaging in a state of flow.

Csikszentmihalyi told me that the great physicist Freeman Dyson would often just sit in his office with his door open. To the casual observer, it appeared that he was doing nothing. But in fact Dyson was searching for the stimulation of interesting hallway conversation. After a week or two of absorbing the buzz, he would retreat behind closed doors to work alone on a new discovery. Creative places—an art scene in Brooklyn, for instance, or Silicon Valley's high-tech district—work in similar ways. They are filled with stimulating cultural offerings, great people to work with and watch, and invigorating outdoor scenes. There is abundant external stimulation to plug into and absorb, but there's also plenty of room for privacy and retreat.

My earlier research along with Ronald Inglehart's has documented the connection between creativity, self-expression, and economic development. But creativity and self-expression also go hand in hand with happiness and well-being. In her research on workplace performance, Teresa Amabile of Harvard Business School discovered that happiness leads to creativity—not vice versa.[9] Controlling for a wide variety of factors, Amabile and her team found that a positive mood could predict creative thinking and workplace innovation; they also found evidence that innovation leads to positive mood.

Finding a place that makes us happy has a powerful effect on our "activation." Such places encourage people to do more than they otherwise would, such as engage in more creative activities, invent new things, or start new companies—all things that are both personally fulfilling and economically productive. This kind of activation, Tinagli found, stems in large part from the visual and cultural stimulation that places can provide—parks and open space, cultural offerings, things she calls "symbolic amenities." This creates a regenerative cycle: the stimulation unleashes creative energy, which in turn attracts more high-energy people from other places, resulting in higher rates of innovation, greater economic prosperity, higher living standards, and more stimulation.

The second has to do with a sense of self. Generally speaking, people derive happiness from being themselves, from cultivating their individuality. Sociologists and psychologists have long pointed out that self-expression is a major source of happiness. A place is a means to that end. It gives us an environment we can adopt and make our own. An undeniable advantage of today's mobile society is that we are not forever tied to the identity of our birthplace—the handed-down norms and customs of our families, religions, and hometowns. We can, if we choose, recreate our identities based on the things that matter to us: work, lifestyle, personal interests, or activities. It might not be conscious, but we seek out places that fit our psychological needs in order to establish ownership over our lives.

The third reason is the flip side of the coin. Place gives us something to which we can belong, providing a sense of pride and attachment. Place offers us characteristics by which to define ourselves and a physical and figurative space in which to live. Some of us root for local sports teams; others are energized by a stunning natural environment; others from their neighbors.

The connection between place and identity is all around us. It's visible even across the bumpers of America's cars. When I first spotted stickers like MVY or ADKS on the back windows of cars, I had no idea what they meant. I also noticed that many of them didn't seem to match their owners' license plates. Then someone explained to me that they are abbreviations for place names (Martha's Vineyard and Adirondacks), most often favored vacation or second home destinations. Newcomers to Manhattan were incensed when the phone company gave them 917 and 646 area codes instead of the coveted 212. Their counterparts on the South Side of Chicago were similarly resentful when they became 773 instead of downtown's 312. Even when we relocate, many of us want to hang on to our old phone number, and not just for convenience; it becomes part of our identity.

Once we determine that a place fits us, we wear it as a badge of honor. Our pride of place comes through in song lyrics, too. Have you ever been to a concert in which the performer substitutes the current city's name for a familiar lyric? He can count on the crowd's roaring appreciation—unless he names last night's city by mistake.

Now that we have a handle on how place affects happiness in general, what is it about our places that we like and dislike? What are the big ticket, and small ticket, items that make us happy with communities—or not?

10

BEYOND MASLOW'S CITY

I N 1943, THE PSYCHOLOGIST ABRAHAM MASLOW SET FORTH the concept of a hierarchy of needs.[1] Maslow's theory, often illustrated in the shape of a pyramid, posits that humans require more than just food, water, air, and sex in order to be fulfilled. These rudimentary—or, "physiological"—needs constitute the base layer of the pyramid. Moving up the hierarchy we find the need for security; the need for love and belonging; the need for self-esteem; and, finally, the need for self-actualization. Only by fulfilling each of the first four layers—what Maslow calls the "deficiency needs," meaning the needs that arise because of deprivation—can we reach the top of the pyramid and fulfill our true potential.

By the time of his death in 1970, Maslow had concluded that his original theory of self-actualization—the method by which humans come to "be all they can be"—was not complete. He broadened the area of self-actualization to include our constant quest for knowledge and perpetual desire for aesthetics and beauty, and created an even higher level called "transcendence," during which people—having satisfied all previous needs—would feel compelled to help others in order to reach fulfillment. These higher-level needs have seemingly little to do with our physiological survival, but in a modern and affluent society, they inevitably shape our psychological development. They motivate us in all ways. They signify the key to a happy and fulfilled life.

The interesting thing is this: everyone seems to want the things promised by the top of the pyramid, regardless of whether prerequisite needs have been satisfied. Maslow's theory implies that fulfilling one level of needs was contingent on having satisfied the preceding one. In other words, before people can fulfill the need for self-esteem, they would have to have already satisfied their basic physiological needs and their need for security. But in a society in which the haves live next to the have-nots, no one sees the top of the pyramid as a luxury. Part of this has to do with the American dream, which in addition to life and liberty promises the pursuit of happiness for all. In this way, the process of self-actualization is viewed as a right, not something to be earned.

But somehow the conversation about place remains stuck in an either-or debate. Even in the face of our affluent, self-expression society, some urban experts and community leaders remain convinced that only basic needs matter. The key to a great community, they contend, lies in good schools, safe streets, and up-to-date infrastructure. Anything else—parks, trails, museums, or other amenities—is a luxury, aimed at the affluent, yuppies, and the privileged classes. Or they say it's something that comes only when a community is already rich. Jobs and basic services are what's needed to generate wealth and income. The rest is what we pay for with the resources so generated. As this chapter will show, they're wrong. The places that make us truly happy don't get trapped in any such tradeoff. They do it all, providing great schools, safe streets, and nice parks, to boot.

This chapter looks at what really matters to people in the places we live. To get beyond the posturing and sloganeering that has dominated the debate to this point, it uses the more than 27,000 responses from the Place and Happiness Survey to identify the key factors that underpin our happiness with place.

The survey covered dozens and dozens of specific community attributes, which we then clustered into five major categories.

- The first is *physical and economic security*—perceptions of crime and safety, the overall direction of the economy, and availability of jobs.
- The second is *basic services*—schools, health-care, affordable housing, roads, and public transportation.
- The third category is *leadership*—the quality and efficacy of elected and unelected (business and civic) leadership and the opportunity for public and local engagement.
- The fourth is *openness*—the level of tolerance for and acceptance of diverse demographic groups including families with children, ethnic and racial minorities, senior citizens, immigrants, and gays and lesbians.
- The fifth cluster is *aesthetics*—physical beauty, amenities, and cultural offerings.

Since the survey collected a wide range of demographic data, we also looked at how what we value in our places is affected by factors like income, education, occupation, age, race, and ethnicity.

What, then, are the things that matter most to Americans when it comes to their communities? While all five factors play important roles, two top the list: aesthetics and basic services, with openness coming in a reasonably close third. (For those who are so inclined, Appendix B summarizes the key statistical findings from the survey.) As we will see, there's no tradeoff here, at least in the minds of the more than 27,000 respondents to the Place and Happiness Survey. It goes without saying that each of these categories matters a great deal.

The Beauty Premium

While our findings on the importance of aesthetics in our communities—their physical beauty and outdoor space—may at first seem controversial, it actually makes a great deal of sense. Most people expect their communities will provide basic services, and most communities do. And as our survey shows, they value basic services highly.

But aesthetics also matter a great deal. The higher people rate the beauty of their community, its physical environment, and recreational offerings, the higher their overall level of community satisfaction. And because we expect our basic services to be provided, we end up valuing aesthetics a little higher. It's analogous to buying a car. When there were huge differences in quality, people gravitated to cars that were high on quality ratings. But now most people expect cars to have a threshold level of quality, so they gravitate to designs, styles, types, and options they like.

In her book *The Substance of Style* and other writings, Virginia Postrel provides powerful insight into the economic appeal and value of aesthetics.[2] "Given a modicum of stability and sustenance," Postrel writes, "people enrich the look and feel of their lives through ritual, personal adornment, and decorated objects." Even primitive people who scavenged for food and lived in caves found ways to adorn their bodies with jewelry and cosmetics and decorate their abodes with baskets and pottery.

Postrel argues that the instinct to make something "special" is not only "emotionally and sensorially gratifying" but also part of a universal and innate desire that all human beings experience.

Barbara Steinfeld was living in Florida in the mid-1990s when she lost her job as a private marketer for the state's tourism industry. While she thought she lived in a tourism mecca in Orlando, she could not find a comparable job despite her best efforts. She had conversations with her husband about where they would most like to live. She had always wanted to move to Oregon, even though she had visited only once for a few days twenty years earlier. Soon after, she came across a job posting for a cultural tourism director at the Portland visitors' bureau, and she described having a eureka moment. "It is what I would love to do in a place I would love to do it." From the moment she took the job, Oregon felt like "putting on an old Birkenstock." She fell in love with "the energy, the unpretentious atmosphere, the natural beauty, the pervasive arts, the involvement of the community in every decision, the superb cuisine." She also loves the climate—"never too hot or too cold, always breathable, fresh and green." And the city's neighborhoods were walkable and the streets felt alive. "I felt like I was on vacation every day walking around for lunch downtown for the first five years." All her life she had lived in places like Florida and the Midwest, where she felt like a "square peg in a round hole." Now she feels truly comfortable for the first time in a place "big enough to have a thriving Jewish community, a gay community, an arts scene, an urban center, great tax-free shopping," and, thanks to urban growth limits and abundant green space, "small enough to feel like a neighborhood."

So what is it about aesthetics that makes us satisfied and happy with our communities? To get why aesthetic beauty resonated so deeply with these residents, the Place and Happiness Survey asked respondents to rank all aspects of their location's physical environment—its overall beauty; its outdoor parks, playgrounds, and trails; even its climate and air quality. We then compared these ratings with people's satisfaction with the community. The results are intriguing. The physical beauty of our communities is the one that matters the most. It's followed by outdoor parks, playgrounds, and trails. Climate and air also matter but are less important than the first two.

So did Maslow have it all wrong? Not entirely, argues Postrel. When his theory is portrayed as a simple pyramid, it can lead to a false conclusion: "That aesthetics is a luxury people only care about when they're wealthy." Postrel points out that there is no pyramid of needs in which moving up requires that one first completely satisfy the needs under it. "The next increment of what we consume changes depending on what we already have . . . The marginal value of some characteristic, such as nutrition or shelter, is high initially—we don't want to starve or freeze to death in a snow storm—but that value drops off faster than the marginal value of other characteristics, including aesthetics." Human beings crave physical beauty. We look for it in so many of the things that surround us, and especially in the places we live.

Economists call this the "beauty premium." People are drawn to and pay more for that which is more aesthetically pleasing. Just consider how much attention home sellers—and home buyers—pay to a house's curb appeal. A 2007 study by economists in Britain and The Netherlands looked for patterns in the appearance of players eliminated from a Dutch TV game show.[3] It found that the beauty premium extends beyond objects. As much as there is a bias toward beautiful people, there is an even greater bias against unattractive people. Even when there appeared no relevant reason to discriminate against the less attractive players, the researchers found that attractive players were "substantially less likely to be eliminated" and that the least attractive player was "almost twice as likely to be eliminated at the end of the first round than any other player." Less attractive players, the study concluded, "are discriminated against, for reasons that are uncorrelated with their performance or behavior during the game." If it is human nature to distance ourselves from unattractive people, despite the psychological damage that such discrimination may inflict, it's hardly surprising that we would treat our communities and their physical surroundings any differently.

In this vein, some people say that the Rustbelt cities may as well pack it in here. How can Pittsburgh or Cleveland compete with places like San Francisco, Seattle, Boulder, or Austin when it comes to beauty, ambiance, natural scenery, and outdoor recreation? Thankfully for Pittsburgh and Cleveland, there is more to aesthetics than pretty parks and mountain vistas. Many older communities have a wonderful mix of natural features and industrial-age buildings. They are filled with old warehouses, historic homes, and terrific neighborhoods. Many have magnificent urban park systems hand-crafted by great landscape designers of the nineteenth and early twentieth centuries.

Having lived in Pittsburgh for nearly two decades, I am a fan of the industrial aesthetic. I found the juxtaposition between the city's three beautiful rivers and its rugged, old, industrial landscape incredibly appealing. Some of my fondest memories of Pittsburgh are of bike riding through the city's industrial corridors and up into its hilly suburbs and exurbs, where climbing skills are really put to the test. Pittsburgh may not be everybody's cup of tea, but my experience living there is a testament to the idea that every place holds appeal for somebody.

Chicago's lakefront renaissance—its incredible twentieth-century architecture and marvelous refurbished neighborhoods—illustrates how older communities can highlight their own brand of aesthetics. Much of this is due to the efforts of

Mayor Richard Daley, who has reached out beyond landmarks like the new millennium park and the improved lakefront to bolster many of the city's neighborhoods by refurbishing smaller community parks and gardens, planting trees, installing public art, and adding hand-painted benches and flower beds.

I recall driving through one such neighborhood on my way to a seminar at the University of Chicago. When my host, Terry Clark, pointed out to me that we were driving through a lower income community, I was perplexed: the lush tree canopy, improved streetscape, and community parks had the visual characteristics even I had come to associate with more affluent communities. At that minute it dawned on me that what made less advantaged communities look "poor" was more often than not their denuded streetscape—a complete lack of trees and green space.

And while many people prefer their place neat and manicured, what I love about Toronto is its "messy urbanism"—highrise condos next to ramshackle Victorians, luxury boutiques next to mom-and-pop shops, sylvan streets than run smack into highly trafficked commercial routes, stunning ravines that cut through dense urban neighborhoods, bike commuters sharing the road with street cars, buses, and luxury sedans.[4]

People Meeting People

Not surprisingly, it turns out that the ability to meet people and make friends is one of the most important factors in determining how happy we are with our communities.

Unfortunately, a growing number of us lack this capability in our lives. A study conducted in 2006 by a team of sociologists from the University of Arizona and Duke University found that the share of Americans who feel socially isolated in their communities (defined by having no one to talk to about personal matters) increased from 10 percent in 1985 to more than 25 percent in 2004.[5] The study found that highly educated middle-class families have been hit hardest, possibly as a consequence of longer commutes and working hours. The authors note that people are spending more time "interacting with multiple computers in the home, instead of with each other." But the biggest change since 1985, the study reports, has been the momentous decline in ties between neighbors. An increasing number of people live alone, and many of them lack friends or family nearby.

That explains why so many people interviewed say they wish they lived in a community that made it easier for them to connect with others and form new relationships. Those who have friends where they live value what they've got. Just ask any group of young singles who live and act together in what author Ethan Watters has dubbed "urban tribes."[6]

It's ironic that a by-product of a globalized world is increased isolation. Little wonder that participants in the Place and Happiness Survey placed such a high value on meeting people and making friends.

Culture Vultures

There is a growing movement in cities around the world to invest in culture as a way of improving their reputations and spurring economic growth. The Place and Happiness Survey found that while not quite as important as physical beauty and sociability, culture and nightlife do play a significant role in place satisfaction.

People today have a broader view of culture than what I've affectionately termed the *SOB*—symphony, opera, and ballet. While those cultural forms remain appealing to many, the most vibrant artistic and cultural communities combine traditional high-culture institutions with street-level art, music, and theater scenes. In a society where many people have little control over their own schedules, time has become one of our scarcest resources. Previous generations seemingly had more time for regular extracurricular activities. Today, it's virtually impossible to plan in advance. Still, even if we lack the flexibility or freedom to fill our schedules with fun events, people like knowing they could go out and do something if they wanted to. The fact that such opportunities are there for the taking—when inspiration strikes or when family and friends come for a visit—is sufficient for many of us.[7]

It All Comes Down to the Basics

Basic services also matter a great deal to our happiness and satisfaction with our communities. The higher people ranked their community's basic services, the higher their satisfaction with that community. At the risk of being redundant, I want to point out again that the findings of the Place and Happiness Survey indicate that there is no tradeoff between aesthetics and basic services: both are important to how happy we are with where we live.

The survey asked people to evaluate several aspects of their communities' infrastructure—its primary and secondary schools, colleges, and universities; its health-care facilities; its job opportunities; its traffic and public transportation options; its housing; and its religious resources.

Of all those factors, primary and secondary schools play the biggest role in community satisfaction. People in a community depend on accessibility to local primary and secondary schools for their children's education; college-aged children are more able to travel greater distances for higher education.

One of the more surprising findings to come out of the Place and Happiness Survey is that people who place the most value on proximity to colleges and universities are, interestingly enough, those with lesser amounts of formal education. One explanation might be that they value the example or aspiration such institutions set for their children. Or maybe they view such institutions as possible options for their own continued education. Or perhaps it is simply because they (and their children) are less mobile, requiring that all access to education—primary through higher—be close by and thus more affordable.

Health-care ranks next: it's a prerequisite to happiness. It is followed closely by the availability of jobs. Not just any job, but a job in one's chosen field. But most communities seem to be doing a poor job of sufficiently meeting that need. According to the survey, just over 17 percent of respondents rated their satisfaction with job opportunities as "very good"; more than a third rated their communities in this respect as "bad" or "very bad." That suggests a potential disconnect between places people want to be in and the kinds of work they would prefer to do. To my mind, this is a key issue—and tradeoff—all of us need to be aware of in choosing a place to live and work.

Religion and spirituality also matter. While a striking 80 percent of survey respondents registered satisfaction ("good" or "very good") with their access to religious and faith-based institutions, we found a reasonable, but not overwhelming, association between religious resources and community happiness.

Communities differ substantially in their religious devotion, though residents of more highly educated populaces (such as Seattle and San Francisco, and unlike those of New Orleans and Detroit) tend to lead more secular lifestyles, opting to forego church for less traditional methods of spiritual or religious practice.

This has not gone unnoticed—as online forums on the topic prove—and many religious leaders and community activists are trying to readjust their agendas to allow for such demographic shifts. One such person, a man named Rod Garvin whom I met at my team's Creative Community Leadership initiative in Charlotte, North Carolina, posted the following questions on his personal blog:

> Are Christians as a whole ready to tackle some tough and uncomfortable questions? What happens when society becomes more accepting of gays and lesbians than the church? Racism and ethnic separation is a global problem, but churches are far more segregated than most corporations and many neighborhoods. Poverty and low wages are driven by economic structures and policies, though personal choices can play a role. Do we have the courage to ask if our capitalist economy can be made better and turn scarcity into abundance?

Creative people, Garvin bemoaned, are leaving organized religion for less hierarchical and more organic forms of spirituality and spiritual expression. And for reasons similar to those at work in other large-scale organizations, organized religions are having great trouble responding to that shift in a forward-looking way. What he told me is that religious groups need to become less "institutional"—formal and rigid—and become creative communities themselves—flexible and responsive to people's spiritual needs as well as their intellectual curiosity.

The Place and Happiness Survey indicates that factors like housing affordability, traffic, and public transportation play a smaller role in community satisfaction overall. However, in cities where housing is very expensive and traffic is bad, they come into play in a big way. More than a third of survey respondents were concerned by the high price of housing in their communities. And 45 percent of respondents said they were dissatisfied with the public transportation options at their disposal. The greatest proportion of these responses came from regions that have experienced sustained growth in recent years and boast high levels of human capital—the means metros discussed in Chapter 5, such as San Francisco and Washington, D.C.

Many people are forced to make a trade-off between location and affordable housing. Such is the case of Tara Beard, who moved to her neighborhood, Midtown Phillips in Minneapolis, because of its affordable housing. "A lot of people don't understand why I live where I do," Beard says. "It is probably the second toughest neighborhood in Minneapolis, and living there can be challenging, frustrating, and scary." But "the price was right."

She adds that she just cannot understand how her coworkers making less than her can possibly afford homes three times the cost of the one she lives in with her family. "We make just under $100,000 a year and spend 30 percent of our income on our mortgage, escrow, and utilities. And that's living in a fixer-upper in a rough neighborhood. The imbalance between housing costs and income levels is astounding. For me, keeping up with the Joneses is less important than living within my means."

Beard and her family are happy with their location on a regional bike trail, less than two miles from her downtown office, and less than a mile from every kind of store she needs. It's close to bus and light rail stops, and the neighborhood is diverse.

"I want to make sure that every day I see someone that looks and acts different than me," Beard says, "to make sure I have the informal interactions with people that I believe help ward away the fear of differences and the tendency to look the other

way. I think it's every person's responsibility to expose themselves to as many different ways of life as possible. It's part of
being a good community member and a contributing citizen. I
hear Spanish or Somali languages spoken in my neighborhood
as often, if not more, than English. I have no doubt in my mind
that this country and all it has to offer belongs to all of us
equally."

But her neighborhood does have its drawbacks. "We frequently hear gunshots, and our lives have been threatened
when we've stood up to drug dealers in the house next door.
The worst thing is the noise," she says. "Honking cars at all
hours of the night, people shouting and whistling up and down
the block while we're trying to sleep. We rarely get to sleep
through the night. I can't walk around my block without seeing a
few prostitutes soliciting and dealers up to no good."

Even so, she adds, living there is worth it. "To me it's a win-
win: I save money, do my part to make the world a better place,
get where I need to go quickly and in a sustainable way, learn all
about different kinds of people, learn about myself and how I
face challenges and fear."

Open City

Gwenn Seemel was born in France and has traveled widely but
ultimately came to settle in Portland. "I dress colorfully," says
Seemel, "and by that I mean both brightly and strangely. I wear
plastic clogs in lime or teal. My sweaters are ordered from old
lady catalogs because I can't find that particular shade of ultra-
marine anywhere else. My scarves and hats are mostly knitted
by my failing grandmother, so that a would-be pointy Peruvian
hat becomes a crocheted head condom with dog ears. My
denim pants aren't blue, but instead paint-dyed to go from yel-
low at my hips to magenta at the cuffs."

When she's in Paris, Seemel says, "people stare at those pants, sneer, and make some snide comment to their companions—and they do so audibly because someone dressed like me couldn't possibly be French. Except that I am French. My cousins there refuse to take me clubbing unless they've approved my wardrobe beforehand." In New York, people are more polite, but hardly encouraging of her eccentric wardrobe. One of her New York friends told her that he'd only ever seen such a combination of colors once before—on a homeless man.

But in Portland, Seemel feels totally at ease with her unique style. "People look at my pants and their gaze travels up the rest of my body to my face, where they make eye contact with me. They smile at me and then laugh *with* me. Some even say 'nice pants.'"

This kind of openness has been a powerful draw for Portland, putting it on the map as an indie-rock Mecca, according to a 2007 article in *Slate* by Taylor Clark.[8] "Sonically," Clark writes, "there's not a whole lot that the twisty pop of the Shins has in common with the 'hyper-literate prog-rock' (to borrow a phrase from Stephen Colbert) of the Decemberists. And virtually none of these groups can be considered 'Portland bands' since, with very few exceptions, they all moved to town *after* gaining some level of fame. . . . You might see Sleater-Kinney drummer Janet Weiss parking her Volvo station wagon in front of Stumptown Coffee Roasters, for instance, but you seldom feel these luminaries exerting any influence on the local music landscape. They all just kind of live here. Which is why it's often quipped that Portland is the place where hipsters go to retire."

This last line is particularly telling. Clearly, if Portland itself isn't breeding the original talent, then there must be something about the community itself that inspires musicians to move there. Clark concludes that the most plausible explanation for the city's influx of rocker migrants is the same one that draws

people like Gwenn Seemel to Portland—its openness and creative vibe, its affordable real estate and aesthetic character. "You
can venture into public dressed like a convicted sex offender or
a homeless person, and no one looks at you askew," Clark writes.
"It's lush and green. Housing is affordable, especially compared
with Seattle or San Francisco. The people are nice. The food is
good. Creativity is the highest law. . . . It might not be enough to
lure the glitterati, but Portland's combination of affordability,
natural beauty, and laid-back weirdness is an independent
artist's dream."

Openness—defined by a communal sense of tolerance and
acceptance of diversity—is the third-ranked factor in the Place
and Happiness Survey. The survey probed openness through
the following questions: "How would you rate your city or area
as a place to live for the following kinds of people?"—

- families with children
- racial and ethnic minorities
- gay and lesbian people
- immigrants from other countries
- senior citizens
- people living below poverty
- young, single people
- recent college graduates looking for work

With every amount of tolerance extended to these groups, the
overall happiness in the community increased. This is not because we all value diversity as an abstract value. Many people are
drawn to open communities on the assumption that it is in those
places where they can most easily be themselves. This conforms
to the research of Ronald Inglehart, whose detailed World Values Surveys of more than fifty countries have found this value of
individual expression to be a defining element of today's society.[9]

And it's here that the Place and Happiness Survey generated another one of its most surprising findings. When people rated their city's openness to various groups, guess which group came in at the bottom of the list? Not immigrants. Not racial or religious minorities. Not gays and lesbians. At the very bottom of the list, alongside "people living below the poverty line," are young recent college graduates looking to enter the job market. That's right. Young, educated folks looking for work. Nearly 45 percent of survey respondents said that their communities were either "bad" or "very bad" places for recent college graduates, while just 7.3 percent said they were "very good."

I find this amazing. All around the country and around the world, I hear community leaders, mothers and fathers worried about losing their young people. When I lived in Pittsburgh, people often bemoaned the fact that the region's biggest export was no longer steel but its talented youngsters. Mayors and chambers of commerce are all too eager to recruit them back after they have spent some time away, getting some skills or sowing their oats, and are ready to settle down and raise a family.

There are several reasons for this seemingly bizarre finding. Young college grads bring new skills into the job market and that can make current workers nervous. They're single, stay up late, and like to have fun. To some people, that means noise and mischief. To others, it means changes in the status quo. That kind of mindset can easily be detected by young people. I heard this in the focus groups I conducted with graduating college seniors and graduate students in the early 2000s. And it's echoed in detailed studies by consultants Rebecca Ryan, Carol Coletta, and Joe Cortright, whose focus groups and interviews similarly find that young college graduates look for communities that will accept them for who they are. They look for lots of other young people around, signals of casual dress and energetic lifestyles, and importantly, the diversity of the overall population and the presence of gays and lesbians.

Openness is clearly a key factor in community satisfaction and in overall happiness, but unfortunately, many communities aren't experiencing much of either. Many survey respondents reported significant obstacles facing some of these groups.

Nearly 45 percent of survey respondents said that their communities were "bad" or "very bad" places for gays and lesbians. Some 40 percent said the same about immigrants. And more than half said that their communities were "bad" or "very bad" places for people living in poverty.

Clearly, there is room for considerable improvement on openness and diversity across these communities. It's not about tolerance for tolerance's sake. As my previous research has shown, places that are intolerant simply do not grow. And, as the Place and Happiness Survey confirms, people in intolerant places are less happy and less fulfilled than those in tolerant and open-minded ones.

Safe and Secure

When Robin Echtle, at age thirty-six, decided to take the great leap and buy a home, she did her homework. "I bought many books," she said, "and even took a first-time home buyer's class over two weekends with twelve other homeowner wannabes." The more difficult question was where to settle down. A self-described "city rat" with a preference for culture, arts, and the bustle of urban life, Robin was drawn to the two largest cities within commuting distance to Seattle: Everett and Tacoma.

A visit to Tacoma sold her on the excitement of the city. She loved the downtown, which at the time was being rebuilt: the "beautiful old buildings," the "quaint and funky" ethnic restaurants, the "three brand spanking new museums," the three historic theaters, the symphony, and most important to her, the opera. But what ultimately sold her on Tacoma was not its rich arts offerings, but the stability of the city. After doing the "math on the market," Echtle concluded that Tacoma—which had a better median income and more job growth than Everett—was the place she wanted to be.

Economic and physical security is the fourth dimension we examined; it includes the overall condition and direction of the economy, the nature and direction of the job market, and social conditions such as general safety. These are deep-seated characteristics that cannot be altered easily or quickly, and are not amenable to direct public or private action. Economic and physical security play an important role in community satisfaction, according to the survey findings, are just slightly less influential than openness.

Other studies have documented the role of aggregate economic growth in individual happiness. In his book *The Moral Consequences of Economic Growth,* the Harvard economist Benjamin Friedman shows how economic growth makes people more conscientious, less likely to commit crimes, more tolerant, and more generous.[10] Increased levels of happiness are also a by-product of such growth, while prolonged economic stagnation or decline can lead to the reverse.

Economic security seems to matter more to community happiness than physical security, according to the survey. (The statistical correlation between economic security and overall community happiness is considerably higher than that for physical security and is one of the highest in the entire survey.) Overall, more survey respondents reported that economic conditions were good than bad—40 percent said good or very good, while 29 percent rated them bad or very bad; the other 40 percent fell somewhere in between. A large share of survey respondents, 57 percent, report that they feel safe or very safe in their communities. Only 9.1 percent reported feeling very unsafe in their communities.

Leaders or Squelchers

Leadership is one of society's great intangible goods. Countless books have been written on the subject, but it remains hard to distill exactly what defines good leadership, how to fully distinguish it from bad leadership, and how to accurately gauge its effect on organizations, nations, and communities.

The Place and Happiness Survey probed the effects of leadership on general community happiness by asking residents for their approval ratings of the local leadership in their area. The correlation between leadership and community happiness, while significant, was on average the lowest of the five major categories.

Not surprisingly, the survey findings indicate that people are happier in cities in which the leadership is positive and forward-looking, with an emphasis on strong ethics and integrity. But the survey also found a sizable split in resident perceptions of leadership. While 60 percent of the survey respondents approved of the leadership in their communities, a staggering 40 percent disapproved. This may well reflect the partisan nature of today's society, in which voters appear to be more polarized than ever before.

But even in today's political climate, not all leaders are polarizing. In Denver, Colorado, approval of local leadership has topped 90 percent. I can understand why. John Hickenlooper, elected mayor in 2003, has become tremendously popular in his city, earning himself the distinction of being one of *Time* magazine's top five big city mayors in the United States after just two

years in office. He has worked hard to provide a positive vision
of the community and to harness the energy of residents across
the city. During his initial days in office, he even appointed his
opponent to the transition team to help make key appointments
to city government. Hickenlooper has succeeded in overcoming
partisan divisions and ideological stalemates, allowing him to focus on what's good for the entire community.

Unfortunately, leadership more often than not works in the
opposite direction by squashing civic energy. Jane Jacobs once
told me that communities everywhere are filled with creative
vigor, but that some of them are run by *squelchers*. Squelchers
are control freaks who think they know what's best for their city
or region, even as their leadership (or lack thereof) causes a
hemorrhage of bright, talented, and creative people. Squelchers, she said, are the kind of leaders that use the word "no" a lot.
They constantly put roadblocks in the way of community energy
and initiatives. I've seen firsthand how these squelchers drain
the life and energy from their communities. They respond to
new ideas with phrases like "That's not how we do things here";
"That will never fly"; or "Why don't you just move someplace
you'll be happy?"

I often wonder what our nation would look like if all the
squelchers in our communities were to be suddenly—and magi-
cally—exposed and immobilized. Would there be anyone left at
the tops of many local governments? Perhaps then we could finally unleash the positive energy that real civic engagement
both inspires and needs.

Smart, Safe, and Green

My friend and colleague, the Dutch urban planner Evert Verha-
gen, likes to tell communities there is a new formula for success

in today's world. Where it was once enough to be "safe and smart," prosperous communities today need to be "smart, safe, and green." I'd add "fair" to his list.

His comments square with my team's analysis of the Place and Happiness Survey, which identifies the following big seven factors as being critical to community satisfaction: a good place to raise children, a good place to meet people and make friends, a place with physical beauty, good schools, parks and open space, a safe place, and a good place for entrepreneurs and new businesses.

And they are additionally confirmed by a statistical factor analysis that Tinagli conducted on all twenty-six dimensions of community satisfaction in the Place and Happiness Survey. Her analysis identified three clusters of factors that are key to our being happy in our communities.

The first cluster includes things that make a community *smart and vibrant*—local universities and colleges, arts and culture, vibrant nightlife, availability of job opportunities in one's field, being a good place to meet people, and being a good place for young college grads, singles, entrepreneurs, artists, and scientists.

The second revolves around *aesthetics and liveability,* and is made up of physical beauty; parks, open space, playgrounds, and trails; climate, and air quality.

The third boils down to essentially *equity* and includes affordable housing, manageable traffic patterns, and being a good place to live for senior citizens and the poor.

We've come to expect our communities to meet our basic needs as a matter of course. We take for granted that our tap water flows when we turn the handle, our trash will be picked up when we put it on the curb. Most of us feel safe when we're walking down the street, and confident that our kids are receiving a good education.

But for better or worse, the bar has been raised. To be truly ful-filled and happy, we want and need more. And at the top of the list are two additional needs: aesthetics and openness. *And they are needs.* They are not just "frills"; they are what we've come to expect from our communities.

That's what residents of New Orleans told us when they re-sponded to the first version of the Place and Happiness Survey implemented just before Hurricane Katrina struck. At the top of their list was the "beauty and physical setting of the city" and the "availability of parks and green space." Churches and reli-gious institutions also proved to be especially critical in the Big Easy. Sixty-one percent of New Orleanians said they spend time in worship, prayer, or meditation every day, and an astounding 56 percent said they had attended church in the past seven days—a higher frequency than in any other city surveyed. Sec-ond to churches and religious institutions, residents felt the "quality of colleges and universities" was their most important consideration.

New Orleans is known for its quixotic mixture of decadence, Southern charm, and innocence, all of which is reflected in the city's nightlife, one of the Big Easy's most important assets. Al-though there is more to New Orleans than Bourbon Street, these cauldrons of musical innovation, joyful celebration, and community allow people to be themselves and—alongside the neighborhood churches—play a critical role in weaving the in-tricate fabric of "third places" outside of work and home where people meet, congregate, and connect.

At the date of this writing, the city is still far from recovery. Rebuilding one of our country's most unique and historic cities is no easy task. But the Place and Happiness Survey—which clearly shows what New Orleanians most value (and now likely miss) most about their city—should give urban planners an idea of where to start. In their haste to focus on buildings and infra-structure—reinforcing the levees, rebuilding the central busi-ness district, and constructing housing—public and private leaders so far have virtually ignored the critical social infrastruc-ture of New Orleans, which is the key to bringing residents back. As a conduit to the myriad of other jazz clubs, neighbor-hood bars, and taverns, and as a major source of tourism in-come, the French Quarter is certainly part of this infrastructure. But it's not the whole story. New Orleanians want and need to connect with each other through core neighborhood institu-tions—their churches, taverns, bars, parks, and schools. They want their personal lives and community relationships back.

Places that rank high in aesthetics and openness do some-thing that is powerful and unique: they level the playing field for all their residents, even in a city like New Orleans, which is both racially and socioeconomically divided. The aesthetics of a place—its physical beauty and natural amenities—are public goods that we can all use and enjoy. A great park is open to every social and demographic category—white, black, Asian, and Hispanic; single and married, gay and straight; rich and poor. As long as there is room, my use of the park does not ex-clude you or anyone else from using it, too. In most cases, the park gets better, safer, and more exciting when more runners, cyclists, roller-bladers, strollers, dog-walkers, young parents with children, picnickers, and sport players of every sort and persuasion congregate together.

Places that are open let us freely express ourselves and be part of a bigger picture, a larger whole. They provide us with the space necessary for personal discovery and self-actualization—for realizing our potential and dreams; for building and raising the family we truly desire. They enable us to be part of a whole and to be ourselves, adding real meaning and fulfillment to our lives.

These survey findings are meant to be guides to what dimensions of a place make the greatest positive impact on an average resident's happiness. But as our same findings illustrate, not every person wants the same thing out of their community, nor do they desire the same things at every stage of their lives. Ultimately, being truly happy with one's place comes down to figuring out what best complements one's lifestyle and core values.

11

CITIES HAVE PERSONALITIES, TOO

I T IS ALL WELL AND GOOD TO KNOW THAT PLACE AFFECTS happiness, that the happiest communities tend to be open-minded, vibrant places where people feel free to express themselves and cultivate their identities, and that these communities tend to foster creativity. But fulfilling the first part of the equation—finding a place that makes us happy—is not always so simple.

The key to finding our happy place largely depends on identifying what it is we most want out of it. As the old adage, "different strokes for different folks," tells us, not all people want or need the same things. Knowing what matters most to you—what your priorities and needs are—is a key part of the battle.

The play between our psychological wants and needs and what our communities can offer I call *fit*.[1] Whatever it's called, it's important to get it right. My wife, Rana, who writes a syndicated relationship advice column with her three sisters, compares the search for a place of one's own to finding the right mate. She says you have to look inward and figure out exactly what makes you tick in order to choose a place that will allow you to grow and develop. And remember, she adds: if you don't remain happy, there's no shame in moving on.

A young graduate assistant also compared relocating to dating. She's already moved plenty of times in her young life, and has had different relationships with each place. She hasn't ever committed to one location; instead, she's dated a few that seemed to fit, at various stages of her life. There is one special city she's gotten to know pretty well. She lived there in graduate school and thinks it might be her true love. But for now, she's thousands of miles away and enjoying where she is.

But for many people, the fit isn't right. According to the Place and Happiness survey:

- About two-thirds (67 percent) of people are happy with where they live, rating their community satisfaction a 4 or 5 on a five-point scale.
- That leaves more than a third of respondents who are ambivalent (24 percent rated their communities 3 out of 5) or unhappy (10 percent gave their communities a 1 or 2 out of 5).
- When asked how they think their communities will fare in five years, 43 percent said they are either ambivalent (26 percent gave their communities a 3 out of 5) or pessimistic (14 percent gave their communities just 1 or 2 out of 5).
- And when asked if they would recommend their community to a relative or friend, 40 percent responded ambivalently (21 percent rated their communities 3 out of 5) or negatively (17 percent gave their communities 1 or 2 out of 5).

Think for a minute about what happens when we pick the wrong place—likely something that has happened to you or someone you know. As with the wrong job or the wrong life partner, the fallout can be profound and depressing. It takes a lot less time and effort to recognize a potential poor fit up front than to have to move again later.

One person I interviewed said that after moving his family to a new city, he immediately sensed it was wrong. He found it hard to resonate with people there. His neighbors were nice enough and of similar age. That wasn't the problem. They just didn't share his attitudes and values, likes and dislikes. The place just didn't feel right. He began to feel negative and angry for inexplicable reasons. Nothing about his environment—despite the nice house and good job—really excited him. He analogized it to feeling like a visitor in his own skin. It took him a while to put it together, but ultimately he realized that he was not somewhere he felt free to be himself and realize his dreams.

He's not the only one. I've heard similar stories from many other people. First they tell me they start getting negative or even angry at their community. They might not even realize the reason for their mood swings, or they think it comes from something else. Eventually they begin to realize that for some reason they don't really fit in where they live.

Being in the wrong place is a theme that appears in our greatest literature and our most slapstick entertainment—mined for comedy and terror and everything in between. Remember Eva Gabor in *Green Acres*, out in the sticks doing farm work in her evening gown?

Or Grandma, Pa, and Jethro in *The Beverly Hillbillies*, showing up in Los Angeles with their beat-up pickup truck and work boots?

How about Paris and Nicole—well, that's the subject of another book.

All of these stories play off a common human endeavor gone wrong—the effort to find the place that best fits us and the way we truly want to live.

The Big Five

The question of psychological fit plays a big role in our place happiness. After writing *Rise of the Creative Class,* I began to suspect that in addition to the more conventional economic and sociological factors behind our decisions, there might also be psychological ones. My interest was piqued in the spring of 2006, when Will Wilkinson, policy analyst at the Cato Institute and managing editor of its online monthly magazine, asked me directly about it after reading an early draft of this book.[2] He wanted to know if I had ever considered how different kinds of personalities might be attracted to and thrive in different kinds of places. Was there a fit between an individual's personality and their community? Are people happier when they find a community that fits them? What happens when one's personality is different from that of their community?

Psychologists say that there are five basic dimensions to personality. This five-factor model, or what psychologists sometimes describe as the "Big Five" dimensions of personality, is straightforward.[3] The first type is openness to experience. Open types have a tendency to enjoy new experiences, especially intellectual experiences, the arts, fantasies, and anything that exposes them to new ideas. People high in openness tend to be curious, artistic, and creative.

The second type is conscientiousness. Conscientious types work hard and have a great deal of self-discipline. They are responsible, detail-oriented, and strive for achievement. Psychologists find that people high in conscientiousness tend to be better than average workers on almost any job, completing tasks competently and efficiently. The third type is extroversion. Extroverts are outgoing, talkative, gregarious, assertive, enthusiastic, and seek excitement. They enjoy meeting new people and tend to maintain a fairly stable, positive mood under most circumstances.

The fourth type is agreeableness. Agreeable types are warm, friendly, compassionate, and concerned for the welfare of others. They generally trust other people and expect other people to trust them.

The fifth type is neuroticism. Neurotic types are emotionally unstable, more likely to experience anxiety, hostility, depression, self-consciousness, and impulsiveness.

While it is tempting to think of people as one or another—we all know people who are extroverts and others who are introverts—the reality is that most people fall somewhere along a spectrum. And while most people have dominant types, everyone possesses some level of each of the five traits. A psychologist might describe Woody Allen as low in extroversion (he seems quiet and reserved), low in agreeableness (aloof and distant), somewhat conscientious (he gets his movies made), high in neuroticism (he's self-absorbed and nervous), but very high in openness to experience. After all, he's a creative, innovative, and artistic filmmaker.

Personality psychologists have empirically verified the five-factor model in scores of research studies, and have found that its five basic traits are rooted in biology, stable over time, and that they are consistent across cultures. Other psychologists who specialize in business and organizations have examined the links between personality type and work. For example, extroverts are found to perform better in sales jobs. Agreeable types do best in jobs that require a great deal of team work. And conscientious types excel at jobs that call for standard tasks. People who are open to experience perform well in creative endeavors and jobs that require flexibility and innovation.

Little research on the relationship between personalities and their home or work environments has examined the relationship between individual personality types and places they choose to live. I felt so inspired by the idea of connecting place and personality that when I was invited to deliver the keynote speech to the Gallup International Positive Psychology Summit in fall 2006, I decided to center my remarks around it. At the conference I felt somewhat out of my element. After all, what did I know about psychology? So I attempted to make light of my being an outsider. I noted that many of the people I had interviewed for my research said they were drawn to places with "energy."

"At first," I said, "I didn't know what to make of this. Bear in mind, when we economists talk about 'energy,' we're usually referring to a physical resource." Could it be, I joked, "that all of those people were simply attracted to places with low gas and electric prices?"

Over time, I explained, I began to understand what they meant. My colleagues and interviewees were talking about energy not in a physical sense but in a psychological sense. They were describing places with vibrant rhythms, lots going on, and other high-energy people.

Fortunately, the joke worked.

I knew my lecture had been a modest hit when afterward, three of the leading positive psychologists in the world—Martin Seligman of the University of Pennsylvania, Christopher Peterson of the University of Michigan, and Mihaly Csikszentmihalyi, the leading authority on the psychology of creativity—approached me and asked if we could all get together.

At the meeting, Seligman zeroed in on the notion of energy. Energy, he explained, is a concept that cuts across biology, physics, and chemistry, and is evident in everything from brain scans to heart rate monitors. "The human body is an energy system, and indeed life itself is based on energy processes, insofar as living things must constantly consume and burn energy."

Think about this stunning fact, he continued. The human brain constitutes only 2 percent of the human body mass, but typically consumes about 20 percent of its total calories. "A good day," he told me, "starts with high energy, positive feelings, and an excited mood. Bad days are marked by low energy and the sluggish, discouraged, and overwhelmed feeling that it brings."

If you want to find places of energy, particularly high-level creative energy, Csikszentmihalyi chimed in, look for concentrations of people who exhibit high levels of curiosity—a point I will return to later in this chapter.

Then Seligman added a clincher: "Biographies of great achievers often note their subjects' remarkable levels of energy, far more crucial to their success than any raw ability."

I asked them, What about place? We know that periods of high achievement, creativity, and innovation have tended to occur in certain cities. Is it possible that what these cities have been able to attract and energize are certain types of personalities?

We agreed to look into this. Seligman and Peterson offered me full access to detailed data drawn from hundreds of thousands of responses to their Values in Action (VIA) personality assessments.[4] Because each entry included information on the respondent's address and zip code, they could be used to determine whether any significant correlation between place and personality existed.

Around the same time, I came across a blog post about a study on the connection between music tastes and personality.

The study was by Sam Gosling, a psychologist at the University of Texas who had become famous for his work on animal personalities, and Jason Rentfrow, a young psychologist at Cambridge University.

Perusing Gosling's Web site, I was captivated by their studies of personality. Gosling and Rentfrow found that they could identify basic personality types simply by asking people what kind of music they liked, or by observing the arrangement and decoration of their dorm rooms or offices. Their findings were intuitive, and they were borne out by the data. How we decorate our homes and offices, which books we buy, the CDs we own, the movies we watch, the clothes we wear, the way we arrange our personal spaces—none of these is a random choice. We base these decisions on who we are, who we want to be, and how we want to be perceived.

Intrigued, I shot off a note to Gosling asking if he knew of anyone who might have undertaken similar work on the relationship between personality and location. Were certain kinds of personalities more likely to move than others? Could it be that cities and regions take on collective personalities of their own, which over time attract certain kinds of people?

Within minutes he responded. He and Rentfrow were already knee-deep in such a project.

Their initial study, entitled "The Geography of Personality," examines the geographic clustering of basic personality traits.[5] Surveying past literature, they note a longstanding interest in cross-cultural personality differences that dates back to the pioneering anthropological studies of Margaret Mead and Ruth Benedict in the early twentieth century.[6]

Since then, the emergence of modern personality studies and the five-factor model of personality have reignited interest in and research on the geography of personality. A 1973 study, which they cite, found that people living in the Northeast, Mid-

west, and West Coast regions of the United States had significantly higher "creative productivity"—characterized by high
levels of creativity, imagination, intelligence, and unconvention-
ality—than those in other regions.[7]

Drawing on this study and others, Rentfrow and Gosling uti-
lized a large database of personality traits from Internet surveys
of more than 600,000 people to explore the distribution and
clustering of personality by state.[8] Their results confirmed that
certain states are high on openness, others on agreeableness,
others on neuroticism, and so on. These personality dimensions
are also associated with key social and economic outcomes.
Openness to experience, for example, was highest in the Northeast and West Coast states and was related to the proportion of
artists and entertainers working in a state, percentages of votes
cast for liberal candidates in presidential elections, support for
same-sex marriage, and patent production.

Rentfrow and I met in Washington, D.C., in the spring of
2007 and decided to combine forces. It was clear from Gosling's
and his research that there was a connection between place and
personality at the state level. Our hunch was that people tend to
sort and cluster in more specific regions, communities, and
neighborhoods.

What Color Is My City?

Since each person who completed the personality survey also
provided their zip code, we were essentially able to link a personality to a location. Thus we could generate maps of the location of more than 350,000 individual personality profiles across
the entire United States. The first set of maps, generated by my
colleague, Kevin Stolarick, covers all the zip codes in the United
States with 30 or more responses. There is one for each of the
five major personality types (see Figure 11.1). The patterns in

FIGURE 11.1 PERSONALITY MAPS

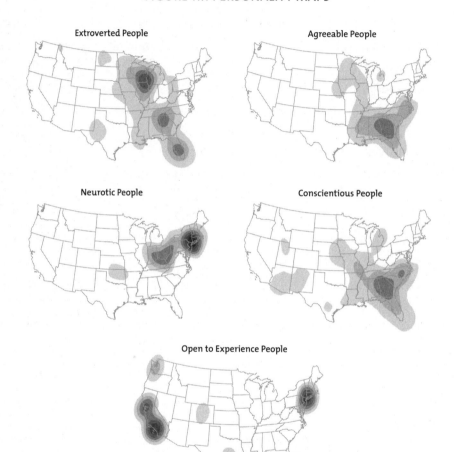

Extroverted People

Agreeable People

Neurotic People

Conscientious People

Open to Experience People

SOURCE: DATA FROM JASON RENTFROW AND SAM GOSLING;
ANALYSIS BY KEVIN STOLARICK; MAP BY RYAN MORRIS

these maps are striking. Each of the five personality types shows up in distinct places.

The map for extroverts shows a strong concentration on a diagonal axis stretching from greater Chicago south through St. Louis, Louisville, Nashville, and Memphis, over to Atlanta, Birmingham, New Orleans, and down through southern Florida. Their concentration flares out from Chicago north to Milwaukee and Minneapolis and west to Omaha, Wichita, and Kansas City, and then east to Cleveland and Pittsburgh.

The map for agreeable and conscientious types show that they track together. The Sunbelt is clearly the dominant place for those two personalities. On both maps, there is a dominant cluster running from Richmond, Virginia, through Charlotte, North Carolina, to Atlanta, down through Orlando, Florida, and then west through New Orleans and north to Jackson, Mississippi, north to Memphis, and back around east to Knoxville. Smaller concentrations of agreeable types can be found around greater Detroit, Minneapolis, and Omaha. Smaller concentrations of conscientious types show up around St. Louis, Detroit, Omaha, Phoenix, Salt Lake City, Albuquerque, and Santa Fe.

The map for neurotic personalities show them clustered heavily in the New York metropolitan area and also in the Midwest industrial heartland stretching from Pittsburgh, Cleveland, Detroit, and Chicago south to Cincinnati, through parts of Indiana, West Virginia, and Kentucky, as well as Wichita, Tulsa, and Oklahoma City.

The first four factors appear to be regionally clustered. Open personalities are more spread out across the country, clustering in the Bos-Wash corridor in the Northeast; Miami, and southern Florida in the Southeast; Houston, Dallas, and Austin, Texas; and Denver, greater LA, the San Francisco Bay area, Portland, and Seattle on the West Coast. This geographic pattern reflects that open people are most likely to reside in large urban areas. Thus, they are likely to seek out and cluster in specific regions that offer new and exciting experiences. Conversely, conscientious and agreeable types, who are less adventuresome and tied more closely to traditional relationships, will tend to spread out from their existing locations.

But regions, even more so than people, aren't made up of just one type of person or personality. They have hundreds of thousands, indeed millions of people with different combinations of personality traits. Thus, if Woody Allen, as a prototypical New Yorker, is low in some traits and high in others, wouldn't New York City follow suit, too? In addition to having a large concentration of open-to-experience personality types, what combination of personality traits define its overall regional personality? How does New York's personality differ from, say, those of Chicago and LA, or Charlotte or Salt Lake City, for that matter? Are there specific configurations of regional personality types that we can identify? If so, can we develop a way to match people to the regions that would best fit their psychological profiles?

To get at this, Stolarick undertook factor analysis—a powerful statistical matching technique—on the hundreds of thousands of data points in the personality survey to identify the main clusters of regional personality types across the United States. His analysis found that all U.S. metropolitan regions break down into three main categories.

The first cluster I call outgoing regions. Scoring high in extroversion, regions in this cluster are low in neuroticism, conscientiousness, openness, and very low in agreeableness. Topping the list here are Chicago and Minneapolis, along with a mix of old industrial regions such as Pittsburgh, Cleveland, Milwaukee, and Detroit, and Sunbelt centers such as Salt Lake City, Fort Worth, San Antonio, Orlando, and West Palm Beach.

Outgoing regions, Rentfrow comments, would likely be a good fit for people who are social and outgoing, who like group activities and functions, who play team sports, and like to be around other people. They are unlikely to appeal to people who prefer very close ties or community involvement, as those preferences are more common among highly agreeable individuals, or to those who constantly need multiple options or enjoy trying new things, which are preferences more common among people high in openness.

The second cluster I call conventional or dutiful regions. Regions in this cluster score high on agreeableness and conscientiousness as well as extroversion, but low in openness and neuroticism. The regions that stand out here are mainly in the Sunbelt: Atlanta, Phoenix, Charlotte, Raleigh, Greensboro, Memphis, Nashville, Tampa, Fort Lauderdale, Jacksonville, Miami, as well as Indianapolis and Portland, Oregon.

Dutiful regions, Rentfrow suggests, would be a good fit for people who are hard working, friendly, trusting, helpful, and compassionate. In some respects, these regions could be thought of as perfect for model citizens. They are places for people who want to fit in and are more conventional or traditional in their outlooks and values; those who value the status quo, obey the rules, and don't typically step out of line. They are places where people trust one another, tend not to challenge authority or each other, are diligent at work and in life, and do what is expected of them. If outgoing regions are good places for people who like to socialize with lots of people, people in dutiful regions prefer to socialize with a relatively small number of close friends and family. Dutiful regions will be a poor fit for those who are artistic and creative and who constantly need to be trying out new and different things.

Experiential regions form the third cluster. Places in this cluster score highly on openness and neuroticism, but low in conscientiousness, extraversion, and agreeableness. Regions in this group include large creative centers such as New York City and its environs, the San Francisco Bay Area (San Francisco, San Jose, and Oakland), LA and San Diego, Boston, Seattle, Washington, D.C., and Baltimore, Denver, Austin, and Dallas, but also Las Vegas, Buffalo, Louisville, and New Orleans.

Experiential regions are a good fit for people who do not need to be around other people, who question authority, and who quest after intense experiences—intellectually, creatively, emotionally, and even physiologically—can you say extreme sports. What's also interesting about this cluster, Rentfrow suggests, is that such regions are likely to be a good fit for people who are creative but perhaps also lost in their own world, socially isolated, aloof, even cantankerous, or who thrive on stress, anxiety, and instability. Experiential regions are a poor fit for people who like to meet new people and make friends easily, have conventional values, are status quo oriented, and prefer to work in stable jobs and on standard tasks.

The bottom line: Regions, like people, have distinct personalities. While opposites sometimes really do attract, and it is always possible to make unusual matches work, most people will be happier and more fulfilled in regions that match their personalities. Since Rentfrow's data included questions on happiness and well-being, we were able to examine the connection between personality, place, and happiness. Were people happier in places with higher concentrations of personality types like themselves? The short answer is a resounding yes. Given the psychological forces clearly at work behind individual people's migration patterns, it seems imperative to keep such geographic personality clusters in mind when contemplating where to live.

Of course, it is always possible to seek out a well-suited neighborhood, even in a region that does not perfectly mirror your tastes and preferences. And clearly, some types of people can and do thrive in places where they are outside the norm. This is especially true of those who like to see themselves as unconventional. As Rentfrow explained in an e-mail:

> In a place like Austin, where the norm is to be open and creative, it's not enough to drink coffee and beer, to smoke American Spirit cigarettes, and listen to Miles Davis. If you're truly open and creative, and desire to be seen as such, it's important to demonstrate this by adopting preferences and habits that are not the norm. After all, being creative and innovative means being unconventional. Furthermore, I think that this group of ultra-creatives, in their efforts to portray themselves as such, may acquire preferences that are not only different, but require a certain degree of commitment; things that require repeated exposure before they can be tolerated and appreciated (it's sort of like a rite of passage). The need to be unique may also be an important determinant of relocating.

But what accounts for the clustering of personality types and the emergence of distinct regional personalities? The first thing that crosses my mind, given my background as an economic geographer, is the historical imprint of economic and industrial structure. Agreeable and conscientious personality types are heavily concentrated in old industrial regions like Pittsburgh and Detroit, where rule-driven mass production industry took root, and also in the Sunbelt, especially along the Interstate 75 corridor that cuts through Ohio, Indiana, and Kentucky, where a large number of newer heavy manufacturing firms like the Japanese and German automotive transplants have located. These industries require agreeable and conscientious people and often orient their hiring accordingly. Extroverted types are concentrated around Chicago, Atlanta, and Charlotte, where lots of sales, business headquarters, and high-level services have located.

Open-to-experience types are clustered in larger cities, especially on the coasts, historically home to diverse economic structures, immigrant populations, and longstanding artistic and bohemian quarters.

While it is admittedly hard to identify what came first—was it an initial concentration of personality types that drew industry or the historical impact of industry structure that shaped and selected for personality?—the overlay between the two is clear. This overlay between personality type and economic structure may pose additional obstacles for older industrial regions. While those regions obviously grew by attracting and mobilizing the agreeable and conscientious personality types that were required to perform standard manufacturing (and in many cases even higher-level service tasks), globalization means that many of those functions have been shifted off-shore—manufacturing has moved to economic centers like Shanghai and other regions in China, and standard services has moved to regions, for example, in India.

The status quo orientation and don't-rock-the-boat values of those regions might not only damp down creativity and innovation in those regions but also encourage an outmigration of the open types who tend to be the source of new creative energy and innovation. Thus the longer-run issues facing these regions may have as much to do with their psychological makeup, or what Rentfrow calls their "psycho-social environment," as their business climate and economic structure.

There are several other reasons why personalities might cluster. The first of these, as Rentfrow and Gosling explain, has to do with the physical environment. It is widely acknowledged that physical environments shape culture and societies. In his seminal book *Guns, Germs, and Steel,* Jared Diamond points out the physical attributes that shaped propulsive growth of northern Europe. Jeffrey Sachs, director of the Earth Institute at Columbia University, has shown that coastal locations have consistently higher rates of economic growth than those inland.[9]

Rentfrow and Gosling argue that physical factors—such as climate and environs—can similarly affect our personalities. Residents of places with cold climates and dark winters exhibit higher incidence of seasonal affective disorder, depression, stress, and anxiety. Other studies have found that people who live in warmer climates commonly display more aggressive behavior. Rentfrow's own research has found a positive correlation between neuroticism and average yearly rainfall.

Social factors also come into play. Political scientists and sociologists have long noted the effect of values and culture on work and economic life. Max Weber famously attributed the growth of capitalism to the "Protestant work ethic." Ronald Inglehart's research on more than fifty nations illustrates the relation between places that value individual self-expression and high incomes and sustained economic growth.[10]

We know that values, beliefs, and attitudes cluster geographically and are sustained over time through social interaction—that's what defines culture. Sooner or later, Rentfrow and Gosling argue, these places (and their inhabitants) will also assume certain personality traits. They refer to these as "social founder effects." That is, people come to acquire personality traits that reflect their practices, lifestyles, and beliefs. Places that tolerate or encourage openness to experience will ultimately attract people who seek environments in which they can feel free to express themselves in whatever way they choose. Even people who are not initially open-minded may, to some extent, internalize some of those values and preferences over time. Eventually, large segments of the population may end up embodying these traits.

Another factor is what Rentfrow and Gosling call "selective migration." Geographic differences in personality, they write, "could have emerged as a result of immigrants selectively migrating to places that satisfied and reinforced their psychological and physical needs." According to the theory, these initial groups establish personality traits that are then passed down to subsequent generations—a notion, Rentfrow and Gosling point out, that is supported by ample evidence. Dubbing this "genetic founder effects," they argue that the migration of like-minded people to certain areas may reduce the amount of variation in the gene pool over time, thereby increasing the proportion of people who possess particular traits.

These effects are reinforced by social pressure and social influence. Clearly, certain kinds of personalities are more attracted to certain kinds of places. We seek out places to live that reinforce and reflect aspects of who we are and who we want to become.

Of course, migration may well be psychologically motivated in the first place. It's not necessarily surprising that certain kinds of personalities would be predisposed to being mobile. People who are open, Rentfrow and Gosling write, "may attempt to escape the ennui experienced in small-town environments by relocating to metropolitan areas where their interests in cultures and needs for social contact and stimulation are more easily met." People who display high levels of openness to experience are by nature the most adventuresome and mobile. Thus it makes sense that they will flock to places that offer lots of exciting experiences and stimuli and eventually (if unwittingly) cluster around one another. As this process occurs, other more conventional regions are gradually drained of open people, which reinforces their non-open personality types while encouraging more open people to leave.

The need to be challenged, to excel, to be the best, can also play a role. Rentfrow writes:

The fact that my musician friends who had successful careers in Austin have since moved to NYC and LA is not some random coincidence; those are the places to be if you really want to excel. It's not easy. On the contrary, there you're competing with the professionals. But that's just it. The people I know who moved there were up for that challenge. Austin was no longer a challenging place for them, so they moved to places where they're forced to rise to the occasion.

Rentfrow uses musicians as his example, but the same can be said of investment bankers who are drawn to New York and London, or young techies and entrepreneurs who move to Silicon Valley.

The effects of personality on mobility hit me one day as I was addressing the top marketing team at Dewar's. They had read *Rise of the Creative Class* and wanted to break the image that all scotch-drinkers are sixty years old, affluent, white, and male. They had found that young creative types, whom they dubbed "urban independents," clustered in places like New York's East Village, D.C.'s Adams Morgan and U Street Corridor, Chicago's Wicker Park, and Los Angeles's West Hollywood, had developed a taste for scotch whiskey. Dewar's began reaching out to their budding clientele, keeping track of their predilections and preferences.

During our meeting, I asked the marketing team a series of questions: Did the Scotch drinkers like loud music and live performance? Did they prefer espresso to lattes?

The answers that came back surprised even me. Yes, the team said, these younger scotch drinkers preferred black coffee and espresso, liked loud music, and favored straight whiskey over mixed drinks.

This all hit a chord. Certain personality types seem to require higher and more intense levels of stimulation—both literally and figuratively. They are drawn to extreme experience—complex music, intense tastes, exciting places, and eccentric people. It's not by chance that people with these qualities happen to cluster in highly stimulating places, I thought. They are inclined, if not programmed, to seek them out.

Analyze This

All of this raises a bigger question. Since personality types cluster geographically, might they also play a role in regional innovation, talent, and economic growth?

Seeing the strong clustering of personality types and learning more about the relationship between psychology and place was causing a subtle but profound shift in my own thinking. All my professional life, I've looked at how social and economic factors shape the world. I'd never really been into psychology—never thought about how personal proclivities might affect innovation or economic development. But all of a sudden it was dawning on me that psychology plays a central role.

For years I had sought to develop better and more refined measures of what economists refer to as human capital or skill. My own measures of the creative class, and of creative occupations, which we discussed earlier, were my attempts to add the kinds of work people do to economists' emphasis on human capital or level of education.

But what if skill is more than education and more than work? Rentfrow suggests that personality involves the capacity to acquire and perform certain tasks competently and effectively. The type of skill economists are interested in, he writes, "implies something that can be acquired with proper training, talent, motivation, and resources." But, he adds, "it's more consistent with personality theory to argue that personality traits predispose people to acquire certain skills. For example, highly conscientious people have a disposition to be detail oriented, plan ahead, or stay organized. Openness influences people's ability to acquire new skills relatively quickly."

Obviously, some people are more creative or more ambitious or more motivated than others. What separates Steve Jobs or Bill Gates from most people is not their level of education or even the work they do; it is this something else. What if that something else is rooted in psychology and personality? Any mother will tell you (mine surely did) that her children came out of the womb with their personalities intact. What if personality itself is a key driver in our capacity to seek out new connections, mobilize resources, innovate, and achieve?

For years I've tried to make out why technology-based growth took off around MIT and Stanford, but not around Carnegie Mellon, where I taught for nearly twenty years. It's surely not the warm sunny weather. It seemed, after all, that there really was something to the old joke.

"How do you make the next Silicon Valley?"

"Take one part great university, add two parts sunshine and three parts venture capital: shake vigorously."

What if Silicon Valley succeeds not just because it is a magnet for highly skilled people but because it attracts those who are also highly motivated, highly ambitious, highly curious, and highly open? The same is true of the people who migrate and succeed in finance in New York or London; the actors and film-makers who make it in LA; and the musicians who thrive in Nashville.

And what about the mobile and the rooted that we discussed in Chapter 5? For years, I've done research on the migration of the young, highly educated, and highly skilled. But what if it's not just educational backgrounds, job skills, or financial resources that shape one's tendency to move? What if the people who move have different personality makeups than those who stay put? What if the means migration we discussed in Chapter 6 is more than the movement of the educated and the talented? What if it is the relocation of certain personality types? And what if these are the same types that are most likely to tolerate risk, try new things, create new innovations, and start new businesses?

It began to dawn on me. Perhaps the same types of people who are most likely to move are also the ones most likely to innovate and start new firms. As more and more of the people leave the places they were born and cluster together, their concentrations become hotbeds of creative endeavor, innovation, start-up companies, and economic growth. The sorting we are witnessing is not just that of education and skill but also of basic personality types.

To get at the effects of this personality sorting on innovation and economic growth, my research team and I matched our datasets on innovation, human capital, and economic growth to Rentfrow and Gosling's data on personality types and Seligman and Peterson's data on psychological strengths. We then conducted a series of statistical analyses (including a rather advanced set of Bayesian linear estimation techniques) to sort out the relationships between personality, innovation, human capital, the creative class, income, and economic growth.

The results were so striking that they shocked us.

First off, we found that the personality variables are indeed capable of explaining a significant portion of the variance in innovation, human capital, income, housing values, and other factors. Of the five personality factors, openness to experience is clearly the most important. It shows consistently significant statistical relationships with each of these factors. But, before turning to it, let's look quickly at the other four personality types.

Neuroticism is negatively associated with top talent in the form of human capital or the supercreative class. In more advanced models, it also turns out to be negatively associated with the creative class, high-tech industry, and wages. In other words, regions with high concentrations of highly educated and ultra-creative individuals tend to be more emotionally stable, less volatile, and more resilient. This suggests, among other things, that these are places where people may be more likely to take risks because they're less concerned about failure.

Agreeableness is associated with jobs in management and health-care. And, while it is positively associated with innovation, high-tech industry, wages, and income in our more advanced models, the effects are quite small. This could mean that the ability to work well with others contributes, albeit slightly, to innovation.

Extraversion is significantly correlated with management and sales jobs, but it too has no effect on human capital overall, high-tech jobs, or regional income.

Conscientiousness is an important characteristic to success in many fields and industries. A management consultant I know likes to say that for every open and creative person who comes up with a new idea, a company needs ten or twenty conscientious ones to carry it out. Psychologists have found that entrepreneurs possess a mixture of openness and conscientiousness, particularly stick-to-itiveness—the ability to persevere in the face of adversity. But as our statistical results show, conscientiousness is not a big factor in regional growth. In fact, it turned out to be negatively associated with innovation, wages and income, and housing values. Then again, as Rentfrow suggested, conscientious individuals tend to be rule-followers; give them a clearly-defined task and they will develop the most efficient procedure for completing it. But when the task is not clearly defined and requires creative thought, someone who is highly

conscientious but not very open will struggle to create something completely original. The way I see it, conscientiousness
alone is not enough to power regional growth. However, it may
play a role in combination with other factors, say, in places
where conscientious personalities mix with open people.

Openness to experience is the only personality type that plays
a consistent role in regional economic development. It is highly
correlated with jobs in computing, science, arts, design, and entertainment; with overall human capital levels, high-tech industry, income, and housing values.

And when we ran Rentfrow and Gosling's personality measures against Seligman and Peterson's strengths inventory, it
turned out that openness is correlated with two particular factors. One is beauty, which helps to explain the strong pull of aesthetic factors we saw in Chapter 10. The other is curiosity—the
factor Csikszentmihalyi initially told me would be the best possible predictor for concentrations of creative people and creative
energy. Peterson's independent analysis of his strengths data and
my own creativity measures found a direct relationship between
character strengths—such as appreciation of beauty, creativity,
curiosity, and a love of learning—and creativity index for cities.[11]
However, Peterson found a negative relationship between creative cities and strengths that connect people to one another—
such as modesty, gratitude, spirituality, teamwork, kindness, and
fairness. It may very well be that creative cities have higher concentrations of people whose basic personality makeup is doing
their own thing. This jibes with my research team's findings
which show that regional creativity and innovation are related to
diversity and openness, but not to social capital of the sort
Robert Putnam has written about. Putnam's most recent research has also found that diversity hinders social capital.[12] This is
all very troubling news for our sense of community and social co-

hesion. The very strengths that make places diverse and creative seem to damage our social capital and community commitment.

The role of personality in regional economic development became even clearer when we ran more advanced statistical tests. Openness to experience had the biggest positive coefficient estimate in every case and was involved in at least eight of the ten top models for every variable. Furthermore, it was the only variable to be positive and statistically significant in every equation. Out of sixty top models generated, openness was a factor in more than fifty.

But the strongest results by far were those that looked at my Gay and Bohemian Indexes and openness to experience—literally off the chart. The finding for openness and the Gay Index was the strongest of our entire analysis. This makes me think that my earlier measures of gay and bohemian concentrations are really proxies for regions with large concentrations of open-to-experience people.

When the *Globe and Mail* wrote a story on my impending move to Toronto in July 2007, a reader commented:

> I just don't see the "gay" component as being all that central to this urban conversion; at least not until well into the later stages. Now, open mindedness; indeed is central! I think we could all agree that open mindedness is a key personality trait of any creative person. But one could easily say that the people who "paved" these places were open minded to many things . . . living outside social norms; an alignment to alternate expectations in life . . . I guess, I'm just wondering why "gay" has been elevated in his thesis.

While I would phrase it differently, this reader has a point. It's not gay and bohemian concentrations in and of themselves that drive regional concentrations of creativity and innovation, but the broader, underlying regional environment of openness to experience that those two measures actually reflect.

The more I consider these results the more I am convinced that the clustering of open-to-experience personalities is a driving factor in regional innovation and economic growth. Openness is a key factor in the ability to attract and capitalize on diversity. At the bottom, regional economic growth requires two dimensions—depth and breadth. Depth comes from specialization and developing deep experience in certain key fields. Breadth comes from diversity and the open-mindedness required to accept, generate, and convert new ideas. Places that are innovative and that can sustain themselves over the long run—places like London, New York, or the San Francisco Bay area—are those that can constantly develop and capitalize on breadth. Their resilience stems from more than the level of education, skill, or technology in those areas. It is part and parcel of their personality profile—their ability to attract and to mobilize open-to-experience people.

Personality plays a significant role in understanding cities, regions, migration, and economic growth. And it is the interplay between the two—personality and place—that is key. "The ways in which personality manifests depends, in part, on the situation one is in," Rentfrow writes. Clearly, personality affects which situations and environments people approach and which ones they avoid, he continues. "But sometimes we find ourselves in situations that we didn't choose. I think it's this aspect that's especially interesting to consider at the regional level," he adds. "If we broaden the situation to include the neighborhoods and cities within which people live, then we can begin considering how the social climate, economic conditions, and available resources in a place interact with the personality traits of the region to affect regional growth."

What does this all boil down to? For cities and regions, it means that their leadership—political, business, and otherwise—must be aware of the powerful role played by psychology. Places really do have different personalities. Those personalities stem from their economic structure and inform and constrain their futures. It's a lot easier to go out and attract a new company, or even build a new stadium, than it is to alter the psychological makeup of a region. Regional leaders must become more aware of how their region's collective personality shapes the kinds of economic activities that it can do and the kinds of people it can attract, satisfy, and retain.

For each of us as individuals, the key is to find the right fit—to think strategically in order to identify our priorities and choose the place that best fits us. As the next part of the book will illustrate, such priorities change as we age and cross the various milestones of our lives.

PART IV

WHERE WE LIVE NOW

12

THREE BIG MOVES

THE IDEA OF A LIFE COMPOSED OF DISTINCT STAGES IS relatively new. For most of human history, we lived with our extended families. Then, relatively recently, people began to move into homes of their own when they got married. So, up until the past two decades, we really made one major move–when we got married and left our parents' home.

Nowadays, people stay single longer, get married later, and live longer lives. Consider the idea of adolescence, which is considered a discrete life stage between childhood and adulthood. The idea of adolescence is a creation of the twentieth century. Before that it simply did not exist. More recently, the postcollege years have come to resemble adolescence in some respects—a new life stage that's been dubbed, somewhat jokingly, "adultalescence."[1] Young adults are encouraged to try new jobs, date different people, and live in different places without having to commit. On the opposite end of the life cycle, "retirement" has come to mean much more than an end to one's career. For many aging adults, it represents an entirely new chance at life!

Each of life's stages brings the opportunity to reconsider how where we live affects our economic status, life-style, and well-being. Most of us can no longer expect a single location to fit our evolving needs as we move from one life phase to the next. The kind of place that's perfect for a single twenty-something primarily interested in establishing a career, making friends, and having fun is not necessarily ideal for a married couple with teenage children. That seems obvious once it's pointed out. If it's not obvious to you, ask anyone who has tried to sleep through a summer night in a neighborhood filled with singles' bars.

While not every life has the same number of stages, life's three big ones—when we graduate from college, when we have children, and when the kids move out—deserve special attention. Today, at each subsequent stage, more and more of us have the ability and means to consider a broader range of options for where to live.

Practically speaking, this means that when we consider where we might want to live, we need to balance two related issues. First, as previous chapters have illustrated, it's in our best interest to be in places with access to great jobs and thriving labor markets that fit our life-style and personality. But we should also want to be in a place that's conducive to our life-stage. Just as places have come to specialize in the kind of job opportunities they offer and amenities they provide, most have also come to specialize in the stage of life they best fit.

To better understand the relationships between place and life cycle and to help people make better choices, my research team developed new rankings of America's metropolitan regions by life stage. To do so, we first identified five distinct life stages.

While most people lump everyone in their twenties and thirties into a single category, my team and I view them as two distinct groups. The first segment is *recent college graduates.* Its members are younger, ages twenty to twenty-nine, just getting out on their own, generally single, and looking for places to start their careers, make friends, have fun, and perhaps find that special someone. The second segment is *young professionals.* They are older, ages thirty to forty-four, established in their careers, have more resources to spend on housing, and tend to be more settled. They include singles, people who are living together, and married couples, but a precondition is that they not have children.

The next phase of life occurs not when people get married but when they have children. The third segment is *families with children.* Although one can define family in many ways, the available data limited our definition to officially "married" couples, one of whom is sixty-four or younger, with children in the household.

Most people think of retirement as the major turning point of this life stage, but at least when it comes to making decisions about location, an equally significant event is when the kids leave home. My team and I divided this demographic into two distinct groups. The fourth segment is *empty-nesters* between the ages of forty-five and sixty-four. The fifth segment is *retirees,* those over the age of sixty-five.

Our rankings, developed by Kevin Stolarick, are based on four key factors. The first is the share of people in that life-stage. I have long been a fan of identifying which populations already exist in a given place, which I think is the single best indicator of whether a place is a good fit for a given group.

The second factor deals with the underlying condition of the economy. This is the only common factor across all five life stages, and it incorporates regional economic growth as well as specific measures for technology, talent, and tolerance.

The third factor has to do with amenities and quality of life factors appropriate to a given life stage. For singles, who go out to meet new people and make friends, we use indices of restaurants and bars, and of arts and cultural activities. For young professionals establishing their careers, we use average commute time and wage growth for knowledge-based and creative occupations. The things that matter to most families with children are good schools and safe streets, so we use indices of the overall crime rate and student-teacher ratio. With the kids out of the house, empty-nesters are looking for new ways to enjoy themselves. We use measures of arts and culture and the availability of recreational activities, such as things like golf courses and marinas. For the older group of retirees, who care about physical safety, weather, and access to high-quality health-care, we use measures of the crime rate, availability of doctors, and weather conditions (average July–January temperature difference).

The fourth factor covers specific cost factors. For most young college grads, rent is their biggest cost. So we use rental affordability, measured as rental costs as a percentage of household income. Young professionals in most places are eager to buy homes. We use home ownership affordability measures as a percentage of household income. For families, we use the overall cost of living index. And we do the same for empty-nesters. Health-care costs become more important as we age. So for retirees, age sixty-five and older, we use an index of health-care costs.

Stolarick compiled these rankings for 167 regions across three distinct size groups: the forty-nine regions with more than a million people; the forty-six regions with 500,000 to 1 million people; and the seventy-two regions with 250,000 to 500,000 people. [2] (Appendix C provides our regional rankings for all households, while Appendix D summarizes them for gay and lesbian households.)

One thing my team learned through our research is that some places are conducive to multiple life stages. This comes out in our ratings, as the next three chapters will show. As background research for this book, my team compiled more than twenty-five individual rankings from a wide range of independent sources, covering everything from best places for families to the most environmentally friendly cities and everything in between. What we found is that a relatively small number of places rank consistently high, regardless of what is being rated.

These generalist places not only rank high for people across a range of life stages; they also do well in terms of economic and other social factors. Highest on the list is the San Francisco Bay area, which appeared among the top-ranked places on twenty of these best places lists. Boston is next, with thirteen mentions. Austin, Minneapolis, Raleigh, and Seattle each have eleven; New York has ten. Among smaller regions, Ann Arbor, Boulder, Madison, Santa Barbara, Portland (Maine), Stamford (Connecticut), and Manchester (New Hampshire) register consistently high scores across the board.

These places do not necessarily offer a one-stop solution for everybody. Few people nowadays would be satisfied to live as my parents did, in the same house (or even neighborhood) for their entire lives. Generalist places are not one-size-fits-all; rather, they are mosaics that offer a range of distinctive and specialized communities attuned to the needs of people at various life stages. They reflect what Jane Jacobs called truly great cities: "federations of neighborhoods" that fit the needs of different kinds of people.

13
THE YOUNG AND THE RESTLESS

F OR MOST OF US, OUR FIRST MOVE IS WHEN WE GO TO
college. We move our most prized and relevant posses-
sions out of our parents' house and embark on a path toward our
own lives and careers.

My own move to Rutgers College fundamentally changed
my life. While many of my friends from high school got themselves into trouble, ended up in jail, or took dead-end jobs, I
found myself in an environment where I felt comfortable being myself and openly pursuing my intellectual interests. For
the first time in my life, I didn't feel social pressure to hide
the fact that I was "smart." It didn't take me long to find a
group of peers with whom I shared intellectual interests—
among us were Mario Batali, who would discuss his dreams to
open his own restaurant, and Eliot Katz, the poet. I lived in a
college town that thrived on music. Virtually every great band
of the time, from the Talking Heads and The Ramones to the

Pretenders and the Gang of Four, passed through New Brunswick, New Jersey.

I liked it so much that I returned after only one year of graduate training at MIT, taking a research job at the Center for Urban Policy Research. Living near my family didn't hurt—I was able to hang out with my younger brother, who was then attending Rutgers, and see my parents and aunts and uncle. And I was also close to many college friends who remained nearby and was able to play with other friends in our band. Living in New Brunswick also enabled me to spend a little time at Columbia University, which I eventually decided offered the right doctoral program for me.

But my first big move came on the heels of my first real job— as an assistant professor at Ohio State University. I rented a Rent a Wreck truck and drove out from New York City to Columbus, Ohio, where I took a small apartment in German Village, and started to build a life.

For many recent college grads life can feel confusing, especially when relatives try to help. Here's a story my editor, Bill Frucht, told me when we were discussing this book.

> After my sister Martha graduated from Cornell and decided she wanted to teach art, my aunt Charlotte, who was the Superintendent of Schools in Rockford, Illinois, insisted she come out for job interviews. This had less to do with helping Martha than with Charlotte wanting to show the family she was successful enough to get her niece a job, but never mind. She scheduled my sister for one half-hour interview a day over five days. The rest of the time Martha was free to roam Rockford's many identical streets full of identical split-level houses, or enjoy local cultural attractions such as the shopping mall and the department store, or watch television.

On the evening of Day Three, Charlotte and her husband took Martha out to their favorite restaurant, where she ordered the lasagna. It was served with a side of mashed potatoes and gravy. That night Martha phoned my mother in tears, wailing, "Aunt Charlotte wants me to take all these jobs, but I can't live here! What do I do?"

After my mother assured her she didn't have to move to Rockford if she didn't want to, Martha canceled her remaining interviews and took the next plane home. That fall she and a friend found an apartment in Cambridge, Massachusetts, where she started her life.

Today, many young people have much broader horizons than Martha or I did. Recent college grads are considering, exploring, and moving to locations across the country and across the world. Many undergraduate students have told me they are seeking jobs and life experiences not just in the United States or Canada, but also in Europe, South America, Africa, or Asia. A good number already have friends and ready-made networks in a number of places abroad.

One such couple, John Trenouth and his girlfriend, lived in more than a dozen different cities in half a dozen countries across three continents before they settled in Vancouver. Both fans of dense and diverse cities, they picked Vancouver because they found it to be physically stunning, all the while combining the "west coast's lifestyle and weather" with "the east coast's authenticity and energy."

"Even grocery shopping is fun," Trenouth says. Instead of going to a single supermarket, they get what they need from the many fruit and vegetable stands, butchers, and bakers that speckle the city. I can say the same about Toronto. As a biracial couple, they are also attracted to the city's diversity and openness, which allows them to feel comfortable together and apart.

The freedom to live wherever we choose—oceans and borders notwithstanding—reflects a relatively recent phenomenon.
Before the late twentieth century, most people stayed fairly
close to home. That's not to say that young people didn't go
away to college, but even those who attended college farther
away tended to return home after graduation. Those who did
move away generally settled in one place and stayed put. Some
of this change can be explained by changes in marital trends. In
the 1950s and 1960s, people married young and traditionally
moved directly from their parents' home to their own new
place, where many stayed for life. For example, my parents
bought their small two-family house in North Arlington, New
Jersey, in 1959 and never left.

These days, fewer and fewer people are marrying young—
postponing marriage until their late twenties or thirties—and
some choose not to get married at all. The upshot of this is that
there is a much longer period of being unmarried, with additional
flexibility and in some cases the necessity to find a place that fits.

Young people are the most likely to move of any demographic
group. The likelihood that one will move peaks at around age
twenty-five and then declines steeply until forty-five and continues to trail off into retirement and old age. A twenty-five-year-
old is three times more likely to move than a forty-five- or
fifty-year-old, according to a 2005 study.[1]

The odds of moving also increase with one's level of education. According to the National Longitudinal Survey of Young
Adults, 45 percent of people with advanced degrees end up
leaving their home state, compared with only 37 percent of
people with a bachelor's degree and just 19 percent of those
with a high school degree.[2]

For young people, this imparts a simple lesson. Because the
ability to move (and the likelihood of moving) slows down so sig-

nificantly with age, the place we choose to locate and settle after college can have a huge effect on our future.

For cities and regions, it means that places that attract young people end up being the winners in the nationwide competition for talent. This does not bode well for cities and regions that seem to believe they will be able to reattract young people who have moved away for fun and adventure once they hit their thirties and decide to settle down and start families. The numbers simply don't add up. Places that lose young people will never be able to recoup, since moving slows down with age. The winning places are the ones that establish an edge early on, by attracting residents in their mid-twenties. These places gain a long-lasting advantage; those that lose out find it all but impossible to catch up.

Rating the best places for singles to live and tracking where they settle has become a growth industry. One list that gets a lot of attention—on which my team consulted—is *Forbes* magazine's.[3] To construct its list, *Forbes* looked at a wide range of city factors: culture, nightlife, prevalence of single people, job growth, and cost of living. Places that consistently top *Forbes*'s list include Denver, Austin, Boston, San Francisco, Washington, D.C., Atlanta, Los Angeles, New York, Chicago, and Seattle.

I took a lot of heat when Pittsburgh, where I lived at the time *Forbes* came out with its first list, ranked dead last. Fortunately, by 2005 Pittsburgh had moved up toward the middle of the pack.

When asked what mattered most about these places, 23 percent of single people surveyed said, "The number of other singles." Just behind in importance was "great career prospects" (20 percent), and much further behind ranked "wild nightlife" and "low cost of living." The findings of *Forbes*'s online survey reinforce the role of being around other singles, in addition to a strong labor market, for young mobile people deciding where to live.

To date, the most comprehensive analysis of where singles live and why comes from a study by Joe Cortright and Carol Coletta called *The Young and the Restless*.[4] Coletta has been interested in this demographic trend for a long time. In the spring of 2003, she hosted the Memphis Manifesto, a gathering of more than a hundred smart and creative young leaders in the country from all kinds of fields, from architecture and law to the nonprofit and documentary film worlds. Now Coletta heads CEOs for Cities, a group that brings together business leaders, mayors, and university presidents to develop new strategies for urban metro economies. Cortright, who is part of the consulting firm Impresa, is one of the country's leading urban analysts.

Cortright and Coletta's study is based on statistical data on where young singles live, as well as in-depth interviews and focus groups on what led them to live where they do. Topping their list of U.S. places with the highest concentration of young residents (between the ages of twenty-five and thirty-four) in 2000 were Austin, Atlanta, Raleigh-Durham–Chapel Hill, Dallas, and Charlotte. Cortright and Coletta also tracked the largest percentages of young people with a bachelor's degree or more. The leading regions are Raleigh (45 percent), Boston (43 percent), San Francisco (41 percent), Washington-Baltimore (41 percent), and Minneapolis–St. Paul (40 percent).

As for the reasons young people move, Cortright and Coletta conclude that while economic growth is important, highly educated young adults place a "higher priority on quality of life factors." Furthermore, their findings show that well-educated young people are "more likely to move to a place with slower job growth than the place they left almost 60 percent of the time."

The Mating Market

But there's another big reason behind these moves—one so basic and obvious it is hard to imagine why so many people ignore it: the basic need to be in a place where you can find a life partner. I call it the mating market.

Let me put it this way: which of these two decisions do you think has a bigger impact on your life—finding the right job, or finding the right significant other?

Getting married might not be everyone's goal in life. But for many of us, finding that special someone is as important as, if not more important than, what we choose to do for a living. While marrying the girl or boy next door is an endearing ideal, it is less and less common in today's society. Where we live has more effect on our chances of meeting our life partner than ever before.

An intriguing study entitled "Sex and the City" by Columbia University economist Lena Edlund found that young women outnumber young men in most urban areas throughout the industrialized world. Since cities offer better labor markets for highly skilled workers, urban job markets should attract more men than women, or at least equal numbers of both genders. Edlund found, however, that while men out-earn women at all ages, young women in the twenty-five to forty-four age range live in more affluent cities. Her answer lies in what she calls the "asymmetries in the marriage market." Men, she writes, "pay women for marriage"—that is, for the relatively higher costs women incur in having and raising children.[5]

As places become more specialized, not just in the jobs and careers they offer but also in the kinds of people they attract and cater to, our odds of meeting that special someone become significantly better in some places than in others. Certain locations have far more single people, as well as more amenities and more activities that bring single people together. And among these favored places, the divergence of urban personalities means that any one person will find many more attractive people in some mating markets than in others. In short, the places to find a mate are clustering like everything else.

I didn't know just how true this was until I posted what I thought was a rather mundane entry on my blog in April 2007. It was just a map (see Figure 13.1), with no text or discussion, with the title "The Singles Map."[6] On it were red dots for places where single women outnumber single men, and blue dots for those where single men outnumber single women. The blog, which I started in 2006, had been puttering along with some thousand or so visitors a day. But within hours of posting that map, the number of hits surged to more than 200,000, and it was linked to a huge array of the most popular Internet sites.

Clearly, people were very interested in seeing which places had the best ratios for their own purposes. According to the map and data, originally published in *National Geographic,* the region with the best ratio for heterosexual men is the New York metropolitan region, which includes New York City and its suburbs in Long Island, Westchester, New Jersey, and Connecticut. Together, those areas house 165,000 more single women than men. Other places where single women outnumber single men include Boston, Washington, D.C., Philadelphia, Baltimore, Miami, Chicago, Detroit, St. Louis, and San Francisco.

On the other hand, the best ratio for heterosexual women was in greater Los Angeles, where single men outnumber single women by 40,000. Other places favorable to single women include San Diego, Portland, Oregon, Seattle, Dallas, Houston, and Austin.

My blog post about the singles map generated a huge number of comments. Some tried to explain the pattern, while others

FIGURE 13.1 THE SINGLES MAP

Circles are sized to reflect how many more singles there are in each metro area, by gender

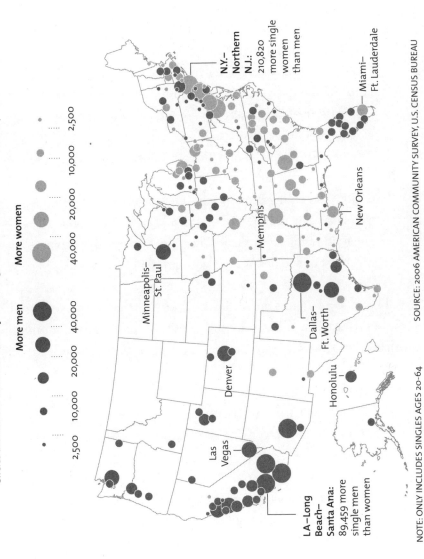

More men

2,500   10,000   20,000   40,000

More women

2,500   10,000   20,000   40,000

N.Y.–Northern N.J.: 210,820 more single women than men

Miami–Ft. Lauderdale

New Orleans

Memphis

Minneapolis–St. Paul

Dallas–Ft. Worth

Denver

Honolulu

Las Vegas

LA–Long Beach–Santa Ana: 89,459 more single men than women

NOTE: ONLY INCLUDES SINGLES AGES 20–64

SOURCE: 2006 AMERICAN COMMUNITY SURVEY, U.S. CENSUS BUREAU

were more personal or even confessional. One commenter wrote the following:

> I'm a single male who moved to San Francisco half a year ago. Coming from Chicago, I can speak with personal conviction to the effects of this graph. When I was in Chicago, it was never long between dates. I moved out here for the new tech boom, jumping head-first into the gold-rush mentality that's driving so many other young single men out here as well.
>
> When I'm hanging out with friends, often times in a large room with few if any women, we routinely turn to the topic of how the dating scene sucks. One of my female friends who's also new to the city says that she's never received so much attention from men in her life. Perhaps this explains why most online dating sites got started in Silicon Valley.

There were many more on this general theme, as you might expect. But a few offered hypotheses based on deeper economic or social patterns. A regular commenter played off the locations of two hit cable-television shows.

> *Sex and the City* takes place at the hub of the #1 female surplus region—New York. Perhaps their frustrations are a reflection of the large single female surplus.
>
> *Entourage* on the other hand is explicitly about young men from Queens, NY migrating to Hollywood, the hub of the #1 male surplus region, Los Angeles, and I believe is based on Boston native Mark Wahlberg's experience.
>
> I agree that the West still holds a "Gold Rush" mentality for young men, and on top of the "Hot Babe" and other beach/surfer dude-oriented aspect of it all, you have the

whole Silicon Valley Type-A nerd culture to draw young men from the East. I think it's also part of the West being the least rooted part of the nation. A young single male who wants to totally throw off his familial and social bonds for more cosmic pursuits would probably like the West better.

I'm not so sure what Texas holds for these young men, but it could be a combination of big oil in Houston, big funkiness in Austin, and just plain big money in Dallas. San Antonio seems to have not joined this club yet. I'm surprised the Southeast is such a female-surplus region, but I supposed their young men migrate West, too. Maybe it's the South's sometimes excessive "rootedness" that pushes the most ambitious young men to flee West.

I won't venture to offer any explanations of my own here, though I will say that I met my wife, Rana, at a speaking event in Lansing, Michigan. She says the high female-to-male ratio there is simple to understand: young men have a greater tendency to move to economic opportunity, while young women stay closer to family.

Demography Is Destiny

Behind this singles map lies a deep and fundamental shift in our nation's demography and family structure. Here are some quick facts to ponder:

- During the 1950s, approximately 80 percent of Americans lived in households headed by married couples.
- Today, that number is just less than half—49.7 percent. That's 55.2 million of the nation's 111.1 million households, according to the Census Bureau.

- Just a quarter of us live in a nuclear family, defined as a married couple with kids at home.
- Some 5 percent of American families are unmarried heterosexual couples living together.
- One in twenty households is someone living alone.
- There are 5 million gay and lesbian people in the U.S., between 2 and 3 percent of the total population.[7]

The fact that the concept of "family" is so diversified poses a problem for some. Until recently, being single into one's late twenties or thirties was seen as odd or worse. In 1957, 80 percent of Americans considered an unmarried woman to be "sick," "neurotic," or "immoral." As late as 1986, 38 percent of Americans thought that being single was not a fully acceptable lifestyle.

It's comical how slow we've been to acknowledge and integrate modern living arrangements. The 1988 edition of the *Handbook of Sociology* uses the phrase "untraditional dyadic relations" to describe all people not part of traditional husband-wife-children families.[8]

I lived through the shift, so I understand how challenging it can be. I grew up with a large extended family at my fingertips. I had ten aunts and uncles on my mother's side, and there were twelve cousins. All of us would gather at my grandmother's house in Newark every Sunday for dinner. I had a similar number on my father's side. Virtually everyone on both sides lived within a five- to ten-mile radius of Newark. North Arlington, where I grew up just five miles away, was a family-oriented town. All the kids knew each other; we participated in the same Cub Scout or Girl Scout activities and played on the same Little League teams. During my childhood, growing up in this world, I came across no divorced people and no adult singles. Neither the concept nor the word *gay* was part of my vocabulary. In fact, I don't remember knowing anyone who was without an extended family much like mine.

Times change. No matter what you call it, our notion of the family is being radically redefined—not by any particular political or ideological agenda but by people themselves. In a recent cross-national survey, 75 percent of Americans said that the main purpose of marriage was something other than having children. My parents or grandparents would have found that unthinkable. Throughout history, marriage has been first and foremost about procreating and having kids, the strong bond that held the family together. In the nineteenth and early twentieth centuries, three-quarters of all households contained children under the age of eighteen. By 1960, the number had dropped to less than half; today it's roughly a quarter.

As mentioned, people are also postponing marriage until later in life. Between 1960 and 2007, the average age of marriage for men rose from twenty-three to twenty-seven, while for women it shifted from twenty to twenty-six. For women with a college degree, it's twenty-seven, and for women with a graduate or professional degree, it's thirty.

And young people today are increasingly choosy. According to the National Marriage Project, 88 percent of singles in 2001 agreed that there is a "special person," often referred to as a soul mate, "waiting for you somewhere out there." What's more amazing is that 87 percent of these never-before-married singles believe they will find that special someone when they're ready to get married.

One consequence of this shift is that since 1960, the number of unmarried couples living together has increased by an astonishing 1200 percent. A quarter of unmarried women between twenty-five and forty-nine are currently living with a partner, and an additional 25 percent did so at some point in the past. "Owning three toothbrushes and finding that they are always at the wrong house when you are getting ready to go to bed wears on you," Amanda Hawn, a twenty-eight-year-old writer who had moved in with her boyfriend, told the *New York Times* in 2006.[10] "Moving in together has simplified life." Roughly half of all first marriages are now preceded by people living together, according to the National Marriage Project at Rutgers University. Some experts now call living together a surrogate for and equivalent to a first marriage.

We are going through a second transition, according to leading demographers. The first occurred during the early to mid-twentieth century and precipitated a golden age for marriage and family life. During that period, more people were married, divorce rates were low, and the age of first marriage for both men and women was lowest in centuries. The second demographic transition, which began in the 1960s and accelerated since the 1980s, is marked by declining rates of marriage, rising divorce rates, falling fertility, and a sharp rise in the age of marriage for both men and women.

So where do people turn for support during the increasingly long period between leaving their parents' house and getting married?

The answer, according to Ethan Watters, is a new surrogate family, the urban tribe.[11] Watters defines it as an "intricate community of young people who live and work together in various combinations, form regular rituals, and provide the same kind of support as an extended family." "If our tribes were maximizing our weak ties within a city," Watters writes, "might we be creating the social science equivalent of dark matter—a force that was invisible but was nonetheless critical to holding everything together?" Furthermore, Watters argues, the urban tribe is especially good at meeting members' needs for self-expression and self-actualization in ways that actual parents and siblings sometimes suppress. But these tribes are not *just* substitutes; on the contrary, they constitute what amounts to our *real* families, in ways the networks we were born into might never be.

Or as a young woman from Chicago put it: "You don't get to pick your family. But you do get to pick your new family—your friends."

Find Myself a City to Live In

Keeping all of these factors in mind, my team and I worked to develop a new rating system and map for the places that best fit people embarking on their adult lives. Recall that we separate young people into two distinct groups: recent college graduates, single, ages twenty to twenty-nine, and young professionals, married and single, ages thirty to forty-four.

San Francisco, Washington, D.C., Boston, LA, and New York top our list of best large regions for young singles (see Table 13.1). But Austin and Minneapolis stand out as best buys. Madison (Wisconsin), Worcester (Massachusetts), Raleigh (North Carolina), and Stamford and New Haven (Connecticut), are the best midsize regions, with Des Moines making the cut as a best buy. Boulder (Colorado), Santa Barbara (California), Trenton (New Jersey), Ann Arbor (Michigan), and Santa Rosa (California), top our list for small regions. Huntsville (Alabama), and Lexington (Kentucky) score as best buys. Contrary to popular belief about what young college grads want, this list includes a number of places far outside America's leading nightlife destinations. In fact, party places such as Las Vegas and Miami rank pretty low on our list.

TABLE 13.1—BEST PLACES FOR SINGLES
(Recent college graduates, ages 20–29)

	All Households		Gay and Lesbian	
	Overall	Best Buy	Overall	Best Buy
Large Regions	San Francisco	Washington, DC	San Diego	Hartford, CT
	Washington DC	Minneapolis	Boston	Austin
	Boston	Austin	Los Angeles	Minneapolis
	Los Angeles	San Francisco	San Francisco	San Jose, CA
	New York	New York	Washington, DC	Washington, DC
Medium-size Regions	Madison, WI	Stamford, CT	Stamford, CT	Stamford, CT
	Worcester, MA	Madison, WI	Worcester, MA	Madison, WI
	Stamford, CT	Raleigh, NC	Portland, OR	Worcester, MA
	New Haven, CT	Worcester, MA	Madison, WI	Raleigh, NC
	Raleigh, NC	Des Moines, IA	Honolulu, HI	Des Moines, IA
Small Regions	Boulder, CO	Trenton, NJ	Boulder, CO	Trenton, NJ
	Santa Barbara, CA	Ann Arbor, MI	Trenton, NJ	Ann Arbor, MI
	Trenton, NJ	Boulder, CO	Santa Rosa, CA	Boulder, CO
	Ann Arbor, MI	Huntsville, AL	Manchester, NH	Green Bay, WI
	Santa Rosa, CA	Lexington, KY	Fort Collins, CO	Norwich, CT

Note: Region names are shortened to core city. See Appendices C and D for full listings.

Source: Analysis and rankings by Kevin Stolarick. Data from the 2005 American Communities Survey of the US Bureau of the Census and other sources.

Now let's turn to the top places for young professionals ages thirty to forty-four (see Table 13.2). Topping our list of large regions are San Jose, Minneapolis, Austin, and San Diego. Denver, Kansas City, and Columbus (Ohio), stand out as best buys. Stamford, Portland (Maine), Madison, Omaha, and Des Moines top our list of midsize regions. Durham (North Carolina) (also part of the Research Triangle), Provo, Reno, Fayetteville (Arkansas), and Boulder top our list for small regions. Lexington (Kentucky), makes the cut as a best buy.

Now let's look at the best places for gay and lesbian people in these early life-stages. The top large regions for young gay and lesbian singles are San Diego, Boston, LA, San Francisco, and D.C. Those pose little surprise, perhaps, but look at the other places that make the list. Minneapolis, Austin, San Jose, and Hartford (Connecticut), stand out as best buys. Stamford, Worcester (Massachusetts), Portland (Oregon), Madison, and Honolulu top the list for midsize regions, with Raleigh and Des Moines coming in as best buys. Boulder, Trenton, Santa Rosa (California), Manchester (New Hampshire), and Fort Collins (Colorado) take the top spots for small regions. Ann Arbor, Green Bay, and Norwich (Connecticut) score as best buys in this category.

Turning to gay professionals ages thirty to forty-four: San Francisco, Hartford, Columbus, Austin, and Minneapolis top our list for large regions. Kansas City, Baltimore, and Seattle make the cut as best buys. Stamford, Portland (Maine), Charleston (South Carolina), Springfield (Massachusetts), and Toledo (Ohio) top our list of midsize regions, with Wichita (Kansas) and Des Moines among the standouts as best buys. Santa Rosa, Green Bay, Fayetteville, Reno, and Manchester lead among small regions. Ocala (Florida), Winston-Salem (North Carolina), Spartanburg (South Carolina), and Green Bay join the

TABLE 13.2—BEST PLACES FOR MID-CAREER PROFESSIONALS,
(Single or married, without children, ages 30–44)

	All Households		Gay and Lesbian	
	Overall	Best Buy	Overall	Best Buy
Large Regions	San Jose, CA	Kansas City	San Francisco	Kansas City
	Minneapolis	Minneapolis	Hartford, CT	Hartford, CT
	Austin	San Jose, CA	Columbus, OH	Baltimore
	San Diego	Columbus, OH	Austin	Columbus, OH
	Denver	Austin	Minneapolis	Seattle
Medium-size Regions	Stamford, CT	Stamford, CT	Stamford, CT	Stamford, CT
	Portland, ME	Des Moines, IA	Portland, ME	Portland, ME
	Madison, WI	Portland, ME	Charleston, SC	Wichita, KS
	Omaha, NE	Omaha, NE	Springfield, MA	Charleston, SC
	Des Moines, IA	Madison, WI	Toledo, OH	Des Moines, IA
Small Regions	Durham, NC	Huntsville, AL	Santa Rosa, CA	Fayetteville, AR
	Provo, UT	Fayetteville, AR	Green Bay, WI	Ocala, FL
	Reno, NV	Durham, NC	Fayetteville, AR	Winston-Salem, NC
	Fayetteville, AR	Lexington, KY	Reno, NV	Spartanburg, SC
	Boulder, CO	Provo, UT	Manchester, NH	Green Bay, WI

Note: Region names are shortened to core city. See Appendices C and D for full listings.

Source: Analysis and rankings by Kevin Stolarick. Data from the 2005 American Communities Survey of the US Bureau of the Census and other sources.

list as best buys. Few if any of these communities would top most people's lists of gay hubs.

To Each His Own Hood

But people don't just choose one region over another and end there. We also have to decide on a specific community or neighborhood. Based on more than twenty years of research, I have developed a typology of neighborhoods by life-cycle stage. More than anything else, this has shown me how many distinct neighborhoods and communities exist.

When I was young, there were far fewer of these choices. There were older urban neighborhoods like the Newark my grandparents and parents were from—the kind of place Philip Roth writes about.[12] There were high-end city neighborhoods like Park Avenue, New York. And there were bedroom suburbs and rural areas. Today, we have a wide array of different kinds of neighborhoods that offer a much wider variety of choices to multiple demographic groups.

For recent college graduates, one obvious choice is to stick around where you went to school, at least for a year or two. Most young graduates eventually move on, but many do choose to stay for at least a while—to engage in research, hang out with friends, or take advantage of a school-related job opportunity. As my own rankings indicate, college towns such as Madison, Ann Arbor, and Boulder are quite successful in attracting this demographic.

This is exactly what I did, after all, and I'm far from the only one. Roger Martin decided to remain in Cambridge for a spell after graduating from Harvard. Since he had already served as captain of Harvard's volleyball team, he jumped at the chance to stay on when the coach announced he was leaving.

Needing a better cover to offer his parents for why he would be staying on, he applied to Harvard Business School and was accepted. What started out as a year in Cambridge morphed into almost two decades. At business school, Roger, some other graduate students, and a few professors, including strategy luminary Michael Porter, decided to create a new consulting firm. In the mid-1980s they launched the hugely-successful Monitor Company, and the rest, as they say, is history.

So one place that's a big draw for recent college grads is the classic *college town*. College towns have remarkable restaurants for their size, great cultural and music scenes, booming foreign populations, and lively third place hangouts. Even large cities are increasing their efforts to retain students after graduation: Campus Philly, for example, is a leading effort to match Philadelphia's more than 90,000 college students with local jobs and improve quality of life in line with their particular needs.[13]

An even bigger trend among young grads is to head for the big city. Between 2000 and 2005, the number of New York City residents with at least a bachelor's degree increased by about 285,000, according to an August 2006 *New York Times* story.[14] Other magnet regions for young graduates are Chicago, Greater Washington, D.C., Boston, the Bay Area, Los Angeles, Minneapolis, Atlanta, Seattle, Austin, and Denver.

Within cities and metropolitan regions, many young singles gravitate toward downtown areas. "All parts of New York City became more educated," the *New York Times* story reports, "but Manhattan and Brooklyn stood out. In Manhattan, more than 57 percent of all residents had at least a bachelor's degree." Without children to worry about, singles are drawn to the density and connective tissue of urban centers, where they can walk or take public transit to work or go out at night, where owning a car is not a necessity, and where there are vibrant mating markets—saturated with places to meet, mingle, and go out on dates.

According to Cortright and Coletta's research, young singles between the ages of twenty-five and thirty-four were 33 percent more likely to live in a close-in neighborhood (within three miles of the city center) than were other demographic groups. In Seattle, 27 percent of people in this age group were clustered within three miles of the central business district; in Denver, it was 25 percent; in Portland, 21 percent; San Francisco, 18 percent; and Chicago, 16 percent. Half of all singles who responded to a Yankelovich survey said that they would consider living in a downtown neighborhood; two-thirds said they would consider living close to downtown; and 69 percent said they would consider living in another urban neighborhood outside of downtown. Only 33 percent of respondents said that they would even consider living in a far-off suburb.[15]

There are several kinds of urban neighborhoods where young people cluster. One increasingly popular option is what I call the *urban mosaic*. A diverse in-city neighborhood, it bears some resemblance to the classic urban neighborhood that Jane Jacobs wrote about, but it has a twist. It offers cheap space, ethnic restaurants with cheaper meals, and dense streets, but may have higher crime rates, less shopping, and less nightlife and open space. Once a magnet for immigrants, working families, and the older poor, they are now attracting twenty- and thirty-somethings drawn mainly by proximity and housing prices. Columbia Heights in D.C. fits the bill. A better example might be Astoria in Queens or the Mission in San Francisco. Unfortunately, urban mosaics—almost by their definition—are neighborhoods in flux. They teeter on the tipping point between poverty and disrepair on the one hand, and total gentrification, which eliminates their diversity, on the other.

Another option is one I call the *hipster haven*. With just the right combination of city grit and posh, hipster havens tend to attract a relatively affluent crowd—that doesn't want to appear *too* affluent. Music scenes, nightclubs, and coffee shops pop up everywhere in their wake, as older residents either cash out or are pushed out. Hipster havens also attract the bridge-and-tunnel crowd on the weekends—people from the suburbs who can't quite stomach city life during the week but like to visit from Friday through Sunday. They come for the small, colorful shops and stay for the sidewalk cafes and the hustle and bustle of a center city neighborhood. Examples of such include Williamsburg in Brooklyn, Chicago's Wicker Park, West Hollywood in LA, Toronto's Queen West, Washington, D.C.'s U Street corridor, Deep Ellum in Dallas, Montrose in Houston, Columbus, Ohio's Short North, and Royal Oak outside Detroit.

During my time in Pittsburgh, I watched as the South Side neighborhood transformed from an older steel community to a vibrant hipster haven filled with shops, restaurants, and housing. As demand has grown and rents risen, rampant gentrification has begun driving out authentic shops, bars, and restaurants. And these places have started to lose some of their creative energy. Plus, the noise is a big deterrent to families.

Not all young people aspire to be hip urban dwellers. Many hold a clear preference for suburban life. Though if asked some will admit that they like older suburbs, which already have many of the amenities typically found in cities. After growing up in the Maryland suburbs of Washington, Dianna Fooksman swore that she "would never move back there, even though it was a great place to grow up." When it was time for college, many of her friends attended school nearby; she headed to New England and spent her summers traveling to major cities across the country. After finishing graduate school in her mid-twenties, she started

looking for a job in arts management. She and her boyfriend considered four regions—Chicago, New York, Boston, and Washington, D.C. The one thing they were certain of, she says, is that
they "didn't want to live *in* the city." To her surprise, they ultimately settled in Columbia, Maryland, which offered a reasonable commute, access to downtown D.C., a small but vibrant
restaurant and bar scene, affordable housing, and a community
in which they could start a family and raise kids.

Older suburbs like Columbia, Maryland, appeal to young
people for these reasons. Some are located on subway or mass
transit lines that make commuting even easier. All in all, they offer younger residents safety, amenities, and access to a mating
market without some of the risks of living in the urban core. Nat-
urally, these types of neighborhoods also fit the needs of many
young professionals in their thirties, whether single or coupled,
many of whom have decided to remain in one place for a while.

But for those whose incomes tempt them into more high-end
living—or for those who just want to *live* like they have a lot of
money (even if they don't)—there is a pricier kind of in-city urban neighborhood: *designer digs.* These places feature upscale
condos, renovated town houses, organic markets, posh grocery
stores, and niche boutiques. Wine bars and high-end restaurants
are the designer digs' equivalent to the ethnic eateries in an urban mosaic, or a hipster haven's dive bars.

I've lived in two such neighborhoods. When I took my first academic job at Ohio State University, I lived in Columbus's remarkable German Village, which I still consider one of the most
strikingly beautiful urban neighborhoods in the United States.
German Village is a truly picturesque place, lined with small, ele-
gant brick houses built by German brewers in the late nineteenth century and dappled with tiny cobblestone streets and
amazing shops that with strong community support had been

saved time and time again from threatening wrecking balls. German Village taught me how important historical preservation is to neighborhoods. I loved it there and made fantastic friends.

In 1987, I moved to Carnegie Mellon in Pittsburgh and settled in Shadyside, an area filled with great historic houses and a vibrant commercial strip. I saw firsthand its transformation from an academic and hippie neighborhood filled with bookstores, "head" shops, delis, "old-man" bars, and antique shops to an upscale retail district boasting Banana Republic, Pottery Barn, Williams Sonoma, and Apple outlets.

There are many such places across North America. To name just a few: Georgetown in D.C.; Back Bay and Beacon Hill in Boston; Philadelphia's Rittenhouse Square; Lincoln Park and the Gold Coast in Chicago; Toronto's Yorkville; San Francisco's Union Square; La Jolla in San Diego; and, of course, Beverly Hills. But there are also a growing raft of designer digs located farther from urban centers that are small towns unto themselves: Carmel and Palo Alto, California; Coral Gables and West Palm Beach, Florida; Scottsdale, Arizona; Birmingham, Michigan; and Vail, Aspen, and Telluride, Colorado. Designer digs can be lovely places, and many once were.

But development pressure, rising rents, and the invasion of chain stores have made them far more homogenous than they were even a decade ago. Designer digs offer wonderful buildings, clean streets, and terrific architecture and renovations, but real estate prices are through the roof, and diversity—particularly economic diversity—is lacking.

The point is to find the place that's best for you, regardless of what others think. That's what John Whiteside did when he moved to Houston from Washington, D.C. His friends were shocked. They couldn't imagine a more different, less appealing place. But he did his homework, visiting Houston a number of times, and he liked what he saw. Only then did he apply for a job transfer.

He liked the city's old houses and tropical foliage, interesting, smart people, its thriving folk art scene, and the visible gay community. He noted "a pervasive attitude that anybody can do anything, create anything, and accomplish anything they want if they're willing to just do it." Since relocating, he's started his own business and built a tight circle of friends outside the "rat race" of D.C. Houston, he says, "won't wow you with natural beauty or charm you with quaintness," he concedes, and will "never be as hip as LA or as brainy as Boston," but "it's endlessly real, dynamic, and interesting."

Giant Sorting Sound

What we are witnessing, for better or for worse, is the growing stratification of communities, countries, and the world at large, which Bill Bishop dubs the "big sort."[16] Various ages, economic affiliations, cultures, and political affiliations once lived in proximity to one another. Now, more and more, we are segregating across virtually every economic and social dimension. It's not just rampant gentrification and the "blanding" of our cities that worry me, it's that the big sort is wreaking havoc on our social fabric, dividing and segregating societies across class lines.

For every young person who moves into an urban mosaic or a hipster haven, it is likely that a lower-income family, or part of that family, has been driven out. For every young professional who finds him or herself living the good life in a designer digs community, many more lower- and working-class households struggle to find affordable rental housing that will allow them to raise their families and make ends meet. City neighborhoods are a perfect microcosm of the rooted versus mobile phenomenon. And its implications are starkest for people with low incomes.

Many have argued that our society's growing economic divide is not born out of outsourcing, immigration, or even wage gaps. While all those things play a role, the real culprit is the divide in human capital and education. "The return for a college education, in percentage terms, is now about what it was in America's Gilded Age in the late nineteenth century," the economics professor and blogger Tyler Cowen writes. "This drives the current scramble to get into top colleges and universities. In contrast, from 1915 to 1950, the relative return for education fell, mostly because more new college graduates competed for a relatively few top jobs, and that kept top wages from rising too high." Starting around 1950, the relative returns to education began to rise. Since 1980 they have skyrocketed.

The reason, Cowen concludes, turns on supply and demand. "For the first time in American history," Cowen wrote in the *New York Times*, "the current generation is not significantly more educated than its parents. Those in need of skilled labor are bidding for a relatively stagnant supply and so must pay more." Furthermore, "evidence suggests that when additional higher education becomes available, it offers returns in the range of 10 to 14 percent per year of college, at least for the first newcomers to enroll."[17]

Class overlays powerfully with race and location. Add to this the even more troubling fact that a large segment of our young population—lower-income youth and African Americans, in particular—no longer live in the urban neighborhoods where they grew up; they live in prison. According to a 2006 Urban Institute report, the real jobless rate for black male high school dropouts in their twenties (including those in jail and not actively seeking work) was 65 percent in 2000, and 72 percent by 2004.[18] The same rate is just 34 percent for white dropouts, and

19 percent for Hispanic dropouts.[19] Using data from 2000, Steven Raphael of the University of California at Berkeley found that among black dropouts in their late twenties, 34 percent were in jail, more than the 30 percent who were working.[20]

Where we live affects how we grow up, how we spend our free time, the educational opportunities available to us, and the people we meet. Being stuck or rooted in place bears on one's financial success in life and one's overall happiness. But clearly, for many, being rooted has graver implications. It means being trapped in a place where options are limited and means to get out and move up are ever sparser.

14
MARRIED WITH CHILDREN

PENELOPE TRUNK, BLOGGER, AND AUTHOR OF *The Brazen Careerist*, has moved around a lot. After growing up in Wilmette, Illinois, she moved to Los Angeles to play professional volleyball, to Boston for graduate school, and then to New York City to embark on her writing career. But after getting married and having her first child, she and her husband knew it was time to move someplace that offered more space, affordable housing, and good schools.

So they conducted a search—a real search. They didn't limit themselves to communities within the New York region but canvassed the entire nation for a place that would best fit them and their young family. After spending six months poring over information on communities and matching them up with statistics about happiness, they ultimately chose Madison, Wisconsin, for its academic ambience, open-minded lifestyle, and ample outdoor amenities. It's one of those generalist places that gets high marks across the board. Life in Madison is far from perfect, as any reader of Trunk's blog knows. It's cold and lacks New York's cultural amenities. She likes to joke that her child's first word was "cow."

Like every other choice in life, the choice of place and location involves being cognizant of what you really need and what you can live without. Understanding these tradeoffs clearly is the key to being happy in your place.

For most of us, our second big move comes when we have kids. At that point certain tradeoffs become clear—schools versus restaurants, safety versus edginess, abundant space to play versus a great music scene. As the last chapter showed, lots of young married couples continue to live in the same neighborhoods they did when they were single. Many still do even when the kids are young. But once the kids are ready to start school, most people bite the bullet and move somewhere that can accommodate the new needs.

In the past, most people chose to move to nearby suburbs, as my parents did when they made the five-mile jump from Newark to North Arlington. Longer-distance moves were generally corporate transfers. But today, many more people are looking at their options through a much wider lens. With flexible careers not so closely tied to any one employer, they are considering places across the country and even across the world.

Valuing Families

Our society doesn't lack self-appointed advocates of families. Pundits and talking heads vie to outdo each other when it comes to supporting families and family values. Many equate the decline of the family with the decay of U.S. society. I should know, because I've felt their wrath. One of the most outspoken critics of *The Rise of the Creative Class* said that my perspective is for

"yuppies, sophistos, trendoids, and gays" and against "real families." Another said I was helping bring about the decline of
Judeo-Christian civilization.

I see no reason to make distinctions between "real" families
and other, presumably less real ones. Every kind of family needs
to be valued and treasured.

Rana and I both come from large, extended families whose
members remain very close. Our house is regularly full of visiting brothers, sisters, aunts, uncles, and their children. But as we
start thinking about a family of our own, I've come to recognize
how hard this is to do in today's society.

Parents across the nation and the world tell me of their
everyday struggles to raise families amid the growing pressures
of work, finances, time, and more. At the top of their list of
needs is affordable, quality child-care. But how many communities provide that? In most places it's up to the individual or, if
they're lucky, their employer to locate it. Imagine the economic
advantage in terms of talent attraction a community could gain
if it actually did what was required to make child-care available
to everyone.

Many parents tell me that one of the things they most want
for their children is cultural diversity. A young woman completing her medical training at the Cleveland Clinic grew to love the
city and her neighborhood. But she added, "I would never stay
in Cleveland to raise my family, because you do not have to go
too far to get to narrow-minded people, fearful of change, who
want to limit the rights of other people."

When we talk about valuing children and families, education is
where the rubber meets the road. A growing number of industry
leaders, academic experts, parents, and kids agree that our current school system is, to use Bill Gates's phrase, "broken."[1] Just
how broken is it? Here's one startling statistic: more than one in
ten U.S. high schools are "dropout factories" where no more

than 60 percent of students who start out as freshmen make it to their senior year, according to a 2007 study by Johns Hopkins University researchers.² If communities were really serious about providing family-friendly environments, they would dig in and fix this problem. There are a handful, such as Providence, Rhode Island, with its innovative MET schools program, that provide learning experiences tied to kids' interests, but most simply try to tweak the traditional model already in place.

The problem is that our educational system meets the needs of the old mass-production economy, which no longer reflects the realities of our creative age. Our school system was built to churn out conformists who could function well in rote factory jobs or rigid corporate hierarchies—*not* in creative, knowledge-based careers that demand innovation and independent thinking. "Our education system looks a lot like the U.S auto industry in the 1970s, stuck in a flabby, inefficient, outdated production model," New York mayor Michael Bloomberg wrote in the *Wall Street Journal* in December 2006.³

The intended purpose of that production model, futurist Alvin Toffler told a leading education magazine in February 2007, was to transmit industrial discipline—not knowledge.⁴ Think of the classic factory assembly line, regulated by the ticking of a clock meant to maintain keep an efficient pace of work. Toffler notes that while precise timing isn't important in agricultural communities, where work ebbs and flows, it is if one's working on an assembly line. If you're late, you mess up the flow of the production. School is structured in a similar way. When the school bell rings, Toffler writes, "you mustn't be tardy. And you march from class to class when the bells ring again."

Today, in an era of standardized testing and of teaching to the test, a huge number of children spend a good deal of their time learning by rote memorization and doing repetitive work reminiscent of the industrial age. This training is sorely out of touch with the needs of the knowledge economy. The public school system we have today, says Toffler, "is designed to produce a workforce for an economy that will not be there."

Most parents want their children in schools whose teachers actively engage students in their work. Both parents and educators are protesting that our industrial-age school system squelches the creativity out of kids. Most education experts report that U.S. schools work reasonably well in the early grades, when children are given more flexibility and latitude in developing learning skills, and that the real problems start when schools begin teaching specific subject matter. That's when U.S. students start to fall behind their European and Asian counterparts.

While many of today's schools are undoubtedly more advanced than the urban parochial school I attended, I can relate to these assessments. I loved school through fourth or fifth grade. But by junior high school, I was bored. I was good at my studies and did well on tests, even with little effort. You could say I "dropped in." My real focus was the garage band I created with my brother and our daily practice sessions in my parents' basement. In high school, I was even more bored.

Many of the smartest kids I ever met dropped out simply because they weren't stimulated enough to stay. It doesn't necessarily take much to keep kids from dropping out: a good education need not be at odds with what keeps kids engaged— whether it be art, fashion, music, technology, or sports.

It's a huge mistake to try to put the blame on teachers. Most teachers I know are hard-working and dedicated. A recent 2006 study by the Gallup Organization found that one way to improve schools is to better engage the teachers.[5] A key to making schools more effective, the Gallup study shows, is to involve teachers integrally in all facets of the educational process, similar to the way successful and productive companies engage their employees.

Parents are coping in a variety of ways. Some are moving considerable distances to find schools that work for them, according to a February 2007 *Wall Street Journal* report.[6] In part, this is made possible by rising affluence and workplace flexibility, which affords some parents considerable geographic latitude with their jobs. The Internet provides ready access to schools across the country, opening up the range of options available to parents who are willing to pick up and move for a better education.

Others are opting out of the system entirely, deciding to home-school their kids instead. Home-schooling, according to *Business Week*'s Michelle Conlin, is "no longer the bailiwick of religious fundamentalists or neo-hippies looking to go off the cultural grid." It's now a growing trend among the educated elite.[7] The number of children being home-schooled grew from 850,000 in 1999 to more than 1.1 million in 2006, according to the U.S. Department of Education.

While the general perception is that people home-school for religious reasons, a more common reason is growing concern over school environments, including negative peer pressure, safety, and drugs. Nearly a third of home-schooling parents surveyed by the National Center for Educational Statistics cited "concern about the environment in other schools" as their primary reason for educating their kids at home. More and more parents, Conlin writes, "believe that even the best-endowed schools are in an Old Economy death grip in which kids are learning passively when they should be learning actively, especially if they want an edge in the global knowledge economy." Parents want more flexibility, more control, and a more direct hand in shaping their child's education.

This trend is heavily influenced by changes born out of globalization: increased workplace flexibility, the rise of free agents who work from home or virtual offices, and the opportunity to live in multiple locations. Home-schooling, Conlin writes, untethers "families from zip codes and school districts, just as the Internet can de-link kids from classrooms, piping economics tutorials from the Federal Reserve, online tours of Florence's Uffizi Gallery, ornithology seminars from Cornell University, and filmmaking classes from UCLA straight onto laptops and handhelds."

Parents who home-school also have available a growing array of resources such as private tutors, cyber communities, online curriculum providers, and parental co-ops.

In recent years, some of the most innovative and successful companies have come to understand that employees with children are far more productive in a family-friendly work environment. Jim Goodnight, the co-founder and CEO of the software company SAS Institute in Cary, North Carolina, likes to say that his most important assets come through the front gate at 9:00 A.M. and leave at 5:00 P.M. Goodnight has to make sure his employees work in an environment that allows them to be as productive and creative as possible.

That's why the company offers a full range of family-friendly services—from on-site health-care and daycare to on-site schools, including a private high school, on-site tutoring, and assistance with standardized tests. This policy underlies the company's extremely high retention rate of employees. Goodnight understands that people simply cannot perform well if they are stressed out about their kids. I know of many people who would gladly trade a pay raise for the kinds of resources offered by a company like SAS.

Competition for talent is growing increasingly international, and these failures may put U.S. communities at real disadvantage. My collaborator Charlotta Mellander, herself a mother in Sweden, says that her country is a "place where society takes a larger responsibility for the family as a whole." She notes her community's good daycare centers: "I don't pay more than $200 per month to have my two kids there 40 hours a week, including meals." A safe environment, she adds, means "kids can have their own interests early on. Seven-year-olds go to their own sports activities. They go to the park with their sleds in the wintertime—without their parents. I'd say that the kids can have more freedom, without depending on the time of their parents."

Toronto, where we live now, is an amazing place for families with children. Our neighborhood is a mile and a half from the university and less than two miles from the downtown core. It has great public as well as private schools, and is filled with families with children. The suburbs versus city tradeoff does not really exist here. As Roger Martin explains:

> In Boston, we lived in the lovely Wellesley Hills. Even though it was an upscale neighborhood, with large single-family houses, we wouldn't have considered letting our 7-year-old son or 10-year-old daughter walk six or seven blocks to a friend's house—or letting our 12-year-old son walk four blocks down to the shopping district on Route 16. It would have felt like being a bad parent.
>
> In Toronto, our youngest has been biking to school since he was 13 years old—and school is about a twenty-minute bike ride along one of the main north-south streets of the city—without inducing even a mild concern. We simply do not worry about their personal safety here.

How many American parents can still say that? In our old neighborhood in D.C., every single child was in private school. Not only were the public schools not up to snuff, the surrounding community was extremely dangerous. We got a feeling for this one day when we came across a map of D.C.-area crime in the *Washington Post*. Our neighborhood was a veritable island on this map surrounded by huge swaths of dots showing murders and other violent crimes all around us.

This was driven home to us our first Halloween in Toronto, so much so that I gave it a name, the "Trick-or-Treater Index," on my blog. During our time in Washington, D.C.—in a solid neighborhood in the city's northwest quadrant—not a single kid came to our door in three years. But on Halloween night in our neighborhood in Toronto, which is closer to the city core and considerably denser than our D.C. neighborhood, our house was mobbed by children of a mosaic of races. A person wrote a comment on my blog, pointing out that Catherine Austin Fitts, a former assistant secretary of Housing and Urban Development, came up with a similar index—the "Popsicle Index"— which she describes as the percentage of people in a community who feel that a child can leave home safely to buy a popsicle. As if that wasn't enough, the day after Halloween the U.S. Census Bureau released a study which found that nearly half of all children in the United States live places where their parents fear that neighbors may be a bad influence, and more than one in five children are kept indoors because they live in dangerous neighborhoods—a number that rises to 34 percent for African Americans and 37 percent for Hispanics.[8]

Here's one more story for you. In the fall of 2006, I was discussing the question of where we choose to live with students, many of whom are from foreign countries, in my graduate seminar at George Mason University. When I asked those from abroad where they thought they might eventually settle, I was shocked by their answers. Most said they wanted to get their degrees and establish their careers in the United States.

But once they married and had children, they expected to return home. Whether they were from East Asia, India, Latin America, Europe, or Africa, they all wanted to raise their children outside the United States. The educational systems were better, they said; their societies were less materialistic; and there was less pressure to work and far more time and consideration for family. And, they added, they would leave the United States even if it meant giving up money and long-term career prospects.

There is a veritable world of options out there for people looking for a great place to raise their families.

The Family Friendlies

OK, enough ranting. Clearly, lots of people note how important it is for regions to be family-friendly. But few studies provide the kind of detailed empirical evidence required to compare how good cities and regions are for families and children.

One ranking done by *Child* magazine, based on indicators of health, crime, environment, housing, employment, and other factors came up with the following top ten cities for families: Denver, Norfolk, Minneapolis–St. Paul, Miami, Orlando, Madison, Anaheim, Rochester, Boston, and San Diego.[9]

Another ranking is the *Kid Friendly Cities: Report Card 2004*, compiled by Population Connection.[10] It is based on measures of health, education, population, and other community factors. Topping its list are Des Moines and Spokane, both of which received A-plus grades, followed by Boston, Madison, Kansas City, Indianapolis, Seattle, Fremont, Yonkers, and Glendale with A's. San Francisco, San Diego, and Minneapolis received A-minuses.

A third, more comprehensive ranking comes from a 2007 study by the Harvard School of Public Health and the Center for the Advancement of Health. The study examined areas with the largest child populations with an eye on race, and measured which communities were best for white, Asian, black, and Hispanic children based on housing, neighborhood conditions, residential integration, education, and health.[11] According to their rankings, the best regions for white children are Ann Arbor, Boston, Chicago, Denver, and Middlesex (New Jersey). For Asian kids, the metro regions of Austin, Baltimore, Monmouth (New Jersey), and Nassau County (New York) top the list. For Hispanic children the top-ranked places are Ann Arbor, Cincinnati, Colorado Springs, Fort Lauderdale, and Jacksonville. And for black children, Colorado Springs, Denver, Middlesex, Nassau, Portland, and Raleigh lead.

Now, have a look at our rankings of the best places for families (see Table 14.1). Although one can define family in many ways, the available data limited our definition to officially "married" couples, one of whom was sixty-four or younger, with children under age 18 in the household. In addition to basic factors—such as prevalence of the same population and the growth factors discussed earlier—we factored in the crime rate and student-teacher ratio.

The Washington, D.C., Boston, San Jose, New York, and San Diego regions top our list of the best large regions for families, with Austin, Minneapolis, Houston, Atlanta, and Dallas coming in as best buys.

Stamford, Worcester, Poughkeepsie, New York, Ventura, and Raleigh take our top spots for midsize regions. Des Moines and Madison make the cut as best buys.

Manchester (New Hampshire), Trenton, Boulder, Provo, and Norwich come out on top for small regions. Fayetteville (Arkansas), Killeen (Texas), and Green Bay score as best buys.

It's high time we got beyond the crude stereotype that all gays and lesbians are swinging city singles. When I think about my own gay colleagues and friends, I have to smile; most of them are older, more conservative, and more committed to their relationships than many of my straight friends. My experience is not an anomaly.

TABLE 14.1 — BEST PLACES FOR FAMILIES
WITH CHILDREN

	All Households		Gay and Lesbian	
	Overall	Best Buy	Overall	Best Buy
Large Regions	Washington DC	Austin	Hartford, CT	Austin
	Boston	Minneapolis	San Francisco	Houston
	San Jose, CA	Houston	Boston	Hartford, CT
	New York	Atlanta	New York	Minneapolis
	San Diego	Dallas	Baltimore	Kansas City
Medium-size Regions	Stamford, CT	Des Moines, IA	Worcester, MA	Worcester, MA
	Worcester, MA	Madison, WI	Stamford, CT	Des Moines, IA
	Poughkeepsie, NY	Raleigh, NC	Portland, ME	Portland, ME
	Ventura, CA	Worcester, MA	Raleigh, NC	Stamford, CT
	Raleigh, NC	Bridgeport, CT	Ventura, CA	Raleigh, NC
Small Regions	Manchester, NH	Manchester, NH	Manchester, NH	Manchester, NH
	Trenton, NJ	Fayetteville, AR	Trenton, NJ	Fayetteville, AR
	Boulder, CO	Killeen, TX	Norwich, CT	Green Bay, WI
	Provo, UT	Boulder, CO	Green Bay, WI	Killeen, TX
	Norwich, CT	Green Bay, WI	Santa Rosa, CA	Roanoke, VA

Note: Region names are shortened to core city. See Appendices C and D for full listings.

Source: Analysis and rankings by Kevin Stolarick. Data from the 2005 American Communities Survey of the US Bureau of the Census and other sources.

Anyone who still wants to draw a distinction between the gay community and traditional child-rearing families will have to deal with the fact that families with children constitute a large segment of the gay population. More than one in four same-sex couples (28 percent) has a child under the age of eighteen, according to detailed research by UCLA demographer Gary Gates and Jason Ost. That's astonishing when you consider that among the U.S. population as a whole, just one in three households has any children. Gay and lesbian couples account for 3.5 of every one thousand households in the U.S. with children.

"As tolerance spreads, gay life is becoming more suburban, contented and even dull," announced a June 2007 article in *The Economist*. "San Francisco is great if you are young, single and looking for a party. But if you want to settle down with a partner, the suburbs and the heartland beckon. Gays who have children—and a quarter of gay couples do—gravitate towards them for the same reasons that straight parents do: better schools, bigger gardens, peace and quiet."[12] According to Gates's research, gay couples are still more likely than straight ones to live in cities, but the gap is closing. In 1990, 92 percent of gay couples were in what the Census Bureau calls "urban clusters," compared with 77 percent of all U.S. households. By 2000, the gap had closed to 84 percent for gay couples and 80 percent for households in general—a striking convergence.

So let's look at the best places for gay and lesbian families with children. Hartford, San Francisco, Boston, New York, and Baltimore top our list for large regions. Austin, Houston, Minneapolis, and Kansas City make the grade as best buys. Worcester, Stamford, Portland (Maine), Raleigh, and Ventura lead for midsize regions, with Des Moines again a best buy. Manchester, Trenton, and Norwich, Green Bay, and Santa Rosa (California), come out on top for small regions. Fayetteville, Killeen, and

Roanoke, Virginia, make the grade as best buys for gay and lesbian families.

From Strollerville to Family Land

When most people think of family-friendly communities, they
imagine a sylvan setting in a small town or upscale suburb—a
place with big houses and big yards. But families live happily in
a wide variety of urban neighborhoods. A 2006 Yankelovich survey found that young married couples with children are as open
to moving to urban neighborhoods close to downtown (51 percent) as to small towns (52 percent) or far-off suburbs (54 percent). On balance, it's true that most young families (73 percent)
prefer to reside in older suburbs close to the city rather than in
them.[13] Forget *Leave It to Beaver:* there are many family-
friendly neighborhoods (with and without cul-de-sacs) worth
imagining.

One such option for young families is a place I call
strollerville. This is a neighborhood full of urban holdovers—
young families who never quite got tired or burned out by city
life. Every city has them. My brother is raising three kids in
Hoboken, New Jersey; the abundance of strollers in the city's
small parks amazes me each time I visit. The same can be said of
Capitol Hill in Washington, D.C., or Toronto's Cabbagetown,
where strollers and children line the streets.

Or St. Louis. When Mark Allgeier and his wife started house
hunting there for their family, they initially looked in the city's
suburbs. But after looking at several communities whose houses
and neighborhoods all felt too generic, they discovered their fit
was actually in Maplewood—an older neighborhood in the city
with unique houses, with a post office, several pubs, a diner, a
church, and a grocery store all nearby. The area felt anything

but generic. "You should see Halloween night here," Allgeier says, when all the kids are out trick or treating.

New York City neighborhoods that used to be singles haunts or even drug bazaars now teem with young mothers and nannies out with their babies. In March 2007, Sam Roberts of the *New York Times* wrote: "Manhattan, which once epitomized the glamorous and largely childless locale for *Sex and the City*, has begun to look more like the set for a decidedly upscale and even more vanilla version of 1960s suburbia in *The Wonder Years*."[14] Roberts points out that since 2000, the number of children under age five living in Manhattan increased by nearly a third (32 percent).

Roberts's *Times* story profiles David Bernard and Joanna Bers, owners of a management and marketing consulting business, who despite growing up in suburbia now live with their twin toddlers on Fifth Avenue. "I like the idea of raising them in the city because they're prepared for pretty much anything. The city challenges you," Mr. Bernard told the *Times*. "It prepares you for life." Bernard and Bers defended New York City as a melting pot, despite the recent boom of white babies: "We were just at the Children's Museum, and I didn't see a lack of diversity there at all," Ms. Bers said, before adding, "We have every intention of sending our kids to P.S. 6. New York is a wonderful place to raise children, especially if there are more of them and more resources devoted to them."

Of course, there is plenty about New York City that would deter many parents from raising a family there. A nice two-bedroom apartment in Manhattan costs $2 million or more. And while P.S. 6 is a public school, it is one of only three on the Upper East Side that is rated acceptable by the Parents' League of New York.

As my college buddy Mario Batali once told me, the best perk about being a celebrity chef was the ability to get his kids into private school. There were a surplus of investment bankers and financial types, but how many schools had the kids of a celebrity chef?

But strollervilles, despite their convenience and urbanity, lack spontaneity when it comes to child-raising. Bill Frucht points out that he and his wife could never just send their kids outside, they had to take them out. The kids could never just go over to a friend's house to see what he was doing—something both Bill and I were doing by age four. Bill or his wife had to make a play date and then go over and chat with the parents until it was time to go home. A steady routine of supervising your children's play can be exhausting for the parents, and it's one reason many of the women pushing the strollers in strollerville are not mothers at all but nannies—which in turn is another reason why living there is so very expensive.

And this is to say nothing about what the near-total lack of un-supervised time does to children's creative development. Much of my childhood, like Bill's, was spent without an adult in sight, which is far less true of kids today. Ironically, today's creative-class parenting styles may actually stunt the creative growth of children.

Strollervilles can also reduce the diversity their parents are trying to achieve for their children. White children now consti-tute the majority among Manhattan's white, black, and Hispanic children—and as of 2005 their parents' income averaged $284,208 a year. By contrast, the average income among other households in Manhattan with toddlers was $66,213 for Asians, $31,171 for blacks, and $25,467 for Hispanics.

Such findings make many ask: what's the point of living in a city whose demographics increasingly resemble those of the suburbs?

Another kind of neighborhood is the *ethnic enclave.* These are primarily immigrant communities, built around specific religious or cultural or ethnic identities. Often its streets give you the impression you're in a foreign country—the groceries, restaurants, churches, and shops all retain a very specific cultural character. Toronto, where we live now, is filled with them. Ethnic enclaves now dot the suburban landscape, too. They are especially popular with families who want to immerse their children in the customs and languages of their home country. Such communities are often fraught with tension, as they endeavor to preserve their culture in the face of competing ways of life; they also tend to be extremely family focused, viewing children as the important legacies of their culture.

My wife, Rana, is Jordanian and grew up in Troy, Michigan, near a huge Middle Eastern enclave. After graduate school she took a job as director of public relations at the Detroit Zoo. Her cousin Suha works as an elementary school teacher in the Detroit public schools, teaching bilingual classes to new Arab immigrants.

On a spring day several years ago, Rana and her cousin arranged for the class to visit the zoo. For weeks, Suha had told her students about her younger cousin. When the class finally arrived, Rana came zipping out to greet them on her zoo-issued golf-cart, wearing a miniskirt and heels, her long hair flowing behind her.

When Suha introduced the class in their bhurkas and traditional Arabic dress, they started to giggle and tease their teacher: "That can't be *your* cousin." The students didn't know any members of their community who dressed and looked like Americans.

Similarly, as young people flood into ethnic enclaves, these communities are seeing their ethnic character fade.

For parents who want some semblance of urban amenities but in a less congested setting, there is the *boho-burb*. These are older suburbs, typically dating from before the great postwar suburban building boom. Often they are on old streetcar, railroad, or subway lines and contain busy commercial strips with cafes, restaurants, boutiques, and shops. Places like Arlington and Alexandria, Virginia; Montclair, New Jersey; Brookline, Massachusetts; Oak Park outside Chicago, and many others. Boho-burbs offer proximity, historic buildings, and teeming retail corridors, but they also share some of the problems of strollervilles: the real-estate prices are sky high, and children often cannot be outdoors unsupervised.

Another variation is the *preservation-burg*. These are 150-year-old places with great Victorian houses built along riverbeds or railway lines and shells of an industrial past. They're some of the most authentic American places, with noble, sturdy houses and the rich patina of history. Formerly centers of transport, manufacturing, and commerce, these areas lost much of their luster and verve by the mid-twentieth century. Now, stocked with sturdy older housing, revitalizing town centers, and reusable warehouse buildings, preservation-burgs are attractive to young families looking for authenticity and a real-town feeling. The Hudson Valley suburbs of New York City fit the bill here, as do the many river towns of Illinois. Grosse Pointe outside Detroit is another; so are Sewickley outside Pittsburgh, and the many quaint towns up and down the Susquehanna River, near Philadelphia. Preservation-burgs offer quaint older housing, but many of them are a bit farther afield and require longer commutes for those who work in or near the urban center.

Family land is still the classic choice for family living. They're filled with soccer moms, patio men, bouncing babies, manicured backyards, and giant gas grills. They offer great schools and manicured lawns.

Peggy Jenkins is a fan of family land. Having lived in Boston, Washington, D.C., and Honolulu, Jenkins ultimately decided to raise her family in Moscow, Idaho. "None of the others hold a candle to Moscow," she says. "Think timber, river, and grasslands, not Napoleon Dynamite and potatoes. And think university—Moscow is home to the University of Idaho, and is only six miles away from Washington State University." The community, she adds, offers something for everyone. There are artists, scientists, nature buffs; people with progressive values and those with more traditional values—all of which adds richness to the community. And Moscow has a cross-section of social classes—a disappearing feature across much of U.S. society. "Kids who live in trailer parks hang out with the kids who live in the mansion on the hill."

While its schools are often better than urban public schools, family land suburbs lack diversity. Commutes can be long and arduous, and the architecture can be mundane. Schools and churches tend to be the nodes that tie these communities together; much of the social life happens in backyards, at private clubs, or otherwise behind closed doors, with the implications that if you're not invited, you may never even know what kinds of groups exist. The lack of a physical town center is often mirrored in the lack of a social center.[15]

Others want to live even farther out. They want a bigger house, with a bigger yard, in a more traditional suburb. These people gravitate to *edge cities,* first made famous by Joel Garreau.[16] Part of Garreau's definition of an edge city was that its population increased at 9:00 A.M. on weekdays—meaning that more people came there to work than left to work, as would be the case in a traditional residential suburb. Edge cities have huge shopping malls and commercial complexes that, to the chagrin of some and the delight of others, serve as their centerpiece. Silicon Valley is a classic edge city with a techie twist. So is Schaumburg, Illinois. Tyson's Corner, Virginia, is considered by many to be the archetypal edge city —it was the model for Garreau's book. Edge cities "are so dispersed across the geography," Garreau writes, "as to challenge the definition."

Many of the fast-growing edge cities of the 1980s and 1990s are struggling today. They're congested and their malls have not aged well. Edge cities now face a number of challenges, the first and foremost being how to transform them into real communities. How to reduce the reliance on cars as the way of getting around? How to increase density? How to make them more pedestrian friendly and accessible by mass transit? How to transform them from subdivisions amid shopping malls to integrated live-work-learn-play communities?

Newurbia is another option. The brainchild of architects like Andrés Duany and Peter Calthorpe, newurbia is a designed community with a traditional feel.[17] The houses are clustered tightly together but surrounded by lots of green space. These places are typically oriented to pedestrian traffic (they restrict the use of cars) and shaped around town centers. One of the most famous examples is Celebration, Florida, on the outskirts of Disney World. But even though they have town centers, these new urbanist communities can lack diversity. Seaside, Florida, Duany's signature project, was the community used in the *Truman Show*—in which Jim Carey's character is unaware that he is living in a constructed reality surrounded by fake friends and family, leading a life intended for the entertainment of those who live outside it.

Then there's *exurbia*. These are the places at the far fringes of major metropolitan centers that have registered remarkable growth over the past two decades. Exurbs are not rural areas as such. They are the far-off peripheries of major mega-regions. Some people go there because they need the space and can't afford the high prices closer in; others go to avoid the hustle and bustle of the city. Ironically, they usually find themselves right back in it, with commute times in excess of 90 minutes each way.

There are tradeoffs involved in each of these types of communities. Strollervilles offer convenience, proximity, urbanity, and diversity, but they are pricey and can be difficult places for children to lead spontaneous lives. Family land suburbs and edge cities offer big yards, plenty of space for kids to play, and great schools, but may lack ethnic and racial diversity. Many who live there or farther afield in exurbs but work in the central city face long commutes, which psychologists now rate as one of life's least satisfying activities. The point is that while each of these kinds of places has something to offer, none of them is perfect. The key is to think through what your family's real needs are and choose what best fits you.

Like Marries Like

It is often said that in order for a marriage to work, love is not enough. Most successful partnerships are also built on shared values, similar backgrounds, and comparable lifestyle preferences. In the last fifty years, women have asserted their right for these things, and the result has been an increase in what some call egalitarian marriages—relationships in which wives are just as smart, wealthy, and career-oriented as their husbands. A *New York Times* article published in the fall of 2006 called attention to a troubling implication of this seemingly progressive shift: "Are we achieving more egalitarian marriages at the cost of a more egalitarian society?"[18]

In other words, while partners have achieved more parity in education and income, the rift between those couples and their less educated, less privileged counterparts has widened, reinforcing existing socioeconomic divides. College-educated men and women today are less likely to marry down—to choose mates who are less educated than they are. According to a 2005 study by sociologists Christine Schwartz and Robert Mare, the chances of a high school graduate marrying someone with a college degree shrank by 43 percent between 1940 and the late 1970s.[19] In this decade, the researchers reported in the journal *Demography,* the percentage of couples who share the same level of education reached its highest point in 40 years.

It's hard to fault people for what Nobel Prize winner Gary Becker termed "assortative mating"—the tendency to pair off with someone like ourselves.[20] And in a world in which highly talented and highly paid people concentrate in the same handful of places, it should come as little surprise that they are marrying each other. Over time, this growing tendency of like marrying like will only reinforce clustering and geographic sorting along class lines, giving the emerging map of social, economic, and cultural segregation even greater permanence.

It stands to reason that assortative mating reflects economic inequality, but recent research also offers evidence that the phenomenon is a driving force behind disparities in wealth as well. A study by economists Raquel Fernández and Richard Rogerson, published in 2001 in the *Quarterly Journal of Economics,* concluded that increased marital sorting (whereby high earners marry high earners and visa versa) "will significantly increase income inequality."[21] Likewise, a 2003 analysis by Brookings economist Gary Burtless found that increased martial sorting between 1979 and 1996 was behind 13 percent of the considerable growth in economic inequality of that period. Burtless cautions, however, that he does not believe assortative mating is necessarily more pronounced than it used to be: men have long married women of their own social class. "Now that women who are in a position to [work or pursue advanced degrees] are attending college and graduate school and joining the professions," writes Annie Murphy Paul in the *New York Times,* "the economic consequences of Americans' assortative mating habits are becoming clearer."

Also behind growing socioeconomic inequality is a growing gap between married couples and single people. Recent studies show that the marital prospects of rich and poor people are diverging. As I noted, marriage has declined across all income groups, but among those who do get married, highly educated couples with high incomes fare far better than those couples with lower incomes. "As marriage with children becomes an exception rather than the norm," the *Washington Post* reported in March 2007, "social scientists say it is also becoming the self-selected province of the college-educated and the affluent."[22]

Class seems to be the best predictor of whether Americans will marry or cohabit, perhaps because marriage is so expensive argues Pamela Smock, a University of Michigan sociology professor.[23] This trend is not limited to the urban poor; it affects suburban and rural areas in equal measure.

Given the simple law of compounding, the end result is easy to see. Over time, highly educated households draw from two increasing incomes, while less skilled and less advantaged people struggle along with one or occasionally none. From where they meet to how they advance in our society, their location and impact are inextricably tied to our increasingly spiky world. Thus, the family, like so many other aspects of our society, is subject to the same kind of sorting brought on by the clustering of like with like.

At the same time, it's getting harder and harder to draw a line between different kinds of families. While culture warriors bloviate about how "yuppies, sophistos, and gays" are undermining old-fashioned "family values," the facts of the matter stand that the best places for traditional families and the best places for gay and lesbian families are often the *same* places. Not only is it high time to pay attention to where you choose to raise your family; it also may be time to rethink what family values really mean.

15
WHEN THE KIDS ARE GONE

O N JANUARY 2, 2005, MARGARET PAYNE CAME TO A REAL-
ization. Strolling along the glistening waterfront in
Tacoma, Washington, past the museum filled with the incredible glass creations of Dale Chihuly, she told her adult daughter:
"I want to live here." Soon after, she signed a lease on a 600-
square-foot loft apartment—but not without first taking a "big
gulp." Payne was about to give up her seventy-five-year-old
house, farm, and more than an acre of gardens in Washington's
Gig Harbor.

"The move has been one of the best decisions of my life," she
says now. "It changed my life!" Initially struck by the city's physical setting—the mix of renovated old buildings, industry, and
water in Tacoma's working harbor—she's since been thrilled by
the energy and connectivity in her new community. She's made
many new friends, and without having to commute to work, she
has time for other things such as volunteering at the Tacoma

Arts Commission and the Peace Community Center. Using some of the proceeds from the sale of her old house, she even bought a small sailboat.

When my wife and I lived in Washington, D.C., many of our neighbors were recent or soon-to-be empty-nesters. On Saturdays and Sundays in the summer, when we would gather by the neighborhood pool, I would invariably overhear at least two kinds of conversations.

The first would be among our neighbors' children—the oldest of whom would be in his or her mid-twenties and back home for a visit—fervently discussing the pros and cons of where they then lived and where they might go in the future.

The second would be among the parents. With their children out of the house or about to leave, they would talk about selling their large houses and moving somewhere else.

But where would they go? Some wanted to move to Georgetown, a mere three miles away, where they could walk to shops and restaurants. Those considering a move beyond D.C. wanted to find a similar kind of neighborhood in a dense, authentic urban center. Not once did I hear anyone mention Florida, Arizona, or any other traditional retirement community—except with disdain.

Our third big move in life often comes once the kids leave home. Many empty-nesters and retirees do consider nearby locations, but a large number are also examining broader options. While fewer of them move than their younger counterparts, Americans over the age of sixty-five are most likely to move the farthest distances: 37.3 percent of them make moves of more than 500 miles, compared, for example, to 25.6 percent of those aged forty-five to fifty-four.

This age group's location choices will become even more significant as more and more of the 80 million baby-boomers, born between 1946 and 1964, head into their sixties.[1] The total share of the U.S. population over age sixty-five (which was less than 5 percent in 1900) is projected to grow from 12.4 percent in 2000 to 18.4 percent by 2025.

If history is any guide, the baby boom's impact will far exceed expectations. From Gidget to Woodstock and Silicon Valley to IRAs, baby-boomers have redefined the lifestyles, consumption patterns, and values of each new life stage they have entered. Their location and habitation patterns are no exception. Boomers spurred the gentrification of urban neighborhoods in the late 1970s and early 1980s, the creation of edge cities in the 1980s and early 1990s, and the revitalization of inner-ring sub-urbs in the late 1990s and 2000s. As they come of age, they will also almost certainly redefine what we used to call the retire-ment community. With greater wealth, higher levels of educa-tion, and more active lifestyles, the country's aging population is headed for an empty-nester and retirement lifestyle different from that of any previous generation. And because of their numbers and accumulated capital, where boomers choose to lo-cate will have an unprecedented effect on the choices open to younger generations as well.

But despite the generation's overall wealth, not all baby-boomers will fare well. According to a major study by William Frey and Ross DeVol, the next few decades' growth of "yuppie elderly"—married, in good health, with substantial accumulated resources, more active lifestyles, and greater locational choices—will coincide with the rise of another group, the "needy elderly," particularly widows over the age of seventy-five especially de-pendent on families and social institutions.[2]

Beyond Leisure Village

So where will retiring boomers go? According to Frey and De-Vol, their location choices are much broader than those of previ-ous generations. Florida and Arizona no longer top the list for retirees. Las Vegas is big, according to their analysis; its rise as a retirement destination is a significant part of its overall growth. Myrtle Beach, South Carolina; Wilmington, North Carolina; and Las Cruces, New Mexico, also register as leading destinations, as do Austin, Atlanta, Raleigh, Denver, Washington, D.C., and Houston. Urban centers also register. Frey's list of cities with the highest baby-boomer-to-child ratios (given in parentheses) includes: San Francisco (2.48); Seattle (2.01); Portland, Oregon (1.48); Washington, D.C. (1.42); Lexington, Kentucky (1.37); Nashville (1.33); Pittsburgh (1.32); Boston (1.29); Denver (1.29); Minneapolis (1.27); Miami (1.27); Atlanta (1.23); and Austin (1.22).

The AARP regularly publishes its own list of the best places to reinvent one's life, based on the availability of jobs and affordable housing, culture and entertainment options, access to outdoor recreation, safety, proximity to universities and educational institutions and health-care, and other factors. Its top-ranked places are Loveland/Fort Collins (Colorado), Bellingham and Spokane (Washington), Raleigh and Asheville (North Carolina), Sarasota and Gainesville (Florida), Fayetteville (Arkansas), Charleston (South Carolina), San Diego (California), San Antonio (Texas), Santa Fe (New Mexico), Iowa City (Iowa), Portsmouth (New Hampshire), and Ashland (Oregon).

Most people think of retirement as the major turning point of this life stage, but at least when it comes to making decisions about location, an equally significant event is when the kids leave home. I've divided this demographic into two distinct groups: empty-nesters, between the ages of forty-five and sixty-four; and retirees, over the age of sixty-five. Now let's have a look at our rankings.

San Francisco, Seattle, Boston, Minneapolis, and Hartford top our list of large regions for empty-nesters. Stamford, Portland (Maine), Madison, Honolulu, and Rochester (New York)

TABLE 15.1—BEST PLACES FOR
EMPTY-NESTERS (AGES 45–64)

	All Households		Gay and Lesbian	
	Overall	Best Buy	Overall	Best Buy
Large Regions	San Francisco	Minneapolis	San Diego	Minneapolis
	Seattle	Seattle	San Jose, CA	Austin
	Boston	San Francisco	Hartford, CT	San Jose, CA
	Minneapolis	Hartford, CT	Baltimore	Hartford, CT
	Hartford, CT	Boston	Boston	San Diego
Medium-size Regions	Stamford, CT	Madison, WI	Stamford, CT	Portland, ME
	Portland, ME	Portland, ME	Portland, ME	Stamford, CT
	Madison, WI	Stamford, CT	Honolulu, HI	Des Moines, IA
	Honolulu, HI	Rochester, NY	Worcester, MA	Madison, WI
	Rochester, NY	Omaha, NE	Rochester, NY	Toledo, OH
Small Regions	Boulder, CO	Boulder, CO	Trenton, NJ	Green Bay, WI
	Trenton, NJ	Charleston, WV	Norwich, CT	Winston-Salem, NC
	Fort Collins, CO	Huntsville, AL	Santa Rosa, CA	Manchester, NH
	Santa Rosa, CA	Fort Collins, CO	Manchester, NH	Charleston, WV
	Norwich, CT	Manchester, NH	Fort Collins, CO	Trenton, NJ

Note: Region names are shortened to core city. See Appendices C and D for full listings.

Source: Analysis and rankings by Kevin Stolarick. Data from the 2005 American Communities Survey of the US Bureau of the Census and other sources.

are top among midsize regions, with Omaha making the cut as a best buy. Boulder and Fort Collins (Colorado), Trenton, Santa Rosa, and Norwich lead among small regions. Charleston (West Virginia), Huntsville (Alabama), and Manchester (New Hampshire) make the list as best buys.

Turning to retirees age sixty-five and over: San Francisco, New York, Boston, San Jose, and Miami top our list for large regions. But Pittsburgh makes the cut as a best buy, along with Tampa. Stamford, Honolulu, Ventura (California), Palm Bay, and Sarasota (Florida) are the highest ranked midsize regions for retirees. Harrisburg and Allentown (Pennsylvania), Portland (Maine), and Cape Coral (Florida) make the cut as best buys. Santa Barbara and Santa Rosa (California), Trenton (New Jersey), and Port St. Lucie and Naples (Florida) lead among small regions. Pensacola (Florida), Roanoke (Virginia), and Erie (Pennsylvania) are best buys.

A growing number of empty-nesters are gay and lesbian. According to research by Gary Gates, more than one in ten (11 percent) of gay and lesbian people are over the age of sixty-four. To meet this need, one of the first low-cost housing developments aimed specifically at gay, lesbian, and transgender retirees opened in Hollywood, California, in March 2007, offering 104 units of affordable housing, a pool, an open courtyard, an activity center, and fully equipped facilities. According to a *Reuters'* article on the opening, the project provides elderly care facilities for gays who "face prejudice and lack the family support systems enjoyed by their heterosexual counterparts" and "are forced to hide their sexual orientation when they enter assisted living facilities after years of living openly as gays."[3] According to Gates, the regions with the largest concentrations of gays and lesbians over the age of sixty-four include Santa Rosa, San Francisco, Santa Cruz, and Riverside (California), Barnstable (Massachusetts) on Cape Cod, Fort Lauderdale (Florida),

TABLE 15.2—BEST PLACES FOR RETIREES
(OVER 65 YEARS OF AGE)

	All Households		Gay and Lesbian	
	Overall	Best Buy	Overall	Best Buy
Large Regions	San Francisco	Pittsburgh	San Diego	San Diego
	New York	Tampa	San Francisco	San Francisco
	Boston	New York	Boston	Orlando, FL
	San Jose, CA	San Francisco	New York	Seattle
	Miami	Miami	Los Angeles	Tampa
Medium-size Regions	Stamford, CT	Palm Bay, FL	Stamford, CT	Portland, ME
	Palm Bay, FL	Harrisburg, PA	Worcester, MA	Stamford, CT
	Honolulu, HI	Portland, ME	Honolulu, HI	Worcester, MA
	Ventura, CA	Allentown, PA	Portland, ME	Palm Bay, FL
	Sarasota, FL	Cape Coral, FL	Charleston, SC	Honolulu, HI
Small Regions	Santa Barbara, CA	Pensacola, FL	Santa Rosa, CA	Manchester, NH
	Trenton, NJ	Port St. Lucie, FL	Trenton, NJ	Killeen, TX
	Santa Rosa, CA	Naples, FL	Manchester, NH	Pensacola, FL
	Port St. Lucie, FL	Roanoke, VA	Norwich, CT	Santa Rosa, CA
	Naples, FL	Erie, PA	Port St. Lucie, FL	Port St. Lucie, FL

Note: Region names are shortened to core city. See Appendices C and D for full listings.

Source: Analysis and rankings by Kevin Stolarick. Data from the 2005 American Communities Survey of the US Bureau of the Census and other sources.

Burlington (Vermont), Goldsboro (North Carolina), and New York City.

Our rankings of the best places for gay empty-nesters and retirees consider where those groups are already located; they also take into account the same amenity and cost factors that are important to heterosexual households. San Diego, San Jose, Hartford, Baltimore, and Boston are the top-ranked regions for gay and lesbian empty-nesters. Minneapolis and Austin take top spots as best buys. Stamford, Portland (Maine), Honolulu, Worcester, and Rochester top the list among midsize regions. Des Moines, Madison, and Toledo make the list as best buys. Among small regions, Trenton, Norwich, Santa Rosa, Manchester, and Fort Collins take top spots for midsize regions. Green Bay, Winston-Salem, and Charleston (West Virginia), score as best buys.

Turning to gay and lesbian retirees over the age of sixty-four: the leading large regions are San Diego, San Francisco, Boston, New York, and LA. Orlando, Seattle, and Tampa make the cut as best buys. Stamford, Worcester, Honolulu, Portland (Maine), and Charleston (South Carolina) top the list for midsize regions, with Palm Bay (Florida) coming on board as a best buy. Santa Rosa, Trenton, Manchester (New Hampshire), Norwich, and Port St. Lucie take the top spots among small regions. Killeen and Pensacola make the cut as best buys.

Generation Ageless

"When it comes to finding a place to live," the *Wall Street Journal* wrote in October 2006, "today's retirees are looking for something completely different."[4] While weather and leisure remain important, retirees are looking for a community "where they can make friends and connections quickly, whether it's a small town or a walkable neighborhood in a big city." They also want to live somewhere that they can indulge post-work passions, a second career, or a newly adopted sport, or be near their grandkids, whether in a mixed-used development, a small town, or an urban center. Empty-nesters and retirees have a wide range of communities to choose from these days. Free from the constraints of full-time jobs and full-time parenting, some even find themselves with the flexibility and means to divide their time among multiple places.

After years of raising kids and taking care of large houses, an increasing share of this demographic is interested in downsizing and returning to the hustle and bustle of urban neighborhoods. "We don't want to be slaves to our house forever," is how one of my former D.C. neighbors put it. Many empty-nesters find themselves drawn to the same neighborhoods that attract young professionals and many people in the gay community. One reason is the obvious: no kids. Another is a common preference for proximity and urban amenities.

A growing number of empty-nesters have become re-singled, and by joining communities where they can make friends and meet other unattached people, they are able to form their own version of midlife urban tribes.

The Rosslyn-Ballston Corridor in Arlington, Virginia, has attracted thousands of such middle-aged people wanting to start over, according to a May 2007 *Washington Post* story.[5] Ray Tenenholtz met a new companion, Kim Slade (both at the age of sixty-three), when he moved to Arlington after separating from his wife of more than thirty-five years. "People like us, who are divorced or widowed or their kids have grown up, we need to have social lives and make new friends," Tenenholtz told the *Post.*

The conflicts that develop when young singles and empty-nesters share the same turf was the subject of a May 2007 feature story in the *Wall Street Journal*, fittingly entitled "Animal

House meets Empty Nest."[6] The story tracked the growing nationwide tendency of condominium projects, originally developed to appeal to twenty- and thirty-somethings, to attract buyers of a much older demographic.

The story also reported on the kinds of tensions that can emerge between these two groups. Julie Lammel, a speech pathologist in her early fifties, described the pool scene at her Nashville building there as an "animal house." "One time I went up there and the twenty-somethings had the whole place monopolized," she told the *Journal,* "and I thought, *Well, not today.*" She helped organize a group of empty-nesters in the building to take over the condo board. That's one side of the tension: younger folks resent what they see as their elders' stodginess and farmers' hours, as well as their effects on real estate prices in supposedly hip young neighborhoods.

College towns are an increasingly popular choice for empty-nesters because they offer access to great health-care, substantial amenities, and diverse, intellectually stimulating communities. Madison, Boulder, and Fort Collins all took spots on our lists. According to Frey and DeVol, Burlington (home to the University of Vermont), Bloomington (Indiana University), State College (Penn State), and East Lansing (Michigan State) have seen significant increases in empty-nesters. They also credit the influx of empty-nesters to Minneapolis and Columbus, Ohio, to the presence of major universities in these cities.

Of course, not all empty-nesters are out for action. Many prefer a less complicated, more pastoral life. After a thirty-year career in communications, Donna moved with her husband, Gene, from Kalamazoo to rural Allegan County in southwestern Michigan. Seeking a more natural, sustainable lifestyle, they were able to buy a five-acre farm where they could raise their own organic vegetables and keep chickens to provide their own organic eggs. For Gene, an amateur blacksmith, this was a chance to build his own forge. For Donna, who makes art from handmade paper grown on their farm, it was a chance to open her own studio, the White Oak Studio & Gallery. Moving to Allegan County also gave the couple an opportunity to tap into the resources of the Blue Coast Artists—an alliance of working artisans who pool resources to market their work to summer tourists, vacationers, and second home owners.

For many empty-nesters and retirees, a key factor in their location choice—and in most everything they do—is proximity to their children and grandchildren. While children may return home after college or when their parents turn ill, an increasing trend is for parents, especially those with means, to follow their kids. Some pick up and move everything—lock, stock, and barrel; for others, a small second home nearby suffices. In many cases, parents come to offer financial assistance or to help out with young families. Sometimes boomer parents want to share the excitement of their children's new lives in a vibrant big city—a prospect their children may feel ambivalent about!

Or how about a joint family move? That's exactly what Tom Hoog and his family did. When Hoog retired as CEO of Hill & Knowlton in New York, he started to think about where he and his wife would move. So they held a family caucus to talk it over with their three adult children. One son lived in Colorado, where the family had originated; another lived in Virginia; and their daughter was in Texas.

In talking it over, Hoog says, it became increasingly clear that "it made sense to reunite the entire family in one place." The place they chose was in the Rocky Mountains outside Denver, close to where they had lived when the kids were growing up. So they built a new home about six blocks from their original house. Their son Michael built a home there; their daughter, Michele, and her family came from Texas; and their son Mark followed. With the grandkids all in the same age range, Hoog adds, "they play on the same little league teams, and the girls go to the same dance studios and are best of friends."

Whatever boomers do, society listens and follows suit.[7] Wherever they go, new kinds of neighborhoods emerge and prices rise. It's no accident that the previous two major moves in boomers' life cycles, in the 1970s and 1980s, coincided with major run-ups in real estate markets. Where boomers flock, bargains disappear, and the neighborhood butcher shop is replaced by a pan-Asian fusion restaurant and a hardware store gives way to a high-end remodeling center. Authenticity quickly comes to acquire a sheen of self-consciousness that, to some, connotes its opposite. Those who lived in these places before feel like an alien culture's invaded, even while some of them make a mint from selling their homes.

Already, the recent back-to-the-city movement among boomers has changed the dynamics of entire communities, making it nearly impossible for subsequent generations to buy in, pushing them to fringe districts or out to the suburbs. Sometimes, if I ask just the right way, my students and younger members of my research team will tell me how they resent what boomers have done, not just by foisting "their music" on them, but by taking over whole parts of cities and pricing them out.

Are we sowing the seeds of generational conflict over location and community? Time will tell.

16

PLACE YOURSELF

WHEN I FIRST ANNOUNCED I WANTED TO WRITE A book that would actually help people choose the best place to live, many colleagues were alarmed. "You're a serious scholar," they said. "Academics don't write self-help books." Except that some do. Leading psychologists, like Martin Seligman, have written extensively on how to better your life by working to your strengths. Dozens of leading medical researchers and clinicians have written useful books, sharing their insights on everything from weight loss to general health management.

After more than twenty years of doing research on place, I felt hopeful that I, too, might be able to impart some information people could actually use. I was heartened when my editor offered his usual sage counsel: "If you really want to give advice, you have to earn it. The way for you to earn it is to write a serious, engaging, and convincing book on why place matters." If you've read this far, I hope you think I've earned that right.

By now I hope you will agree that place matters even more today than it did before. Despite all those predictions about how new technologies—the car, the cell phone, and, of course, the Internet—would free us from the constraints of location, allow work to be moved all over the world, and enable us to live most anywhere we want, location remains a key factor in the global economy.

When we look at where innovation and economic activity really occur, it turns out that only about two or three dozen places across the world really make the cut. By any measure of past, present, or future economic growth—population, economic activity, innovation, location of scientific talent—these mega-regions tower above their neighbors. And behind all these trends lies the great power of the clustering force: the tendency of creative people to seek out and thrive in like-minded groups, and the self-perpetuating economic edge that comes from their doing so. But place is not important only to the global economy, it is also important to your life.

I started this book by saying that most of us devote a great deal of thought to two key questions: what we do for a living and whom we make our life partner. All of us, regardless of the career we ultimately choose, intermittently agonize about where to work and how to best nurture and advance our careers. Some of us take even more time making sure we find the right person with whom to spend our lives and create a family.

But few of us spend sufficient time strategically considering the third question: *where* to live. In researching this book, it became clear to me that this third question is at least as important as the other two.

As we've seen, where we reside has more and more relevance to the kinds of work available to us. In a large number of professions, jobs have become geographically specialized, concentrating in certain places. What matters most to people is not unlimited job or career opportunity, but enough solid options to provide real flexibility and choice.

Where we live can determine other aspects of our economic stability, too. Take buying a house, which is the single biggest financial investment most of us ever make. The performance of real estate markets—the growth and appreciation of housing investments—varies widely from place to place. This does not mean one should choose a place to live solely on the basis of potential real estate returns, which is sort of like marrying for money. But so long as housing remains one of life's largest investments, it's better to know how different markets stack up on this score.

In addition to the state of our finances and our professional life, where we choose to live can hugely determine how happy we are in our personal lives. Where we live can determine whom we meet, how we meet them, and our opportunities for spending time with our friends and loved ones.

Perhaps even more important, place can determine how happy we are with ourselves. In addition to economic and cultural specialization, the clustering force has resulted in the geographic concentration of personality types. Different kinds of places suit distinct types of people. Someone who thrives in Manhattan may not flourish in Boise, Idaho, and vice versa. Understanding which places best fit one's personality ought to be at the top of every person's to-do list.

So in finding the best place for you to live, it's important to weigh five key factors.

First, you need to think about how the place you live will affect your job and career prospects. As we have seen, many kinds of jobs are clustering and concentrating in particular locations. Before you settle on a place, it's very important to look closely at how it matches up with your short-run and long-run career goals.

Second, it's crucial that you have a good sense of how important it is to you to have close friends and family near by, and of what you will give up if you move far away. In Chapter 5, we discussed one study which says that leaving close friends behind is worth as much as six figures in monetary compensation. Whether you think that number is reliable or not, it helps focus the mind on how where you choose to live can affect your relationships with family and close friends.

Third, you need to be honest with yourself about the kind of place that best suits your lifestyle. Some of us like the buzz and energy of the big city; others like the ease of living in the suburbs; still others want to be part of nature and the great outdoors. What are the hobbies, activities, and lifestyle interests that bring you true joy? I'm a cyclist and would not even think about living somewhere where the road-riding wasn't great. If you're a skier you probably want to be close to snow-capped mountains. If you're a surfer, sailor, or beach-bum, you'll want to be close to a great coastline.

Fourth, it's important to think carefully about how the place you choose to live matches your personality. If new experiences are your thing, you'll want to be in a place that provides intense stimulation. If you're an extrovert, you'll want to be around lots of other people who are easy to meet and befriend. If you're conscientious, you'll want to be around other people who take work seriously and honor their commitments.

Fifth and finally, you'll want to make sure your place fits your particular life-stage. If you're single, you'll want to be in a place where you can make friends and find people to date. If you're married with children, you'll want a community that's safe and offers great schools. If you're an empty-nester, you'll want a place not too far away from your kids where you can engage in interests and hobbies you really love.

Most of all, be aware of the tradeoffs involved. It's vital to weigh how important each of these five dimensions is to you when narrowing down the places on your list and ultimately making your choice.

Finding a place that best fits us isn't easy—as nothing that's truly important in life is—but it can be done. To help you better assess your priorities and options, I've come up with a basic framework, some real-world tools, and a ten-step plan to help you narrow the field and make your decision.

Step One: Get Your Priorities Straight

If you ask people what's most important to them in a partner or a job, chances are they will have a well-rehearsed response ready. Our relationship with place is no less intimate and should not be neglected, slighted, or taken for granted. Figuring out what your priorities are is the first and most fundamental step before deciding where to live.

Consider what's really important to you by asking yourself some basic questions about the place you live or might want to live.

- What do you like most and least about where you're living now?
- Where are the places you'd most like to live? If the place you live now isn't on this list, you need to give this special attention.
- Is it important to you to find a job in a specific field, or are you thinking about a career change?
- What stage of life are you in, and does that figure into your expectations?
- What's most important to you right now—your work? Finding a mate? Your physical environment? Your family?

- How important to you are outdoor activities and the natural environment?
- To what degree do climate and weather matter?
- How much do cultural activities like access to art, film, theater, and music mean to you?
- Do you crave experiences? Do you need to be around other people, or do you like being alone?
- Do you prefer the hustle and bustle of the big city, a comfortable suburb, or a rural community? Do you want to be closer to the action or farther from the frenzy?
- What are your deal-makers? Deal-breakers?

Take out a piece of paper and a pen and write down your preferences in these and any other key dimensions of your life. Consider nothing too big or too trivial.

Step Two: Generate a Short-List

For most people, simply giving these questions some preliminary consideration will lead to a surprising number of revelations. But my team and I have developed some basic tools that can also help you identify the broad metropolitan regions that may fit you best.

To narrow down your list of places, use the location calculators we've provided at whosyourcity.com (or use the link at creativeclass.com). One I like a lot is Bert Sperling's "Find Your Own Best Place" Web site.[1] Use these calculators to generate a list of five to ten possible places—that is, broad metropolitan regions—that are possible good fits for you. Don't be upset if these tools fail to generate a perfect set of matches. I've used a whole slew of them in researching this book, and sometimes they come up with places that don't really seem to fit me. If that happens to you, try them one more time, paying particular attention to your answers. If they still generate places that don't really fit you, take an even simpler approach: write down the places where you'd most like to live.

Step Three: Do Your Homework

It would be great if you could simply push a button and be instantly matched with your perfect place, but it's not quite that simple. There's a ton of pertinent information about the place that's best for you that can't be crammed into any computer program.

So, once you have your short-list in hand, my team and I have developed a framework that will help you assess your options. It's organized around what I call the *Place Pyramid* (see Figure 16.1), which reflects the research in this book.

At the base of the pyramid is opportunity. Next in line are basic services like education, health care, and so forth. Leadership forms the midpoint of the pyramid. Then come values, and on top there's the aesthetics and quality of places. As Chapter 11 has shown, each level is important. Most of us will be happiest when we find a place that meets our needs and preferences across the entire pyramid. The goal is to live in a place that fulfills your needs from bottom to top. When considering a potential move, it's crucial to assess how your new community will stack up against your needs at each level.

Where detailed statistical information is available, I'll tell you where to get it and how to use it. But for many things you need to know more about, there simply isn't any quantitative data available. You'll need to collect qualitative information—read local papers, talk to people there, and go out and see for yourself. In

FIGURE 16.1 THE PLACE PYRAMID

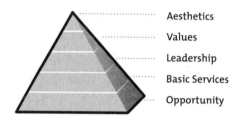

Aesthetics

Values

Leadership

Basic Services

Opportunity

many cases, collecting information this way will give you deeper and better insights into the places you're considering. The real power is in the combination of both types of data—hard statistical facts and your own personal assessments. If the numbers all say a place is perfect but your gut says it's not for you, take notice. Remember that the bottom line is your happiness.

To help you collect this information, my team and I have designed a tool we call the *Place Finder*, which I've included as an appendix to this book (see Appendix E). It may look simple, but, trust me, it reflects countless studies and decades of research. (You can download as many versions of it as you like from whosyourcity.com or creativeclass.com). I see it as a way to help you organize your thoughts, consider your priorities, collect and analyze quantitative and qualitative information, and ultimately compare, rate, and rank places. Fill out each box on the form using a 1–5 scale, with 1 as the lowest value and 5 the highest. Even after you've collected statistical information, there's plenty of room for your personal judgment. Enter the score that best reflects your assessment, your needs, your observations, and your sensibilities.

Step Four: What Do They Offer?

The first step in your assessment starts at the base of the pyramid: what are the economic opportunities the places on your list offer? If there aren't any, it might be hard to afford to live there. There's a wealth of statistical information on this out there. Business magazines like *Forbes*, *Money*, and *Business 2.0* provide annual listings of the best places for business and for jobs and careers. Local newspapers and business magazines provide more detailed assessments of the local economy. Check out the local business media as well as the local chamber of commerce's Web site. Most major cities also have bloggers who write regularly on local economic conditions.

Jobs

How do your places stack up in the specific job opportunities they offer. Consider the following questions: Do you want a job in the field you're in now, or do you want to change careers? Are you a risk-taker, or do you like to play it safe? Do you want to work for a company, or launch one? A great place to get detailed information on the job market is the Bureau of Labor Statistics. It has a fantastic Web site with profiles on a range of jobs and their salaries for more than 800 specific occupations, in every metropolitan region in the United States.[2] It's the baseline data my team and I use in our own research. It can tell you how many jobs there are in the places on your list and how much they pay. Use it to compare one place to another.

Don't forget the cost of living. Some places are more expensive than others, and your paycheck won't stretch equally everywhere. Make sure to calculate comparative costs so you know how far your salary will really go. There are calculators available online that will help you tally the precise cost-of-living

differences among the locations you're considering. They also
enable you to see what kind of salary you would need in order
to maintain your current lifestyle in other places. These sites
(salary.com is just one example) also give you objective, fact-
based tools with which to negotiate your salary, which is especially important if part of why you're moving is for a new job.

Professional Development

Whether or not you're on a fast career track, access to professional development and lifelong learning opportunities are important to everyone—if only to make sure our minds remain
active as we age! Studies have shown time and again that expanding one's mind can add years onto your life. Access to such
opportunities may depend, in part, on proximity to great colleges, universities, and graduate programs. But learning outside
of formal educational institutions through seminars, networks,
executive training programs, and professional development offerings can be even more important. Take note of where graduate programs are located (see guides such as *US News and
World Report,* or *Business Week*); survey local newspapers,
trade magazines, and Web sites for announcements on continu-
ing-education courses and seminar offerings. Make sure to see
for yourself what the community has to offer. Visit local colleges
and graduate programs and talk to people in programs that
might fit your needs.

Networks

In a similar vein, studies have also shown that people who feel
disconnected or isolated age at an accelerated pace; they're also,
not surprisingly, unhappier people. Plugging in, building networks, meeting people, and creating support structures—those
are all things that not only further professional development but
also contribute significantly to overall well-being. But in this re-

spect, as in most others, not all places are created equal. Do you know people who are already in these networks: if so, talk to them. Ask yourself: is this a place I can easily plug into, or is it the kind of place I'll run into real resistance?

Step Five: Getting the Basics Right

Next, take a long look at the quality of the community's basic services like education, safety, health care, housing, and the like. This, you will recall, is one of the most important dimensions a place has to offer. And it can vary a great deal across them.

Education

The quality and range of schools is certainly critical for parents of school-age children, but it's something everyone needs to look at—because the quality and proliferation of educational opportunities can indicate the quality and proliferation of other things, too, including safety. Unfortunately, there's no comprehensive or reliable data on schools. Some publications attempt to zero in on the best. *Newsweek* publishes an annual list of the top schools, as does *US News and World Report.* But these metrics can be hard to trust. After all, children thrive in different kinds of environments. I know plenty of parents who relocated for better access to high-quality public schools only to later transfer their kids to more specialized private schools. You'll need to dig this information out yourself. Local newspapers and magazines frequently list a community's top schools based on test scores and other measures. But you absolutely have to visit schools and talk to parents and children in them before you make your decision.

Health and Safety

Of course you need to consider safety and health; they're as basic as it gets. Fortunately, data on crime and safety are readily available from the FBI's Uniform Crime Reports.[3] Check the local papers, too, all of which tend to provide regular crime reports. Make sure to get a sense of the quality of local police, fire, and law enforcement. Are people who live there satisfied? Do police, firefighters, and EMTs respond in a timely fashion? Are they too aggressive for your taste?

Health is another key to happiness; having access to quality, affordable health care is critical. As we have seen, its importance varies with your age and life stage. Are doctors readily available? Are they taking new patients? Do they take insurance? You might think that is a strange question, but when we lived in Washington we found it was not only hard to find health care providers who were taking on new patients but virtually all of them also demanded payment up front in cash. What are the major health care centers nearby? Is there a trauma center? What about university-affiliated research hospitals? How long are waits at the emergency room? How healthy is the community overall? Here again you'll want to talk to people who live there about their health care experience. It doesn't hurt to visit local hospitals and take a look at the emergency room, especially on a busy Friday or Saturday night.

Housing

It's imperative that you have a good sense of the housing market, given the wide discrepancies out there. Even if you're a renter, you'll need to know if you will *ever* be able to buy a house in an area where you would want to live. Pay attention not only to current prices but also to historical trends and projections for the future. Start with information on housing prices from the Census Bureau's American Community Survey Web site.[4] *Business Week* and *Money* do regular rankings of housing prices by zip code. Zillow.com and other real estate Web sites provide extensive information on property values in the form of viewable maps. Many states have multi-listing services you can access online for free. And even when they don't, many real estate agencies have their own listings online and links to others as well. Go to open houses to get a good sense of what's available in your price range.

Getting Around

The ability to move easily—to get to and from work or anywhere else for that matter—is a significant factor in an individual's daily sense of well-being. Two of the biggest stressors related to place are long commutes and traffic jams, according to psychologists who study happiness. A study by Daniel Kahneman and his collaborators based on detailed diaries of people's daily activities found that commuting was the least enjoyable activity in anyone's day. (Not surprisingly, "intimate relations" topped their lists!)[5] Can you afford a house within a reasonable commuting distance, or will you have to drive long distances? Is there a subway, train, or other form of mass transit available? Can you live in a neighborhood where you can walk or use a bike for most activities? If you have to drive, how bad is the traffic? The American Community Survey has detailed data on commute times on its Web site. There are specialized reports that tell you where the most congested points are in major regions. To get a day-to-day sense of what traffic patterns are like during rush hour, visit local Web sites and watch local news. And above all else: try out your potential commute in advance.

It's also important to consider transportation and connectivity in a broader sense. How accessible is your location to the world? Is there a major hub airport nearby? If travel is part of your job or lifestyle, how many direct flights are there to your key destinations? How easily can you—and others—get in and out? What are the lines like at security?

Don't forget about the wired world. Colleagues of mine who moved to Paris in 2006 spent more than a month there without basic Internet or phone service. In this day and age, and particularly in this global economy, being cut off from the wired world can feel like a death sentence.

Step Six: Does the Place Get It?

Next, assess the leadership in the places on your list. Statistical analysis and polls of resident perceptions are one way to do it. But the best way to get a feel for leadership is simply to read the local media, especially the alternative papers and local bloggers. When possible, read up on the political history of a place; past events will undoubtedly inform its present context. Who are the political and business leaders? What are their track records, their popularity? Do they reflect the kind of diversity you want to see? Do their values and visions fit yours? Do they address issues that are important to you? Are decisions about the community discussed and made out in the open or behind closed doors? Are there opportunities for citizens to be involved? Talk to residents: How informed and engaged are they? How do they feel about their leadership? Is the leadership open-minded and inclusive, or dominated by squelchers? Go to community meetings, observe leadership in action, ask residents for their assessments.

Step Seven: Values Check

The next step is to look closely at the values prevalent in the places on your list—things like tolerance, trust, and self-expression. These are things many people neglect when moving to a new place, but as we've seen, they are among the things that matter most to how happy you'll ultimately be.

Tolerance .

Like people, places have varying abilities to welcome and absorb newcomers—particularly those who are different from its current residents. Some places, like New York City or Toronto, have a large number of new immigrants from around the world. Others are more insular, making it harder for newcomers to fit in and feel welcome. Some are warm and friendly, others a bit more aloof. You need to figure out how important this is to you, and how well (or not) you may fare in a new place. Talk to people who live there. Better yet, walk down the streets. Do you see the kinds of people you want—and need—to be around?

Trust

Trust—not only between people but also between people and institutions—is hard to measure, but not impossible. There are signs everywhere. Do people make eye contact with each other on the street? Do they hide their handbags or briefcases when they sit down? Does someone's "word" still seem to matter in everyday business transactions? Do people lock their doors when they leave their houses or cars? Do people treat each other with respect? How are children treated? What about young singles, families, the elderly, or people with disabilities? Are some groups marginalized? When we moved from D.C. to Toronto we were amazed by how polite people are, that cars stop for pedestrians, and that virtually no one raises their voice or blows their horn. When you visit, pay close attention to how people respect and treat one another.

Self-expression

Here again, places vary a lot. Some welcome self-expression, others remain more conformist. How strong is your need to be yourself? What role does individuality play in your daily life? Is it important to you to find a place where you can be unique and reinvent yourself should you so desire? Do you see visible signs of self-expression on the street, or do people seem to be cookie-cutter versions of one another?

Step Eight: Come on City Light My Fire

Now it's time to find out whether the places you're looking at really have the spark you need. To remind you, the Place and Happiness Survey found aesthetics and "energy" to be among the most important determinants of how happy people are with their places. Take it seriously.

Beauty and the Eye of the Beholder

All of us are drawn to beauty, but remember the old adage about beauty being in the eye of the beholder. Each of us looks for different things in the places we live. Some consider a pleasant aesthetic to be a gritty urban streetscape. Others prefer well-manicured parks. What do you find beautiful? How do the places on your list match your own sense of beauty? Does their appearance really excite you and make you feel alive?

How Real Is It?

In a mass-produced and mass-marketed world, many people crave authenticity. If you're one of them, ask yourself the following: How authentic is the place? Does it have unique neighborhoods and shops, or is everything generic? What gives it true soul? How does it value and promote its history, uniqueness, physical structures, and culture? Decide for yourself what really matters to you and rank your places accordingly.

The Fun Factor

Places are not just about work. What are the things you really love to do—arts and culture; music or theater; spectator sports or participant sports; running or cycling; rock climbing or fishing? Is it a place where you can do the things that matter most to you? And what about things you might want to do, someday? An avid cyclist may one day choose a different form of exercise. People in their twenties who like clubs and nightlife may become symphony or jazz buffs in their thirties, or find themselves coaching soccer when kids come along. Talk to people who share your interests and hobbies. Better yet, do you see people doing the things you love? I can quickly tell a place is for me if I see lots of cyclists buzzing along in their riding gear.

Buzz

Every city has its own energy level or buzz. Are you inspired by high energy and lots of activity, or do you prefer a slower speed? What is the energy of the place? Does it jibe with your own ideal pace of life? Does its energy level match your own?

Step Nine: Tally It Up

Now that I've reminded you of all the things you need to consider and why, it's important to remember: no place is perfect. Don't drive yourself crazy by seeking the ultimate match.

Now tally your score, and compare your places. Use your scores to weigh the pros and cons of each place. There are no right or wrong answers here. Remember: the objective is to find the place that fits you best.

Step Ten: Go There

Few of us would ever make an important decision like taking a job or getting married purely based on what someone—or something—told us to do. Deciding where you'll live is no different. I'm always shocked at the number of people I meet who tell me they relocated without visiting their new home first. Would you take a job before assessing how you might get along with your superiors and peers? Would you marry someone before going out together?

Don't get me wrong. I know there are exceptions to this rule. For that matter, I know someone who swears that the longer you date someone, the less likely you are to marry him or her!

But there's no good reason *not* to take better precautions if you can. Talk to people you know there. Talk to them. According to a Yankelovich survey published in 2006, people highly value the information they get from friends or family who live in a community.[6]

And then go visit them. My personal rule of thumb is to visit at least three places on your list before making a final decision. According to the same Yankelovich survey, visiting for the weekend was by far the best means to a useful assessment. My own advice is to take more than just a weekend—spend enough time to get to know the place. Believe me, you owe it to yourself, your family, and your future.

While you're there, make sure to consider how you would feel about the community in future stages of your life. Visit a neighborhood you might like to live in now, and a neighborhood you might like to live in ten years from now. Ask yourself some questions and think about how you might feel in the future. Can I see myself walking down this street every day? Can I take the noise level? Is it too crowded or too empty? Too gritty or too ersatz? What would start to get on my nerves? What places would I visit a lot? How would I get around?

Most important, if a place doesn't feel right for any reason while you're actually there, don't hesitate to reject it based on your gut feeling, regardless of how it ranks on your list. Realize that your intuition is telling you something important. It's how you feel about the place—and how it makes you feel.

Finally: Choose

Now that you've done your homework, collected more information than you ever thought existed, compiled all your scores, talked to people and made your visits, it's time to pick your place. Take a deep breath. Where you choose to live is one of the top three decisions, if not the single most important decision, you'll ever make.

It's a lot to think about—quite a tall order, for sure. But if you do it right, finding the best place for you will vastly improve every facet of your life.

Choose wisely.

Acknowledgments

A book like this is truly a team effort. I am fortunate to have a team of research collaborators who are second to none. First and foremost, I thank my longtime collaborator Kevin Stolarick, my colleague once again at Martin Prosperity Institute who is the source of much of the statistical material and data in this book. I am also grateful to Charlotta Mellander of the Jönköping International Business School, who has worked with me on a series of research projects for this book and for her detailed comments on various drafts of the manuscript.

I also want to thank a number of others who have collaborated on research for this book. Tim Gulden developed the light emissions and mega-regions data and built the maps for Chapters 2 and 3. Rob Axtell—whom I've known since my earliest days at Carnegie Mellon—built the model of emergent cities in Chapter 4. Darby Miller-Steiger helped to design and implement the Place and Happiness Survey; and Irene Tinagli and David Wilson collaborated on the analysis discussed in Chapters 9 and 10. Jason Rentfrow provided the personality data and collaborated on the research reported in Chapter 11. The book has also benefited from several capable research assistants: Scott Jackson, who worked on the analysis of music scenes; Brian

Knudsen; and Ryan Sutter, who worked on the personality and location research.

Two great editorial assistants made this book a much better read. Jesse Elliott worked side by side with me on the first draft of the manuscript, before moving on to record and tour with his band, These United States; Abigail Cutler took over on the second draft; her deft editorial hand improved the tone, tightened the arguments, and helped to make this a much better book. Amanda Styron and Abby Liebskind worked on the references, assisted with data collection, checked over the facts, and did a myriad of tasks whenever asked. Ryan Morris designed the book's graphics. Kim Ryan proofread the technical appendices.

Susan Schulman, my agent, believed in this project and helped to see it through. Bill Frucht is a terrific editor and much more. He is a collaborator and friend whose intelligence and energy make my ideas much better. Courtney Miller and Jodi Marchowsky shepherded the manuscript deftly through the production process. The entire Basic Books team is professional, effective, and a delight to work with. I thank each and every one of you.

Don Peck of the *Atlantic Monthly* helped me to shape my ideas on the spiky world and the means migration. Will Wilkinson provided helpful comments on an early version of this manuscript. There are so many friends and colleagues who support my efforts in myriad ways. Among them, Elizabeth Currid, Martin Kenney, and Gary Gates stand out as people I have worked with consistently over the years and whose intelligence, interaction, and comments strengthen my own thinking.

I could not imagine a better place to work than the Martin Prosperity Institute. Roger Martin is the best dean around. He is brilliant, committed to big ideas, and tireless. He came up with the idea for the institute and got it funded. I thank the entire Rotman team for their collegiality, support, and professionalism. I'd also like to thank Geoff Beattie for believing in this idea from the beginning, and our funders—particularly Premier Dalton McGuinty and the Province of Ontario, and Joseph Rotman—for their commitment to this work.

My team at the Creative Class Group (CCG) keeps me grounded in the real world. David Miller was in on the early brainstorming sessions for this book. Steven Pedigo worked on various datasets for this book and handled organizing them, so that they could be turned into graphics.

I've met so many people in my travels who work tirelessly to bring change to their workplaces and their communities; their efforts keep my ideas grounded in the real world, inspire me, and give me energy. I thank Alberto Ibargüen and the Knight Foundation for supporting some of our community capacity-building initiatives around the United States.

I am fortunate to have a large extended family that is the source of great comfort and joy. My brother Robert, his wife, Ginny, and nieces Sophia and Tessa and nephew Luca; the Kozouz clan: Zak and Ruth Kozouz, and Reham, Markis, and Adiev Alexander; Dean and Ruba Alexander; Leena, Adam, Christian, Melia, and Sophia Hosler; Tarig and Anastasia, and Ramiz and Christina Kozouz; and my DeCicco cousins too numerous to mention who bring incredible joy to my life.

At the end of the day, I owe my deepest debt of gratitude to my wife, Rana. Her energy and enthusiasm are boundless; her passion for life is incredible; her quirky sense of humor keeps me in stitches. And, by the way, she also runs the CCG, deals with the lawyers and accountants, the Web site and IT people, and manages our entire CCG team—basically giving me the time, space, and flexibility to focus on my research and writing. I am beyond lucky to have her as my life partner and soul-mate.

Appendices

Appendix A: Mega-Regions of the World

Name (Ranked by LRP)	Population (Millions)	Population Rank	LRP ($Billions)	Innovation/ Patents (Rank)	Star Scientists (Rank)
Greater Tokyo	55.1	4	2,500	2	24
Bos-Wash	54.3	5	2,200	8	2
Chi-Pitts	46.0	9	1,600	9	14
Am-Brus-Twerp	59.3	3	1,500	22	18
Osaka-Nagoya	36.0	14	1,400	7	22
Lon-Leed-Chester	50.1	6	1,200	25	10
Mil-Tur	48.3	7	1,000	34	23
Char-lanta	22.4	18	730	16	9
So-Cal	21.4	22	710	13	4
Frank-Gart	23.1	17	630	21	12
Barce-Lyon	25.0	16	610	24	20
Tor-Buff-Chester	22.1	19	530	19	7
Seoul-San	46.1	8	500	6	32
Nor-Cal	12.8	28	470	3	1
So-Flo	15.1	25	430	17	17
Fuku-Kyushu	18.5	24	430	23	19
Paris	14.7	26	380	4	16
Dal-Austin	10.4	30	370	14	13
Hou-Orleans	9.7	32	330	15	5
Mexico City	45.5	10	290	35	32

Cascadia	8.9	33	260	10	3
Rio-Paulo	43.4	12	230	32	32
Hong-Zhen	44.9	11	220	28	31
Sapporo	4.3	37	200	27	32
Vienna-Budapest	21.8	21	180	26	29
Tel Aviv-Amman-Beirut	30.9	15	160	31	21
Prague	10.4	29	150	12	25
Buenos Aires	14.0	27	150	33	32
Denver-Boulder	3.7	40	140	5	6
Phoenix-Tucson	4.7	36	140	11	15
Shanghai	66.4	2	130	30	32
Taipei	21.8	20	130	36	30
Lisbon	9.9	31	110	36	28
Beijing	43.1	13	110	29	32
Delhi-Lahore	121.6	1	110	36	32
Glas-burgh	3.8	39	110	18	8
Berlin	4.1	38	110	1	11
Singapore	6.1	34	100	36	27
Madrid	5.9	35	100	20	26
Bangkok	19.2	23	100	36	32

Source: Data by Tim Gulden; analysis and rankings by Charlotta Mellander. For full sources and methodology see, Richard Florida, Timothy Gulden, and Charlotta Mellander, "The Rise of the Mega-Region," *Cambridge Journal of Regions, Economy, and Society*, 1, 1, 2008.

Note: Ranking based on the 40 mega-regions with LRP (light-based regional product) of $100 billion or more. Rankings for innovations and star scientists are adjusted for population.

Appendix B: Key Results from the Place and Happiness Survey

FACTOR	MEAN RANKING	Correlation			
		OVERALL PLACE HAPPINESS	CITY SATISFACTION	RECOMMEND TO FRIENDS AND FAMILY	OUTLOOK FOR THE FUTURE
AESTHETICS AND LIFESTYLE	3.65	.622	.581	.579	.503
Aesthetics	3.88	.560	.534	.510	.456
Beauty and physical setting	4.00	.499	.475	.463	.395
Outdoor parks, playgrounds, trails	4.06	.445	.424	.413	.355
Air quality	3.76	.389	.371	.341	.333
Climate	3.70	.373	.358	.340	.300
Lifestyle	3.35	.457	.412	.438	.367
Meet new people and make friends	3.65	.528	.486	.500	.422
Cultural offerings	3.38	.342	.309	.329	.272
Nightlife	3.08	.289	.254	.281	.233
BASIC SERVICES	3.46	.603	.545	.558	.509
Primary and secondary education	3.55	.468	.443	.427	.384
Health care	3.83	.410	.383	.380	.334
Job offerings	3.15	.401	.365	.380	.327
Faith institutions	4.23	.346	.334	.334	.265
Higher education	3.93	.321	.292	.305	.261

	Mean				
Housing	3.03	.310	.257	.278	.293
Traffic	3.33	.306	.266	.257	.299
Public transportation	2.77	.188	.161	.179	.162
OPENNESS	**3.03**	**.509**	**.455**	**.475**	**.427**
Families with children	3.75	.558	.506	.516	.466
Senior citizens	3.49	.466	.432	.418	.394
Young singles	2.94	.384	.337	.373	.310
Recent college graduates	2.69	.375	.322	.361	.314
Racial and ethnic minorities	3.19	.252	.219	.236	.218
Immigrants	3.00	.201	.177	.188	.175
Gay and lesbian people	2.75	.176	.156	.171	.140
People living in poverty	2.49	.169	.142	.153	.155
ECONOMIC AND PERSONAL SECURITY	**1.72**	**.497**	**.454**	**.441**	**.437**
Overall Economic Security	0.66	.440	.393	.390	.395
Economic conditions	3.24	.548	.514	.495	.458
Good time to find a job	NA	.294	.265	.267	.256
Economy getting better	NA	.256	.206	.221	.260
Personal security	3.54	.409	.394	.354	.352
LEADERSHIP	**NA**	**.432**	**.408**	**.377**	**.376**

Note: Mean score is based on 1–5 scale where 1 is the lowest and 5 the highest N=27,885

Appendix C: Regional Rankings by Life Stage for All Households

RANKINGS FOR LARGE U.S. REGIONS (more than 1 million people)

	Singles (ages 20–29)		Professionals (ages 29–44)		Families with children		Empty-Nesters (ages 45–64)		Retirees (over 65)	
	Overall	Best Buy	Overall	Best Buy	Overall	Best Buy	Overall	Best Buy	Overall	Best Buy
Atlanta-Sandy Springs-Marietta, GA	39	48	56	44	22	11	91	68	100	107
Austin-Round Rock, TX	13	6	8	10	19	2	59	21	94	101
Baltimore-Towson, MD	54	48	42	27	51	66	17	16	37	40
Birmingham-Hoover, AL	141	128	141	100	95	59	120	95	74	78
Boston-Cambridge-Quincy, MA-NH	5	13	28	53	5	20	6	12	5	19
Buffalo-Niagara Falls, NY	75	74	102	86	96	115	82	105	66	75
Charlotte-Gastonia-Concord, NC-SC	80	62	40	23	90	47	103	71	122	140
Chicago-Naperville-Joliet, IL-IN-WI	39	36	91	102	16	14	62	68	43	45
Cincinnati-Middletown, OH-KY-IN	123	85	73	54	81	51	98	66	108	74
Cleveland-Elyria-Mentor, OH	103	96	109	104	85	73	80	73	46	35
Columbus, OH	43	26	12	9	88	85	80	81	121	126
Dallas-Fort Worth-Arlington, TX	80	73	44	48	40	12	116	88	119	89
Denver-Aurora, CO	27	16	10	18	40	35	33	28	80	89
Detroit-Warren-Livonia, MI	106	84	129	122	99	104	109	115	107	82
Hartford-West Hartford-East Hartford, CT	39	21	35	31	21	32	10	9	23	36
Houston-Sugar Land-Baytown, TX	105	75	71	55	33	6	112	77	94	93
Indianapolis, IN	85	53	67	32	70	51	95	73	119	91
Jacksonville, FL	133	137	83	46	111	84	75	47	71	49
Kansas City, MO-KS	92	72	17	5	42	23	50	18	84	64
Las Vegas-Paradise, NV	66	95	82	105	135	140	88	98	127	120
Los Angeles-Long Beach-Santa Ana, CA	6	19	84	118	26	50	38	67	15	22
Louisville, KY-IN	146	119	139	109	128	109	78	60	124	113

Memphis, TN-MS-AR	124	130	93	76	147	129	129	112	143	131
Miami-Fort Lauderdale-Miami Beach, FL	86	114	116	130	115	120	88	101	10	13
Milwaukee-Waukesha-West Allis, WI	68	54	59	73	93	75	35	17	84	104
Minneapolis-St. Paul-Bloomington, MN-WI	25	5	6	6	15	5	9	3	88	83
Nashville-Davidson--Murfreesboro, TN	84	56	88	52	99	61	68	24	125	91
New Orleans-Metairie-Kenner, LA	78	86	134	98	127	111	107	100	60	28
New York-Northern New Jersey-Long Island, NY-NJ-PA	7	12	85	117	9	26	11	23	2	7
Oklahoma City, OK	118	91	60	16	132	97	134	103	130	115
Orlando-Kissimmee, FL	62	93	65	74	92	100	64	79	49	25
Philadelphia-Camden-Wilmington, PA-NJ-DE-MD	42	47	95	85	29	42	40	60	24	42
Phoenix-Mesa-Scottsdale, AZ	59	70	81	60	87	78	114	111	78	79
Pittsburgh, PA	111	77	124	90	86	56	41	14	34	2
Portland-Vancouver-Beaverton, OR-WA	35	42	20	37	77	95	32	43	69	99
Providence-New Bedford-Fall River, RI-MA	24	26	53	78	47	65	46	80	39	53
Richmond, VA	118	112	46	18	54	57	74	81	59	61
Riverside-San Bernardino-Ontario, CA	112	132	134	143	46	58	138	138	60	68
Sacramento--Arden-Arcade--Roseville, CA	45	69	44	78	44	61	96	115	31	43
Salt Lake City, UT	71	51	23	24	55	49	127	123	136	107
San Antonio, TX	128	121	108	61	103	66	137	114	112	100
San Diego-Carlsbad-San Marcos, CA	17	41	9	36	14	28	42	81	16	23
San Francisco-Oakland-Fremont, CA	2	11	30	69	37	66	2	7	1	11
San Jose-Sunnyvale-Santa Clara, CA	16	23	2	8	7	25	19	37	7	19
Seattle-Tacoma-Bellevue, WA	21	18	38	57	65	75	5	4	26	50
St. Louis, MO-IL	108	67	72	29	112	102	71	59	41	18
Tampa-St. Petersburg-Clearwater, FL	127	138	93	67	130	117	93	89	28	3
Virginia Beach-Norfolk-Newport News, VA-NC	114	123	36	45	70	74	109	118	80	70
Washington-Arlington-Alexandria, DC-VA-MD-WV	3	4	13	16	3	13	14	22	22	23

RANKINGS FOR MEDIUM-SIZED U.S. REGIONS (500,000–999,999 people)

	Singles (ages 20–29)		Professionals (ages 29–44)		Families with children		Empty-Nesters (ages 45–64)		Retirees (over 65)	
	Overall	Best Buy	Overall	Best Buy	Overall	Best Buy	Overall	Best Buy	Overall	Best Buy
Akron, OH	34	31	60	62	68	47	52	25	64	47
Albany-Schenectady-Troy, NY	20	14	27	32	25	44	22	29	25	31
Albuquerque, NM	45	40	50	34	74	69	49	41	68	85
Allentown-Bethlehem-Easton, PA-NJ	90	76	112	115	34	39	42	58	36	6
Augusta-Richmond County, GA-SC	121	104	124	86	72	41	101	76	90	66
Bakersfield, CA	100	110	77	96	67	88	127	131	110	114
Baton Rouge, LA	76	70	127	81	117	94	130	109	117	98
Boise City-Nampa, ID	51	44	14	14	20	10	70	52	70	66
Bridgeport-Stamford-Norwalk, CT	10	1	1	1	1	9	1	4	2	9
Cape Coral-Fort Myers, FL	100	116	52	22	113	112	73	77	21	8
Charleston-North Charleston, SC	36	57	22	25	97	96	54	54	51	68
Colorado Springs, CO	23	22	23	40	26	18	55	32	79	107
Columbia, SC	62	57	48	21	83	53	64	31	76	81
Dayton, OH	89	78	41	35	113	89	67	39	75	62
Des Moines, IA	33	9	11	2	17	1	45	11	98	60
El Paso, TX	125	122	87	63	48	27	133	117	72	52
Fresno, CA	74	87	63	88	64	93	119	129	106	119
Grand Rapids-Wyoming, MI	70	44	85	71	52	64	88	101	109	95
Greensboro-High Point, NC	91	99	98	93	101	89	85	68	82	106
Greenville, SC	106	81	78	41	74	44	118	93	73	70

City										
Harrisburg-Carlisle, PA	72	43	53	28	30	33	29	33	31	4
Honolulu, HI	19	35	101	119	60	99	8	15	8	12
Knoxville, TN	93	65	53	13	74	35	68	20	54	14
Lakeland, FL	117	125	118	77	107	107	121	125	27	25
Little Rock-North Little Rock, AR	100	94	58	15	109	71	86	49	98	57
Madison, WI	4	2	4	11	12	3	7	1	53	51
McAllen-Edinburg-Mission, TX	131	142	64	48	53	22	131	97	102	85
New Haven-Milford, CT	15	15	34	68	32	54	27	47	18	33
Omaha-Council Bluffs, NE-IA	60	34	5	7	49	19	42	10	102	72
Oxnard-Thousand Oaks-Ventura, CA	36	64	48	80	10	24	25	44	11	19
Palm Bay-Melbourne-Titusville, FL	78	101	57	38	66	72	36	36	6	1
Portland-South Portland-Biddeford, ME	22	24	3	3	18	17	4	2	20	5
Poughkeepsie-Newburgh-Middletown, NY	26	32	78	107	8	16	22	29	44	47
Raleigh-Cary, NC	18	3	29	25	11	4	36	26	65	76
Rochester, NY	30	28	39	51	24	29	12	6	37	27
Sarasota-Bradenton-Venice, FL	83	107	74	50	110	115	21	18	12	17
Scranton--Wilkes-Barre, PA	57	38	106	91	80	92	111	120	47	15
Springfield, MA	29	36	26	47	58	89	38	64	62	97
Stockton, CA	72	91	104	129	59	78	116	127	114	128
Syracuse, NY	30	19	80	69	55	46	51	39	50	16
Toledo, OH	48	29	60	75	126	113	57	45	113	102
Tucson, AZ	47	50	36	39	105	103	46	41	58	63
Tulsa, OK	104	82	75	43	69	34	93	53	90	88
Wichita, KS	86	52	43	20	57	37	104	89	90	58
Worcester, MA	9	8	19	41	4	8	29	50	19	31
Youngstown-Warren-Boardman, OH-PA	129	98	100	65	98	85	57	45	63	46

RANKINGS FOR SMALL U.S. REGIONS (250,000–499,999 people)

	Singles (ages 20-29)		Professionals (ages 29-44)		Families with children		Empty-Nesters (ages 45-64)		Retirees (over 65)	
	Overall	Best Buy	Overall	Best Buy	Overall	Best Buy	Overall	Best Buy	Overall	Best Buy
Anchorage, AK	65	83	90	132	94	138	26	85	153	164
Ann Arbor, MI	12	10	32	99	34	61	22	50	48	53
Asheville, NC	88	113	138	113	119	131	87	107	33	37
Atlantic City, NJ	94	134	155	165	102	144	115	144	118	147
Beaumont-Port Arthur, TX	164	163	152	138	165	160	166	162	146	144
Boulder, CO	1	17	21	82	13	30	3	8	42	76
Brownsville-Harlingen, TX	162	166	154	157	121	77	167	155	132	105
Canton-Massillon, OH	154	148	161	160	121	124	113	124	100	112
Charleston, WV	150	144	165	149	138	123	33	13	56	44
Chattanooga, TN-GA	157	146	104	65	149	139	102	91	130	130
Columbus, GA-AL	144	153	157	158	163	158	153	147	161	162
Corpus Christi, TX	120	141	167	164	158	137	152	134	151	132
Davenport-Moline-Rock Island, IA-IL	96	61	107	82	144	143	79	92	145	127
Deltona-Daytona Beach-Ormond Beach, FL	147	160	143	147	157	161	126	140	39	55
Duluth, MN-WI	113	106	131	125	142	149	31	57	135	143
Durham, NC	28	33	7	30	77	80	76	84	57	96
Erie, PA	116	114	132	139	91	110	76	98	67	37
Eugene-Springfield, OR	43	100	166	167	164	167	72	121	86	135
Evansville, IN-KY	159	140	119	95	134	126	145	139	138	132
Fayetteville, NC	160	164	122	144	160	153	165	164	167	167
Fayetteville-Springdale-Rogers, AR-MO	132	136	17	12	38	15	142	126	123	111
Flint, MI	125	101	164	162	162	162	149	158	166	161

Fort Collins-Loveland, CO	80	117	67	124	34	69	14	33	111	128
Fort Smith, AR-OK	167	165	158	142	150	120	162	150	165	163
Fort Wayne, IN	134	97	132	101	115	80	124	96	154	138
Green Bay, WI	54	39	66	111	39	31	106	104	147	141
Hickory-Lenoir-Morganton, NC	161	158	147	135	125	122	151	151	139	153
Huntington-Ashland, WV-KY-OH	165	157	145	110	146	146	147	145	90	117
Huntsville, AL	52	25	30	4	63	43	55	27	77	73
Jackson, MS	95	120	103	89	152	136	141	130	125	118
Kalamazoo-Portage, MI	77	66	120	131	128	132	100	113	142	156
Killeen-Temple-Fort Hood, TX	158	162	96	111	43	21	158	146	133	123
Kingsport-Bristol, TN-VA	166	156	163	146	155	132	136	110	97	80
Lancaster, PA	129	131	129	134	50	105	60	119	83	94
Lansing-East Lansing, MI	53	59	137	153	81	114	122	135	150	151
Lexington-Fayette, KY	54	30	51	55	61	60	62	64	115	121
Lincoln, NE	122	105	25	72	83	55	83	56	157	146
Lubbock, TX	64	118	114	106	154	127	157	142	163	156
Manchester-Nashua, NH	36	79	69	127	2	7	20	35	51	56
Mobile, AL	142	147	150	151	166	162	163	159	149	125
Modesto, CA	136	154	162	166	130	155	155	166	160	165
Montgomery, AL	137	109	111	63	155	150	146	141	148	122
Naples-Marco Island, FL	109	135	97	97	106	135	28	73	16	30
Norwich-New London, CT	49	68	110	137	28	87	18	63	30	87
Ocala, FL	162	167	136	102	161	166	161	165	45	65
Ogden-Clearfield, UT	135	127	127	141	62	83	160	163	164	148
Pensacola-Ferry Pass-Brent, FL	155	159	140	122	120	106	96	86	29	10

(continued on next page)

RANKINGS FOR SMALL U.S. REGIONS (250,000–499,999 people), *continued*

	Singles (ages 20–29)		Professionals (ages 29–44)		Families with children		Empty-Nesters (ages 45–64)		Retirees (over 65)	
	Overall	Best Buy	Overall	Best Buy	Overall	Best Buy	Overall	Best Buy	Overall	Best Buy
Peoria, IL	98	60	116	91	118	118	99	106	116	103
Port St. Lucie-Fort Pierce, FL	153	161	160	156	148	157	105	132	14	29
Provo-Orem, UT	67	88	15	58	23	38	154	156	152	137
Reading, PA	148	128	149	155	73	119	108	136	94	83
Reno-Sparks, NV	58	101	16	82	141	156	92	128	134	154
Roanoke, VA	143	126	123	114	107	82	64	37	35	34
Rockford, IL	145	132	76	128	136	142	156	160	159	160
Salem, OR	138	139	121	150	145	158	148	161	139	155
Salinas, CA	97	145	91	148	79	134	140	157	55	116
Santa Barbara-Santa Maria, CA	8	44	33	108	31	98	53	122	2	37
Santa Rosa-Petaluma, CA	14	54	47	120	45	108	16	72	13	58
Savannah, GA	61	110	98	116	137	148	143	152	137	152

Shreveport-Bossier City, LA	156	151	153	139	167	165	159	153	141	134
South Bend-Mishawaka, IN-MI	140	150	155	151	151	128	132	108	155	150
Spartanburg, SC	139	123	113	94	153	145	144	137	156	158
Spokane, WA	68	90	142	154	143	147	61	87	143	159
Springfield, MO	149	152	143	136	140	130	150	143	158	149
Tallahassee, FL	32	63	124	126	139	151	139	148	127	139
Trenton-Ewing, NJ	10	7	89	133	6	40	13	62	9	41
Utica-Rome, NY	115	108	146	144	133	154	135	154	104	136
Vallejo-Fairfield, CA	109	149	148	163	88	141	122	149	89	142
Visalia-Porterville, CA	151	155	151	161	123	152	164	167	162	166
Wilmington, NC	49	89	115	120	159	164	48	94	104	145
Winston-Salem, NC	99	79	69	59	124	100	83	54	87	124
York-Hanover, PA	152	143	159	159	103	125	125	133	129	107

Note: N=167

Source: Analysis and rankings by Kevin Stolarick. Data from the 2005 American Communities Survey of the U.S. Bureau of the Census and other sources.

Appendix D: Regional Rankings by Life Stage for Gay and Lesbian Households

RANKINGS FOR LARGE U.S. REGIONS (more than 1 million people)

	Singles (ages 20–29)		Professionals (ages 29–44)		Families with children		Empty-Nesters (ages 45–64)		Retirees (over 65s)	
	Overall	Best Buy	Overall	Best Buy	Overall	Best Buy	Overall	Best Buy	Overall	Best Buy
Atlanta-Sandy Springs-Marietta, GA	59	70	90	73	43	24	90	70	100	109
Austin-Round Rock, TX	16	6	9	15	16	1	22	3	63	63
Baltimore-Towson, MD	30	25	16	6	13	26	7	13	24	16
Birmingham-Hoover, AL	146	139	149	113	116	86	143	127	121	119
Boston-Cambridge-Quincy, MA-NH	7	15	35	61	8	22	10	23	8	23
Buffalo-Niagara Falls, NY	90	84	97	76	86	115	99	119	95	103
Charlotte-Gastonia-Concord, NC-SC	96	74	52	31	97	53	103	60	113	133
Chicago-Naperville-Joliet, IL-IN-WI	62	57	119	125	30	32	63	70	61	73
Cincinnati-Middletown, OH-KY-IN	124	77	95	72	98	66	112	86	128	100
Cleveland-Elyria-Mentor, OH	81	80	88	82	72	58	83	77	47	45
Columbus, OH	31	14	6	7	60	53	43	34	72	84
Dallas-Fort Worth-Arlington, TX	73	71	47	56	49	18	91	53	107	76
Denver-Aurora, CO	31	23	20	26	46	43	50	45	78	74
Detroit-Warren-Livonia, MI	109	89	133	127	115	119	135	130	124	113
Hartford-West Hartford-East Hartford, CT	21	4	4	4	4	7	6	8	17	28
Houston-Sugar Land-Baytown, TX	80	59	53	39	34	6	75	33	67	56
Indianapolis, IN	92	66	95	60	91	74	87	65	120	94
Jacksonville, FL	111	124	84	42	95	72	76	54	65	36
Kansas City, MO-KS	65	44	13	2	29	15	42	14	69	41
Las Vegas-Paradise, NV	82	108	93	110	130	127	57	73	111	114
Los Angeles-Long Beach-Santa Ana, CA	10	21	65	102	30	50	14	28	14	16
Louisville, KY-IN	140	117	142	117	127	111	101	87	138	126

Memphis, TN-MS-AR	118	123	57	38	135	115	99	81	122	108
Miami-Fort Lauderdale-Miami Beach, FL	69	105	106	120	106	120	73	93	15	14
Milwaukee-Waukesha-West Allis, WI	98	81	81	92	101	88	84	73	127	129
Minneapolis-St. Paul-Bloomington, MN-WI	28	9	9	10	17	10	11	2	77	63
Nashville-Davidson--Murfreesboro, TN	79	60	115	74	113	80	59	24	123	90
New Orleans-Metairie-Kenner, LA	122	116	137	98	127	117	136	121	97	60
New York-Northern New Jersey-Long Island, NY-NJ-PA	17	20	92	116	9	29	16	35	9	14
Oklahoma City, OK	131	96	69	26	140	106	140	113	140	130
Orlando-Kissimmee, FL	52	78	35	42	62	65	26	29	31	7
Philadelphia-Camden-Wilmington, PA-NJ-DE-MD	46	49	62	52	21	31	33	42	21	36
Phoenix-Mesa-Scottsdale, AZ	75	89	103	77	98	102	109	103	98	90
Pittsburgh, PA	118	79	126	83	89	64	104	78	74	31
Portland-Vancouver-Beaverton, OR-WA	26	35	22	30	66	77	29	35	43	69
Providence-New Bedford-Fall River, RI-MA	23	31	27	44	23	42	27	45	29	55
Richmond, VA	133	120	91	50	82	93	126	124	98	104
Riverside-San Bernardino-Ontario, CA	94	117	68	100	45	61	105	115	27	32
Sacramento--Arden-Arcade--Roseville, CA	31	51	15	33	23	39	40	55	18	18
Salt Lake City, UT	128	119	101	53	119	85	134	105	118	110
San Antonio, TX	31	62	28	64	26	46	56	89	26	43
San Diego-Carlsbad-San Marcos, CA	2	13	34	71	30	62	2	10	1	3
San Francisco-Oakland-Fremont, CA	12	15	3	12	6	20	18	40	3	4
San Jose-Sunnyvale-Santa Clara, CA	15	10	38	57	51	56	4	5	15	30
Seattle-Tacoma-Bellevue, WA	77	47	30	9	81	69	45	31	30	9
St. Louis, MO-IL	77	61	42	34	78	69	117	108	132	105
Tampa-St. Petersburg-Clearwater, FL	129	137	89	57	121	118	106	100	40	12
Virginia Beach-Norfolk-Newport News, VA-NC	104	120	33	35	60	58	91	96	83	58
Washington-Arlington-Alexandria, DC-VA-MD-WV	13	11	43	54	15	35	35	60	33	49

RANKINGS FOR MEDIUM-SIZED U.S. REGIONS (500,000–999,999 people)

	Singles (ages 20–29)		Professionals (ages 29–44)		Families with children		Empty-Nesters (ages 45–64)		Retirees (over 65)	
	Overall	Best Buy	Overall	Best Buy	Overall	Best Buy	Overall	Best Buy	Overall	Best Buy
Akron, OH	54	54	85	85	85	63	65	43	96	79
Albany-Schenectady-Troy, NY	25	23	43	48	33	46	40	55	33	45
Albuquerque, NM	42	33	64	44	79	71	62	55	86	90
Allentown-Bethlehem-Easton, PA-NJ	92	74	120	119	53	58	78	92	54	25
Augusta-Richmond County, GA-SC	127	100	122	75	76	40	95	63	92	67
Bakersfield, CA	120	122	74	93	96	112	125	131	104	111
Baton Rouge, LA	109	96	138	88	125	105	132	109	117	98
Boise City-Nampa, ID	55	46	41	41	40	21	61	44	74	69
Bridgeport-Stamford-Norwalk, CT	1	1	1	1	3	8	1	4	2	2
Cape Coral-Fort Myers, FL	130	131	77	37	110	112	107	105	59	56
Charleston-North Charleston, SC	36	52	7	8	36	30	25	17	12	20
Colorado Springs, CO	48	50	77	93	71	49	97	82	93	111
Columbia, SC	66	64	46	23	70	41	51	21	65	61
Dayton, OH	99	86	70	67	112	98	97	80	115	95
Des Moines, IA	28	8	25	10	20	3	34	6	90	44
El Paso, TX	89	92	31	20	36	16	93	64	46	27
Fresno, CA	61	76	14	28	54	78	66	95	62	83
Grand Rapids-Wyoming, MI	84	58	121	96	73	88	82	100	108	93
Greensboro-High Point, NC	95	99	102	91	103	92	63	52	104	117
Greenville, SC	115	89	110	69	107	76	126	99	103	96

Harrisburg-Carlisle, PA	70	43	71	47	44	46	59	68	41	13
Honolulu, HI	18	28	58	80	52	91	9	22	7	7
Knoxville, TN	83	62	47	16	67	27	68	26	45	11
Lakeland, FL	113	125	99	49	87	100	101	104	31	29
Little Rock-North Little Rock, AR	114	107	111	65	123	86	110	76	116	81
Madison, WI	11	2	20	31	18	11	21	7	39	50
McAllen-Edinburg-Mission, TX	101	128	18	13	56	19	112	67	86	62
New Haven-Milford, CT	46	52	94	115	65	97	66	98	50	86
Omaha-Council Bluffs, NE-IA	67	41	23	24	63	25	46	12	109	82
Oxnard-Thousand Oaks-Ventura, CA	39	64	55	89	12	33	36	62	12	23
Palm Bay-Melbourne-Titusville, FL	71	98	62	36	68	68	76	84	21	6
Portland-South Portland-Biddeford, ME	8	12	2	3	7	4	3	1	10	1
Poughkeepsie-Newburgh-Middletown, NY	42	55	112	135	19	35	49	68	57	72
Raleigh-Cary, NC	22	7	40	29	10	9	23	15	42	53
Rochester, NY	24	26	32	39	22	23	14	10	35	26
Sarasota-Bradenton-Venice, FL	85	110	73	51	108	123	47	58	19	22
Scranton--Wilkes-Barre, PA	53	35	87	70	64	67	89	100	48	19
Springfield, MA	27	38	8	19	34	51	31	51	51	88
Stockton, CA	64	83	45	79	58	80	68	94	78	96
Syracuse, NY	44	30	74	65	59	44	48	37	53	21
Toledo, OH	35	17	11	18	74	57	20	9	86	65
Tucson, AZ	40	39	24	22	79	74	27	18	68	74
Tulsa, OK	56	42	38	14	47	17	52	16	64	54
Wichita, KS	57	35	17	5	47	28	54	30	89	47
Worcester, MA	4	5	12	25	2	2	13	18	5	5
Youngstown-Warren-Boardman, OH-PA	88	68	37	16	49	37	38	20	54	42

RANKINGS FOR SMALL U.S. REGIONS (250,000–499,999 people)

	Singles (ages 20–29)		Professionals (ages 29–44)		Families with children		Empty-Nesters (ages 45–64)		Retirees (over 65)	
	Overall	Best Buy	Overall	Best Buy	Overall	Best Buy	Overall	Best Buy	Overall	Best Buy
Anchorage, AK	37	45	107	144	90	134	30	91	134	155
Ann Arbor, MI	20	18	105	151	84	122	72	107	70	84
Asheville, NC	76	105	124	96	69	103	84	110	36	51
Atlantic City, NJ	137	149	163	165	139	162	128	155	152	161
Beaumont-Port Arthur, TX	167	167	159	147	166	164	167	166	162	160
Boulder, CO	3	19	51	112	28	52	23	48	56	99
Brownsville-Harlingen, TX	151	161	108	125	133	96	148	127	110	80
Canton-Massillon, OH	142	138	145	154	92	109	119	122	104	116
Charleston, WV	143	134	158	137	98	84	53	38	73	66
Chattanooga, TN-GA	161	147	154	130	160	152	156	142	161	152
Columbus, GA-AL	163	164	164	164	164	166	163	156	163	167
Corpus Christi, TX	101	130	151	152	145	114	129	96	133	100
Davenport-Moline-Rock Island, IA-IL	125	82	118	89	152	142	118	123	159	145
Deltona-Daytona Beach-Ormond Beach, FL	144	163	128	139	153	158	137	148	60	89
Duluth, MN-WI	126	111	127	123	136	139	86	111	157	156
Durham, NC	49	56	67	104	132	126	121	116	85	118
Erie, PA	97	95	81	99	57	83	57	88	74	39
Eugene-Springfield, OR	115	146	167	167	167	167	130	148	143	157
Evansville, IN-KY	157	134	109	78	126	124	144	138	139	128
Fayetteville, NC	150	162	122	145	143	132	145	141	151	159
Fayetteville-Springdale-Rogers, AR-MO	103	115	26	21	27	12	111	83	81	59
Flint, MI	132	103	152	158	151	150	138	143	146	149

Fort Collins-Loveland, CO	14	31	85	141	41	80	19	45	78	100
Fort Smith, AR-OK	165	165	144	114	137	108	157	136	149	158
Fort Wayne, IN	123	84	139	107	121	94	108	73	142	125
Green Bay, WI	38	21	19	62	13	13	37	25	71	68
Hickory-Lenoir-Morganton, NC	154	148	145	132	104	110	142	140	118	142
Huntington-Ashland, WV-KY-OH	164	156	132	83	137	132	151	151	130	138
Huntsville, AL	100	67	113	67	116	101	131	111	129	123
Jackson, MS	136	143	143	135	157	143	161	144	137	130
Kalamazoo-Portage, MI	111	93	130	142	146	140	114	120	150	161
Killeen-Temple-Fort Hood, TX	108	142	74	93	38	13	115	85	37	33
Kingsport-Bristol-Bristol, TN-VA	166	155	157	140	155	125	152	133	136	122
Lancaster, PA	104	112	115	124	41	104	32	89	83	76
Lansing-East Lansing, MI	115	113	162	163	140	145	147	158	155	151
Lexington-Fayette, KY	62	40	77	81	77	79	71	70	91	105
Lincoln, NE	41	28	55	101	114	95	70	40	152	136
Lubbock, TX	138	152	135	128	163	150	166	146	165	164
Manchester-Nashua, NH	8	34	49	122	1	5	17	32	11	10
Mobile, AL	152	150	148	149	161	157	165	159	154	132
Modesto, CA	147	159	155	162	149	165	150	167	147	165
Montgomery, AL	153	136	130	86	158	156	153	145	159	141
Naples-Marco Island, FL	135	144	129	129	118	135	81	118	28	52
Norwich-New London, CT	19	27	97	133	11	55	8	50	20	69
Ocala, FL	159	166	77	46	148	154	148	162	44	78
Ogden-Clearfield, UT	144	140	153	157	83	106	158	160	158	139
Pensacola-Ferry Pass-Brent, FL	149	157	133	109	105	99	124	113	57	34

(continued on next page)

RANKINGS FOR SMALL U.S. REGIONS (250,000–499,999 people), *continued*

	Singles (ages 20–29)		Professionals (ages 29–44)		Families with children		Empty-Nesters (ages 45–64)		Retirees (over 65)	
	Overall	Best Buy	Overall	Best Buy	Overall	Best Buy	Overall	Best Buy	Overall	Best Buy
Peoria, IL	107	73	136	106	108	120	123	126	135	124
Port St. Lucie-Fort Pierce, FL	139	160	141	146	120	136	80	117	23	36
Provo-Orem, UT	91	109	53	105	38	44	154	157	145	127
Reading, PA	141	126	149	155	88	128	115	139	112	105
Reno-Sparks, NV	58	103	29	103	146	159	96	135	114	147
Roanoke, VA	106	87	104	86	54	33	74	48	38	48
Rockford, IL	158	145	140	159	156	161	164	163	167	166
Salem, OR	87	94	66	118	129	147	88	131	100	134
Salinas, CA	72	133	60	138	92	137	119	150	51	121
Santa Barbara-Santa Maria, CA	51	102	81	143	94	138	94	137	48	120
Santa Rosa-Petaluma, CA	6	48	5	63	25	88	12	66	4	35
Savannah, GA	74	126	113	131	150	149	139	147	126	148

Shreveport-Bossier City, LA	162	154	155	134	165	163	162	151	156	144
South Bend-Mishawaka, IN-MI	155	158	165	161	162	148	146	129	166	163
Spartanburg, SC	134	113	71	59	144	131	133	125	141	146
Spokane, WA	45	69	125	150	124	130	44	58	125	150
Springfield, MO	156	153	161	156	159	152	160	154	164	153
Tallahassee, FL	60	100	160	160	154	160	155	165	130	140
Trenton-Ewing, NJ	5	3	61	110	5	38	4	39	6	39
Utica-Rome, NY	147	141	147	148	134	155	141	161	144	154
Vallejo-Fairfield, CA	67	129	100	152	74	129	79	134	25	87
Visalia-Porterville, CA	121	132	50	108	111	146	122	153	102	143
Wilmington, NC	49	88	117	120	130	141	39	78	94	137
Winston-Salem, NC	86	72	58	55	102	72	55	27	82	115
York-Hanover, PA	160	151	166	166	142	144	159	164	148	134

Source: Analysis and rankings by Kevin Stolarick. Data from the 2005 American Communities Survey of the U.S. Bureau of the Census and other sources.

Appendix E: Place Finder

Rate each category on a 1–5 scale where 1 is lowest and 5 is highest		Current Place	Option 1	Option 2	Option 3
OPPORTUNITY					
Economic Conditions	How are overall economic conditions?				
Job Market	Does the place offer good jobs and good salaries in your field?				
Professional Development	How available are the professional development resources that you need in your life and career?				
Networking	Do you have a professional network already established; If not, how easy is it to access and build one?				
	Subtotal				
BASIC SERVICES					
Education	Does the place offer educational options that meet the needs of you and your family?				
Health and Safety	Does the place meet your criteria for safety and healthcare?				
Housing	Does the place have housing that you like at a price you can afford?				
Connectivity	Is the place connected—locally, globally, and digitally—in the ways that most matter to you?				
	Subtotal				
LEADERSHIP					
Politicos	Do political leaders inspire your trust and confidence?				
Business	Are business leaders the type you admire and have confidence in?				
Diversity	Is leadership diverse – by gender, race, age, ethnicity, sexual orientation and other factors?				
Access and engagement	How open and inclusive is the decision-making process?				
	Subtotal				

	Current Place	Option 1	Option 2	Option 3
VALUES				
Tolerance — How are people of different races, ethnicities, religions, and lifestyles treated?				
Trust — Do people generally trust one another?				
Self-expression — Can you be yourself there?				
People Climate — How does the place value people?				
Subtotal				
AESTHETICS AND LIFESTYLE				
Physical Beauty — How do you rate the physical and natural beauty of the place?				
Authenticity — Does the place have a unique character?				
Amenities — Does the place have the arts, lifestyle, and recreational amenities you need?				
Buzz — How does the "energy" of the place match yours?				
Subtotal				
TOTAL				

Notes

Chapter 1

1. Books and articles on happiness are a veritable growth industry. See, for example, Darrin McMahon, *Happiness: A History*, Atlantic Monthly Press, 2006; Jonathan Haidt, *The Happiness Hypothesis*, Basic Books, 2005; Martin Seligman, *Authentic Happiness*, Free Press, 2004; Richard Layard, *Happiness: A New Science*, Penguin, 2005.

2. See Jason Schachter, *Why People Move: Exploring the March 2000 Current Population Survey*, U.S. Census Bureau, Current Population Report, May 2001. These data are updated annually and are available on the Census Web site.

3. Charles Tiebout, "A Pure Theory of Local Expenditures," *Journal of Political Economy* 64, 5, 1956, pp. 416–24.

4. In particular, the work of Jane Jacobs: *The Death and Life of Great American Cities*, Vintage, 1992 (first ed., 1961), *The Economy of Cities*, Vintage, 1970 (first ed., 1969), and *Cities and the Wealth of Nations*, Vintage, 1985 (first ed., 1984). Much of my own research on this subject is summarized in *The Rise of the Creative Class*, Basic Books, 2002.

Chapter 2

1. Thomas Friedman, *The World Is Flat,* Farrar, Straus and Giroux, 2005.

2. The original article is Frances Cairncross, "The Death of Distance," *The Economist* 336, 7934, September 30, 1995. She later published an influential book by the same title, *The Death of Distance,* Harvard Business School Press, 2001 (first ed., 1997). Also, "Conquest of Location," *The Economist,* October 7, 1999.

3. Edward E. Leamer, "A Flat World, A Level Playing Field, a Small World After All or None of the Above? Review of Thomas L. Friedman, *The World Is Flat." Journal of Economic Literature* 45, 1, 2007, pp. 83–126

4. Urbanization data are from "World Population Prospects: The 2006 Revision Population Database." Population Division, Department of Economic and Social Affairs, United Nations 2007. Available at: esa.un.org/unpp.

5. "Q&A with Michael Porter," *Business Week,* August 21, 2006. www.businessweek.com/magazine/content/06_34/b3998460.htm.

6. Richard Florida, "The World is Spiky," *Atlantic Monthly*, 296, 3, October 2005.

7. Gulden used the light that is visible from space at night as a basis for estimating economic activity. He calibrated the light data using estimates of Gross Regional Product (GRP) compiled for the lower forty-eight U.S. states. He translated this physical economic activity into standard units by renormalizing the total for each nation to agree with that nation's 2000 GDP in 2000 U.S. dollars at current market exchange rates. He then overlaid the light maps with detailed population maps from the LandScan 2005 population grid, developed by Oak Ridge National Laboratory. The result is consistent estimates of economic activity for every 30 arc-second grid cell (less than 1 square kilometer) in the world. For more on this methodology, see Richard Florida, Timothy Gulden, and Charlotta Mellander, "The Rise of the Mega-region," *Cambridge Journal of Regions,*

Economy and Society, 1, 1, 2008. See also William Nordhaus et al., "The G-Econ Database on Gridded Output: Methods and Data," Yale University, May 12, 2006; Nordhaus, "Geography and Macroeconomics: New Data and New Findings," *Proceedings of the National Academy of Sciences,* 103, 10, March 7, 2006, pp. 3510–17. Data on economic output or Gross Regional Product for U.S. regions is from Global Insight, *The Role of Metro Areas in the U.S. Economy,* Prepared for the United States Conference of Mayors, January 13, 2006.

8. Gulden estimated global patents for every region in the world by combining data from the U.S. Patent and Trademark Office (USPTO), which provides the exact city location of the inventor with data from the World Intellectual Property Office (WIPO) on national patents. Because inventors from around the world file for patent protection in the United States, and the USPTO tracks the city of residence of the inventor, he was able to count the number of U.S. patents for each city in the world. These data on patenting by U.S. region were developed by Phil Auserwald and his research team at George Mason University's School of Public Policy, who made them available to us. While this file provides a fine portrait of inventions in U.S. cities, it undercounts (sometimes radically) inventions in other countries because not every inventor files for a U.S. patent. Gulden compensated for that by using the USPTO data to estimate the relative importance of the cities within each country. He then took the number of patents reported to WIPO by each national patent office as granted to domestic inventors and reallocated them to cities using the weights derived from the USPTO data. He assumed that inventors who patent in the United States have the same spatial distribution as inventors who patent domestically. This may overstate the importance of major cities (where access to the world patent system might be easier), but that is not a large source of bias. For more on this methodology, see Florida, Gulden, and Mellander, "The Rise of the Mega-Region," 2008.

9. AnnaLee Saxenian, *Silicon Valley's Immigrant Entrepreneurs,* San Francisco: Public Policy Institute of California, 1999. Vivek Wadhwa, AnnaLee Saxenian, Ben Rissing, Gary Gereffi, "America's New

Immigrant Entrepreneurs: Part 1," Duke University, University of California, Berkeley, and Pratt School of Engineering, January 4, 2007. See also Rafiq Dossani, "Chinese and Indian Entrepreneurs and Their Networks in Silicon Valley," Stanford University, Shorenstein APARC, March 2002.

10. See Martin Kenney, "The Globalization of Venture Capital: The Cases of Taiwan and Japan," November 17, 2004; "A Life Cycle Model for the Creation of National Venture Capital Industries: Comparing the U.S. and Israeli Experiences," November 14, 2004; "Building Venture Capital Industries: Understanding the U.S. and Israeli Experiences," November 26, 2003; "Venture Capital Industries in East Asia," December 4, 2002. All available at http://hcd.ucdavis.edu/faculty/kenney/.

11. More information on IPO's available from the U.S. Securities and Exchange Commission. SECLaw.com has a complete IPO Information Center at: http://www.seclaw.com/centers/ipocent.shtml.

12. These data may be somewhat skewed because they exclude citations in many non–English language journals. That said, the vast majority of global scientific discourse is conducted in English. Authors publishing in other languages are not likely to be cited often enough to show up on this map. See Michael Batty, "The Geography of Scientific Citation," *Environment and Planning A*, 35, 2003, pp. 761–70. An earlier version dated December 19, 2002, has more detailed data and maps. It can be downloaded from his site: http://www.casa.ucl.ac.uk/people/MikesPage.htm.

13. Lynne Zucker and Michael Darby, "Movement of Star Scientists and Engineers in High-Tech Firm Entry," Working Paper No. 12172, National Bureau of Economic Research, September 2006.

14. Mike Davis, *Planet of Slums*, Verso, 2006.

15. Peter J. Taylor and Robert E. Lang, "U.S. Cities in the 'World City Network,'" Brookings Institution, February 2005.

16. "Magnets for Money," *The Economist*, September 13, 2007.

17. Benjamin Barber, "McWorld vs. Jihad," *Atlantic Monthly*, 269, 3, 1992. See also his *Jihad vs. McWorld: How the Planet Is Both Falling Apart and Coming Together and What This Means for Democracy*, Crown, 1995.

18. Tairan Li and Richard Florida, "Talent, Technological Innovation and Economic Growth in China," February 2006. Available at creativeclass.com.

19. Jonathan Watts, "Thousands of Villagers Riot as China Enforces BirthLimit," *Guardian,* May 22, 2007.

20. Tao Wu, "Urban-Rural Divide in China Continues to Widen," Gallup Organization, March 28, 2007.

21. Rafiq Dossani, "Origins and Growth of the Software Industry in India," Stanford University, Shorenstein APARC, September 2005. Available at http://aparc.stanford.edu/people/rafiqdossani.

Chapter 3

1. David Ricardo, *Principles of Political Economy and Taxation,* Cosimo Classics, 2006 (first ed., 1817).

2. Jane Jacobs, *The Economy of Cities,* Vintage, 1970 (first ed., 1969); also Jacobs, *Cities and the Wealth of Nations,* Vintage, 1985 (first ed., Random House, May 1984).

3. Jean Gottman, *Megalopolis,* Twentieth Century Fund, 1961.

4. Kenichi Ohmae, *The End of the Nation State: The Rise of Regional Economies,* Simon and Schuster, 1995. See also his "The Rise of the Region State," *Foreign Affairs*, Cpring 1993.

5. John Gapper, "NyLon, a Risky Tale of Twin City States," *Financial Times*, October 24, 2007.

6. Robert Lang and Dawn Dhavale, *Beyond Megalopolis: Exploring America's New Megalapolitan Geography,* Brookings Institution, July 2005. See also Edward Glaeser, "Do Regional Economies Need Regional Coordination?" Harvard Institute of Economic Research Discussion Paper 2131, March 2007.

7. To do this, Gulden set a light threshold that captures the essence of the geographic pattern of U.S. mega-regions described by Lang and Dhavale and other researchers who use more complex methods, such as population, income, or measures of commuting patterns to identify mega-regions. He found that while these factors are critically important

for understanding the functioning of a mega-region, contiguous development is a good enough proxy for economic integration that it can meaningfully be used in this context. After determining the threshold that gives the best approximation for established U.S. mega-regions, he then applied the same threshold to the nighttime lights dataset for the rest of the world. This produced tens of thousands of lighted patches representing the full range of settlement sizes – from the largest mega-regions covering thousands of square kilometers to small villages and other light sources that are on the order of a single square kilometer. He then closed the remaining small gaps, merging lighted areas that are separated by less than 2 kilometers. For more on this methodology see, Florida, Gulden, and Mellander, "The Rise of the Mega-region," 2008.

8. "The Texas Triangle as Megalopolis," Federal Reserve Bank of Dallas, Houston Branch, April 2004. http://www.dallasfed.org/research/houston/2004/hb0403.html.

9. On Montreal, see Kevin Stolarick and Richard Florida, "Creativity, Connections and Innovation: A Study of Linkages in the Montréal Region," *Environment and Planning A* 38, 10, 2006, pp. 1799–1817.

10. Dominic Wilson and Roopa Purushothaman, "Dreaming with BRICs: The Path to 2050," Global Economics Paper No. 99, Goldman Sachs, October 1, 2003.

Chapter 4

1. Robert Lucas, "On the Mechanics of Economic Development," *Journal of Monetary Economics* 22, 1988, pp. 3–42.

2. Adam Smith, *The Wealth of Nations*, Bantam, 2003 (first ed., 1776).

3. Or, as Ricardo chose to explain it:

> To produce the wine in Portugal, might require only the labor
> of 80 men for one year, and to produce the cloth in the same
> country, might require the labor of 90 men for the same time.
> It would therefore be advantageous for her to export wine in

exchange for cloth. This exchange might even take place, notwithstanding that the commodity imported by Portugal could be produced there with less labor than in England. Though she could make the cloth with the labor of 90 men, she would import it from a country where it required the labor of 100 men to produce it, because it would be advantageous to her rather to employ her capital in the production of wine, for which she would obtain more cloth from England, than she could produce by diverting a portion of her capital from the cultivation of vines to the manufacture of cloth.

David Ricardo, *Principles of Political Economy and Taxation,* Cosimo Classics, 2006 (first ed., 1817).

4. Joseph Schumpeter, *Theory of Economic Development,* Harvard University Press, 1934 (first ed., 1911).

5. Joseph Schumpeter, *Capitalism, Socialism and Democracy,* Harper, 1975 (first ed., 1942). Thomas McCraw has written an illuminating biography of Schumpeter, *Prophet of Innovation: Joseph Schumpeter and Creative Destruction,* Belknap Press, 2007.

6. Robert Solow, "Technical Change and the Aggregate Production Function," *Review of Economics and Statistics* 39, 3, August 1957, pp. 312–20.

7. Paul Romer, "Increasing Returns and Long-Run Growth," *Journal of Political Economy* 94, 5, October 1986, pp. 1002–37; Romer, "Endogenous Technological Change," *Journal of Political Economy* 98, 5, October 1990, pp. S71–102. David Warsh's *Knowledge and the Wealth of Nations,* W.W. Norton, 2006, provides a lively and informative summary of Romer's ideas and the theory of growth more broadly.

8. Bill Steigerwald, "City Views: Urban Studies Legend Jane Jacobs on Gentrification, the New Urbanism, and Her Legacy," *Reason,* June 2001.

9. See the discussion of Jacobs's ideas in David Ellerman, "Jane Jacobs on Development," *Oxford Development Studies* 32, December 4, 2004, pp. 507–21.

10. Geoffrey West, Luis Bettencourt, Jose Lobo, Dirk Helbing, and Christian Kuehnert, "Growth, Innovation, Scaling and the Pace of Life in Cities," *Proceedings of the National Academy of Sciences* 104, 17, April 24, 2007, pp. 7301–6.

11. George K. Zipf, *Human Behaviour and the Principle of Least-Effort,* Addison-Wesley, 1949; George K. Zipf, *The Psychobiology of Language,* Houghton-Mifflin, 1935.

12. Robert Axtell and Richard Florida. "Emergent Cities: Micro-foundations of Zipf's Law," March 2006. Available at creativeclass.com.

Chapter 5

1. A comprehensive 2005 study of the subject found that wages and salaries for Americans in the middle of the national income distribution rose 11 percent between 1966 and 2001. The rise in wages and salaries for top earners was a staggering 617 percent. That means that over thirty-five years, wages and salaries rose at least as fast as nationwide productivity for only a tenth of U.S. laborers. As Cornell University economist Robert Frank points out in his 2007 book *Falling Behind,* the richest 1 percent of Americans saw their share of national income rise from 8.2 percent in 1980 to 17.4 percent in 2005. "More astonishing still," noted journalist Clive Crook in a 2006 article for the *Atlantic Monthly,* is that "from 1997 to 2001, the top 1 percent captured far more of the real national gain in wage and salary income than did the bottom 50 *percent.* And even within that highest percentile, the gains were heavily concentrated at the top." See Ian Dew-Becker and Robert Gordon, "Where Did the Productivity Growth Go? Inflation Dynamics and the Distribution of Income," presented to the Brookings Institution, September 2005. Robert Frank, *Falling Behind: How Inequality Harms the Middle Class,* University of California Press, 2007. Clive Crook, "The Height of Inequality," *Atlantic Monthly,* 298, 2, September 2006, pp. 36–37.

2. Herbert Muschamp, "Checking in to Escapism," *New York Times,* November 2, 2002.

3. Bethan Thomas and Danny Dorling, *Identity in Britain: A Cradle-to-Grave Atlas,* Polity Press, 2007. See also Lucy Ward, "Where You Live Can Be Crucial to Your Future," *Guardian,* September 8, 2007.

4. Jason Schachter, *Why People Move: Exploring the March 2000 Current Population Survey,* U.S. Census Bureau, Current Population Report, May 2001.

5. "Pick a Place to Live, Then Find a Job," *Wall Street Journal,* January 27, 2002.

The original study is by Next Generation Consulting, *Talent Capitals: The Emerging Battleground in the War for Talent: A White Paper,* 2002. The May 2006 survey was commissioned by CEO's for Cities and conducted by the Segmentation Company, a division of Yankelovich, *Attracting the Young College-Educated to Cities,* CEOs for Cities, May 11. 2006. Available at http://www.ceosforcities.org/rethink/research/files/CEOsforCitiesAttractingYoungEducatedPres2006.pdf.

6. See, Nattavudh Powdthavee, "Putting a Price Tag on Friends, Relatives and Neighbors: Using Surveys of Life Satisfaction to Value Social Relationships," *Journal of Socio-Economics,* 2008.

7. Albert O. Hirschman, *Exit, Voice and Loyalty,* Harvard University Press, 1970.

Chapter 6

1. "The World Goes to Town," *The Economist,* May 3, 2007.

2. Alfonso Hernandez Marin, "Cultural Changes: From the Rural World to Urban Environment," *United Nations Chronicle,* November 4, 2006.

3. Kenneth Jackson, *Crabgrass Frontier,* Oxford University Press, 1987; Robert Bruegmann, *Sprawl: A Compact History,* University of Chicago Press, 2005.

4. Joel Garreau, *Edge City,* Anchor, 1992.

5. David Brooks, *Bobos in Paradise,* Simon and Schuster, 2001; and his *On Paradise Drive,* Simon and Schuster, 2004.

6. Edward Glaeser and Christopher Berry, "The Divergence of Human Capital Levels across Cities," Harvard Institute of Economic Research, August 2005.

7. Richard Florida, "Where the Brains Are," *Atlantic Monthly* 298, 3, October 2006, p. 34.

8. Joseph Gyourko, Christopher Mayer, and Todd Sinai, "Superstar Cities," National Bureau of Economic Research Working Paper No. 12355, July 2006.

Chapter 7

1. Dan Pink, *Free Agent Nation,* Warner Books, 2001.

2. Peter Drucker, *Post-Capitalist Society,* Harper Business, 1993. Also, Drucker, "Beyond the Information Revolution," *Atlantic Monthly* 284, 4, October 1999, pp. 47–57; Drucker, "The Next Society," *The Economist,* November 1, 2001, pp. 1–20. Fritz Machlup is often credited with the term "knowledge worker" from his 1962 book *The Production and Distribution of Knowledge in the United States,* Princeton University Press, 1962.

3. See, Richard Florida, *The Rise of the Creative Class,* Basic Books, 2002. Data updated by Kevin Stolarick.

4. "The World's Richest People," *Forbes Magazine,* March 8, 2007.

5. Richard Florida, Charlotta Mellander, and Kevin Stolarick, "Inside the Black Box of Economic Development: Human Capital, the Creative Class, and Tolerance," *Journal of Economic Geography,* 8, 5, 2008.

6. The correlations between occupation and per capita income are as follows: computer and math (.659); business and finance (.549); arts, entertainment, and media (.511); sales (.480); engineering and architecture (.472); science (.393); law (.390); and management (.358).

7. The correlations with regional income are as follows: healthcare occupations (.052); education occupations (.055).

8. See for example, Alfred Weber, *Theory of the Location of Industries,* University of Chicago Press, 1929 (first ed., 1909).

9. Michael Piore and Charles Sabel, *The Second Industrial Divide,* Basic Books, 1984.

10. Alfred Marshall, *Principles of Economics,* Cosimo Classics (abridged ed.), 2006 (first ed., 1890).

11. Michael Porter, "Clusters and the New Economics of Competition," *Harvard Business Review,* November–December 1998; "Location, Clusters, and Company Strategy," in Gordon Clark, Meric Gertler, and Mayrann Feldman (eds.), *Oxford Handbook of Economic Geography,* Oxford University Press, 2000; and "Location, Competition and Economic Development: Local Clusters in a Global Economy," *Economic Development Quarterly* 14, 1, February 2000, pp. 15–34.

12. Joseph Cortright and Heike Mayer, "Signs of Life: The Growth of Biotechnology Centers in the US," Brookings Institution, Center for Metropolitan Policy, 2001.

13. Venture capital data are from PriceWaterhouseCoopers Money Tree. Available at https://www.pwcmoneytree.com/MTPublic/ns/index.jsp.

14. Pui-Wing Tam, "New Hot Spot for High Tech Firms Is the Old One," *Wall Street Journal,* October 5, 2006.

15. Ann Markusen and Greg Schrock, "The Distinctive City: Divergent Patterns in Growth, Hierarchy and Specialization," *Urban Studies* 43, 8, July 2006, pp. 1301–23.

16. Maryann Feldman and Roger Martin, "Jurisdictional Advantage," National Bureau of Economic Research, October 2004.

17. Dan Fitzpatrick, "Extreme Commuters at PNC Raise Eyebrows," *Pittsburgh Post-Gazette,* August 7, 2005.

18. Robert D. Putnam, *Bowling Alone: The Collapse and Revival of American Community,* Simon and Schuster, 2000.

19. Andrew Hargadon, "Bridging Old Worlds and Building New Ones: Toward a Micro-sociology of Creativity," in Leigh Thompson (ed.), *Creativity and Innovation in Groups and Teams,* Lawrence Erlbaum Associates, 2007.

20. AnnaLee Saxenian, *Regional Advantage,* Harvard University Press, 1994.

21. Mark Granovetter, "The Strength of Weak Ties," *American Journal of Sociology* 78, 6, May 1973, pp. 1360–80.

22. Richard Caves, *Creative Industries: Contracts between Art and Commerce,* Harvard University Press, 2002. See also Elizabeth Currid's detailed analysis of the interweaving of design, music, and art scenes in contemporary New York, *The Warhol Economy,* Princeton University Press, 2007.

23. See Terry Nichols Clark, "Making Culture Into Magic: How Can it Bring Tourists and Residents?" *International Review of Public Administration,* 12 January 2007, pp. 13-25. Also see Terry Nichols Clark, Lawrence Rothfield, and Daniel Silver (eds.), *Scenes* (book draft), University of Chicago, 2007. Also see Richard Lloyd and Terry Nichols Clark, "The City as an Entertainment Machine," *Research in Urban Sociology: Critical Perspectives on Urban Redevelopment* 6, 2001, pp. 357–78.

24. Scott Jackson, "The Music Machine: The Impact of Geography, History and Form on Music Innovation in the United States 1970–2004," George Mason University, May 2007.

25. "Jack White Leaves 'Super-Negative' Detroit," *USA Today,* May 25, 2006.

Chapter 8

1. The data on housing trends here are from the U.S. Bureau of the Census, *American Community Survey.* Available at http://www.census.gov/acs/www/.

2. Peter Coy, "The Richest Zip Codes–and How They Got That Way," *Business Week,* April 2, 2007.

3. Joseph Gyourko, Christopher Mayer, and Todd Sinai, "Superstar Cities," National Bureau of Economic Research, Working Paper No. 12355, July 2006.

4. Robert Shiller, "Superstar Cities May be Investors' Superstardust," *Shanghai Daily,* May 22, 2007. Available at www.taipeitimes.com/News/editorials/archives/2007/05/20/2003361715.

5. Robert Shiller, "Historic Turning Points in Real Estate," Yale University, Cowles Foundation for Research in Economics Discussion Paper No. 1610, June 2007. Available at http://cowles.econ.yale.edu/P/cd/d16a/d1610.pdf. Detailed data from the Case-Shiller Home Price Index are available at http://macromarkets.com/csi_housing/sp_caseshiller.asp. See also Shiller's *Irrational Exuberance,* Princeton University Press, 2005.

6. Roger Lowenstein, "Pop Psychology," *New York Times,* March 18, 2007. For an interesting perspective on bubbles in general, see Daniel Gross, *Pop! Why Bubbles Are Great for the Economy,* Collins, 2007.

7. Ryan Avent, "Are Superstar Cities Super Investments?" *The Bellows,* May 22, 2007. Available at www.ryanavent.com/blog/?p=403.

8. Richard Florida and Charlotta Mellander, "There Goes the Neighborhood: How and Why Artists, Bohemians and Gays Affect Housing Values," 2007. Available at creativeclass.com.

9. John D. Landis, Vicki Elmer, and Matthew Zook, "New Economy Housing Markets: Fast and Furious—But Different?" *Housing Policy Debate* 3, 2, 2002, pp. 233–74.

10. Jennifer Roback, "Wages, Rents, and the Quality of Life," *Journal of Political Economy* 90, 6, 1982, pp. 1257–78.

11. Edward Glaeser, Jed Kolko, and Albert Saiz, "Consumer City," *Journal of Economic Geography* 1, 1, 2001, pp. 27–50; also Glaeser and Joshua Gottlieb, "Urban Resurgence and the Consumer City," *Urban Studies* 43, 8, 2006, pp. 1275–99.

12. Maya Roney, "Bohemian Today, High-Rent Tomorrow," *Business Week,* February 26, 2007.

13. Ann Markusen and Greg Schrock, "The Artistic Specialization and Economic Development Implications," *Urban Studies* 43, 10, 2006, pp. 1661–86.

14. Tim Hartford, "Undercover Economist: On the Move," *Financial Times,* March 9, 2007.

15. Andrew Oswald with David Blanchflower and Peter Sanfey, "Wages, Profits and Rent-Sharing," *Quarterly Journal of Economics* 111, 1, February 1996, pp. 227–52.

Chapter 9

1. Claudia Willis, "The New Science of Happiness," *Time,* January 9, 2005.

2. Kahneman believes that well-being can be accurately assessed through the use of a detailed daily reconstruction method to gauge happiness. See, for example, Daniel Kahneman, Alan B. Krueger, David A. Schkade, Norbert Schwarz, and Arthur A. Stone, "Survey Method for Characterizing Daily Life Experience: The Day Reconstruction Method," *Science* 306, 5702, December 3, 2004, pp. 1776–80. See also Daniel Kahneman, Alan B. Krueger, David Schkade, Norbert Schwarz, and Arthur A. Stone, "Would You Be Happier If You Were Richer? A Focusing Illusion," Princeton University, Center for Economic Policy Studies, 2006.

3. Daniel Gilbert, *Stumbling on Happiness,* Knopf, 2006.

4. Edward Diener and Martin E. P. Seligman, "Beyond Money: Toward an Economy of Well-Being," *Psychological Science in the Public Interest* 5, 1, 2004, pp. 1–31.

5. Nick Paumgarten, "There and Back Again," *New Yorker,* April 16, 2007.

6. The correlation coefficients between overall happiness and various factors are as follows: financial satisfaction (.369), job satisfaction (.367), place satisfaction (.303). Compare with income (.153), home-ownership (.126), and age (.06). The regression coefficients (from an ordered probit regression) are as follows: financial satisfaction (.342), place satisfaction (.254), job satisfaction (.254). Compare with income (.039), age (-.06), and education (-.09).

7. The overall correlation between income and community satisfaction is relatively weak (.15).

8. Mihaly Csikszentmihalyi, *Flow: The Psychology of Optimal Experience,* Harper Collins, 1990; and *Finding Flow: The Psychology of Engagement with Everyday Life,* Basic Books, 1997.

9. See Teresa Amabile, et al., "Affect and Creativity at Work," *Administrative Science Quarterly* 50, March 2005, pp. 367–403.

Chapter 10

1. Abraham Maslow, "A Theory of Human Motivation," *Psychological Review,* 50, 1943, pp. 370–96. Also see his, *Motivation and Personality,* Harper Collins, 1987 (first ed., Harper, 1954). For more, see www.maslow.com/.

2. Virginia Postrel, "Why Buy What You Don't Need: The Marginal Appeal of Aesthetics," *Innovation,* Spring 2004; "The Economics of Aesthetics," *Strategy and Business,* Fall 2003; *The Substance of Style: How the Rise of Aesthetic Value Is Remaking Commerce, Culture, and Consciousness,* HarperCollins, 2003. More is available at http://www.vpostrel.com/.

3. Michèle Bhaskar and Jeroen van de Ven, "Is Beauty Only Skin Deep? Disentangling the Beauty Premium on a Game Show," Discussion Paper, University of Essex, Department of Economics, January 2007.

4. James Rojas, "A Messy, Inspiring Urbanism," *National Post,* October 18, 2007. http://www.canada.com/nationalpost/news/toronto/story.html ?id=4e82b4f5–941a–421ea50c–18bd1d6dbff8&k=1731.

5. Miller McPherson, Lynn Smith-Lovin, and Matthew E. Brashears, "Social Isolation in America: Changes in Core Discussion Networks over Two Decades," *American Sociological Review* 71, 3, June 2006, pp. 353–75.

6. Ethan Watters, *Urban Tribes: Are Friends the New Family?* Bloomsbury USA, 2004.

7. Richard Lloyd and Terry Nichols Clark, "The City as an Entertainment Machine," *Research in Urban Sociology: Critical Perspectives on Urban Redevelopment* 6, 2002, pp. 357–78.

8. Taylor Clark, "The Indie City: Why Portland Is America's Indie Rock Mecca," *Slate,* September 11, 2007. Slate.com/id/2173729/.

9. Ronald Inglehart, *Modernization and Postmodernization: Cultural, Economic and Political Change in 43 Societies,* Princeton University Press, 1997. For more detail on the World Values Survey, see http://www.world valuessurvey.org/.

10. Benjamin Friedman, *The Moral Consequences of Economic Growth,* Knopf, 2005.

Chapter 11

1. Psychologists have found that there are three main factors that shape the fit between people and their environments. The first they call "selection." That is, people seek out social and physical environments that satisfy and reinforce their psychological needs. The second is "evocation"—people unconsciously elicit reactions from their social and physical environments that are a result of their psychological makeup. And the third is "manipulation." People essentially adjust and tailor their environments to reinforce and express their psychological qualities. See David Buss, "Selection, Evocation, and Manipulation," *Journal of Personality and Social Psychology* 53, 6, 1987, pp. 1214–21.

2. Will Wilkinson, "In Pursuit of Happiness Research: Is It Reliable? What Does It Imply for Policy?" Cato Institute Policy Analysis, April 11, 2007. Available at http://www.cato.org/pub_display.php?pub_id=8179. For more information and his blog, see http://willwilkinson.net/.

3. For more on psychologists' five-factor model of personality, see esp. Lewis Goldberg, "An Alternative Description of Personality: The Big-Five Factor Structure," *Journal of Personality and Social Psychology* 59, 1990, pp. 1216–29; Goldberg, "The Development of Markers for the Big-Five Factor Structure," *Psychological Assessment* 4, 1992, pp. pp. 26–42; Paul Costa and Robert McCrae, *Revised Personality Inventory (NEO-PI-R) and NEO Five Factor Inventory (NEO-FFI) Professional Manual,* Psychological Assessment Resources, 1992. See also http://www.centacs.com/quickstart.htm.

4. For more information on Seligman's and Peterson's Values in Action survey, see www.authentichappiness.sas.upenn.edu/questionnaires.aspx.

5. Peter J. Rentfrow, Sam Gosling, and J. Potter, "The Geography of Personality: A Theory of Emergence, Persistence, Expression of Regional Variation in Personality Traits," *Perspectives on Psychological Science,* 2008.

6. Margaret Mead, *Sex and Temperament in Primitive Societies,* Morrow, 1935; Ruth Benedict, *The Chrysanthemum and the Sword: Patterns of Japanese Culture,* Houghton Mifflin, 1946.

7. S.E. Krug, and R. W. Kulhavy, "Personality Differences Across Regions of the United States," *Journal of Social Psychology* 91, 1973, pp. 73–79.

8. If you are so inclined you can take the test, or just have a look at it. See http://www.outofservice.com/bigfive/.

9. Jared Diamond, *Guns, Germs and Steel,* W. W. Norton, 1997; Jefery Sachs and Jordan Rappaport, "The United States as a Coastal Nation," *Journal of Economic Growth* 8, 1, March 2003, pp. 5–46.

10. Max Weber, *The Protestant Ethic and the Spirit of Capitalism,* Dover, 2003 (first ed., 1905); Ronald Inglehart, *Modernization and Post-modernization: Cultural, Economic and Political Change in 43 Societies,* Princeton University Press, 1997.

11. Peterson analyzed data for the fifty largest U.S. cities, those with populations of 300,000 and above, giving him a sample of 203,000 people. The highest positive correlations for cities ranking high on my creativity index measures and his character strengths were for: curiosity (.43), love of learning (.36), appreciation of beauty, and creativity (.29). Conversely, the highest negative correlations were for modesty (−.65), spirituality (−.59), gratitude (−.59), teamwork (−.57), perseverance (−.52), hope (−.50), kindness (−.49), and fairness (−.48). The correlations between the creativity index and meaning were negative (−.39) for presence of meaning and positive (.30) for search for meaning. See Christopher Peterson and Nansook Park, "Why Character Matters," prepared for the International Positive Psychology Summit, October 6, 2007.

12. See Gary Gates, "Racial Integration, Diversity, and Social Capital: An Analysis of Their Effects on Regional Population and Job Growth," Williams Institute, UCLA School of Law, April 2003. Brian Knudsen, Kevin Stolarick, Denise M. Rousseau, and Richard Florida, "Bridging and Bonding: A Multi-dimensional Approach to Regional Social Capital," Carnegie Mellon University, 2005. Robert Putnam, "E Pluribus Unum: Diversity and Community in the Twenty-First Century," *Scandinavian Political Studies*, 30, 2, 2007, pp. 137–74.

Chapter 12

1. For a history of the concept of adolescence see, Jon Savage, *Teenage: The Creation of Youth Culture*, Viking Adult, 2007. Granville Stanley Hall, *Adolescence: Its Psychology and Its Relations to Physiology, Anthropology, Sociology, Sex, Crime, Religion and Education*. D. Appleton and Co., 1904. For a witty take on "adultalescence" see William Safire, "Lingo of Adultalescence," *New York Times Sunday Magazine*, September 30, 2007, p. 46.

2. Our initial rankings were developed for *Kiplingers* magazine and were featured in their June 2007 issue. But we have since revised our methodology along two lines. The *Kiplingers* rankings included cost factors. Our new rankings are done with and without those cost factors to identify the best regions regardless of cost, and then also to see where the best values were. Also, the earlier *Kiplingers* rankings covered all households without regard for sexual orientation. Our updated rankings provide a breakout for gay and lesbian households.

Chapter 13

1. See Joseph Cortright and Carol Coletta, *The Young and the Restless in the Knowledge Economy*, CEOs for Cities, December 2005.

2. National Longitudinal Survey of Young Adults, Bureau of Labor Statistics. Available at http://www.bls.gov/nls/.

3. Lacey Rose and Leah Hoffmann, "The Best Cities for Singles," *Forbes*, July 25, 2006.

4. Cortright and Coletta, "The Young and the Restless in the Knowledge Economy," December 2005.

5. Lena Edlund, "Sex and the City," *Scandinavian Journal of Economics* 1, 107, 2005, pp. 26–44.

6. "Singles Map," *National Geographic*, February 2007.

7. Gary Gates and Jason Ost, *Gay and Lesbian Atlas*, Urban Institute Press, May 2004.

8. Neil J. Smelser, *Handbook of Sociology*, Sage Publications, August 1988.

9. Much of the statistical data in this section is drawn from the National Marriage Project at Rutgers University. See, for example, *The State of Our Unions*, Rutgers University, 2007, and a wide range of other studies, data, and information available at http://marriage.rutgers.edu/.

10. Sam Roberts, "In the United States, the Married Are in the Minority," *New York Times*, October 15, 2006.

11. Ethan Watters, *Urban Tribes: Are Friends the New Family?* Bloomsbury USA, 2004.

12. For example, his *American Pastoral*, Houghton Mifflin, 1997.

13. More information about the Campus Philly initiative can be found at http://www.campusphilly.org/about_section/about.html.

14. Patrick McGeehan, "New York Area Is a Magnet for Graduates," *New York Times*, August 16, 2006.

15. The Segmentation Company, a division of Yankelovich, *Attracting the Young College-Educated to Cities*, CEOs for Cities, May 11, 2006. Available at http://www.ceosforcities.org/rethink/research/files/CEOsforCitiesAttractingYoungEducatedPres2006.pdf.

16. Bill Bishop, *The Big Sort*, Houghton Mifflin, 2008.

17. Tyler Cowen, "Incomes and Inequality: What the Numbers Don't Tell Us," *New York Times*, Economic Scene, January 25, 2007.

18. Ronald Mincy, *Black Males Left Behind*, Urban Institute Press, 2006.

19. Eckholm, Erik, "Plight Deepens for Black Men, Studies Warn," *New York Times,* March 20, 2006.

20. Steven Raphael, "The Socioeconomic Status of Black Males: The Increasing Importance of Incarceration," in Alan Auerbach, David Card, and John Quigley (eds.), *Poverty, the Distribution of Income, and Public Policy,* Russell Sage Foundation, 2005.

Chapter 14

1. See, U.S. Census Bureau, A Child's Day: 2004, *Selected Indicators of Child Well-Being,* http://www.census.gov/population/www/socdemo/2004_detailedtables.html. Sam Roberts, "Census Reveals Fear over Neighborhoods," *New York Times*, November 1, 2007.

2. Bill Gates, "Prepared Comments for the National Education Summit on High Schools," February 26, 2005. Available at http://www.gatesfoundation.org/MediaCenter/Speeches/CoChairSpeeches/Billg Speeches/BGSpeechNGA–050226.htm.

3. According to the study, 1,700 high schools, 2 percent of all U.S. high schools, are places where no more than 60 percent of entering freshman make it to their senior year. Nancy Zuckerbrod, "1 in 10 Schools Are Drop Out Factories," *Associated Press,* October 29, 2007. http://www.huffingtonpost.com/huff-wires/20071029/dropout-factories/.

4. Michael R. Bloomberg, "Flabby, Inefficient, Outdated," *Wall Street Journal,* December 14, 2006.

5. James Daly, "Future School: Alvin Toffler Tells Us What's Wrong— and Right—with Public Education," *Edutopia Magazine,* February 2007.

6. Gary Gordon with Steve Crabtree, *Building Engaged Schools: Getting the Most Out of America's Classrooms,* Gallup Press, 2006.

7. Suein Hwang, "Anxiety High: Moving for Schools," *Wall Street Journal,* February 20, 2007.

8. Michelle Conlin, "Meet My Teachers: Mom and Dad," *Business Week,* February 20, 2006. Also see *Homeschooling in the United States: 2003*, National Center for Education Statistics, February 2006.

9. Megan Othersen, Roxanne Patel, and Sandra Gordon, "10 Best Cities for Families." *Child Magazine.* Available online at http://www.child.com.

10. Available at www.kidfriendlycities.org.

11. Dolores Acevedo-Garcia, Nancy McArdle, Theresa Osypuk, Bonnie Leftkowitz, Barbara Krimgold, "Children Left Behind: How Metropolitan Areas Are Failing America's Children," Harvard School of Public Health and the Center for Health Advancement, January 2007.

12. "Out and Proud Parents," *The Economist,* June 28, 2007.

13. The Segmentation Company, a division of Yankelovich, *Attracting the Young College-Educated to Cities,* CEOs for Cities, May 11, 2006. Available at http://www.ceosforcities.org/rethink/research/files/CEOsforCitiesAttractingYoungEducatedPres2006.pdf.

14. Sam Roberts, "In Surge in Manhattan Toddlers, Rich White Families Lead Way," *New York Times*, March 23, 2007.

15. See James Howard Kunstler, *Geography of Nowhere: The Rise and Decline of America's Man-Made Landscape*, Free Press, 1996.

16. Joel Garreau, *Edge City: Life on the New Frontier,* Anchor, 1992.

17. See Andres Duany, Elizabeth Plater-Zyberk, and Jeff Speck, *Suburban Nation: The Rise of Sprawl and the Decline of the American Dream,* North Point Press, 2001.

18. Annie Murphy Paul, "The Real Marriage Penalty," *New York Times*, November 19, 2006.

19. Christine Schwartz and Robert Mare, "Trends in Educational Assortative Marriage from 1940 to 2003," *Demography* 42, 4, November 2005, pp. 621–46.

20. Gary Becker, *A Treatise on the Family*, Harvard University Press, 1991.

21. Raquel Fernández and Richard Rogerson, "Sorting and Long Run Inequality," *Quarterly Journal of Economics* 116, 4, November 2001, pp. 1305–41. See also Feng Hou and John Miles, "The Changing Role of Education in the Marriage Market: Assortative Marriage in Canada and the United States since 1970," Statistics Canada, May 2007. Available at http://www.statcan.ca/english/research/11F0019MIE/11F0019MIE2007299.pdf.

22. Blaine Harden, "Numbers Drop for the Married with Children: Institution Becoming the Choice of the Educated, Affluent," *Washington Post,* March 4, 2007.

23. Pamela Smock, "The Wax and Wane of Marriage: Prospects for Marriage in the 21st Century," *Journal of Marriage and Family* 66, 4, 2004, pp. 966–73. See also Sarah Avellar and Pamela Smock, "The Economic Consequences of the Dissolution of Cohabiting Unions," *Journal of Marriage and Family* 67, 2, 2005, pp. 315–27.

Chapter 15

1. See Leonard Steinhorn, *The Greater Generation: In Defense of the Baby Boom Legacy,* St. Martin's, 2007.

2. William H. Frey and Ross C. DeVol, "America's Demography in the New Century: Aging Baby Boomers and New Immigrants as Major Players," Milken Institute Policy Brief, March 2000.

3. Gay and Lesbian Elder Housing Group. See http://www.gleh.org/.

4. Pete Lydens, "Forget Golf Courses, Beaches and Mountains," *Wall Street Journal,* October 2, 2006.

5. Daniela Deane, "Clarendon Area's Urban Energy Helps Melt Midlife Ordeals Away," *Washington Post,* May 21, 2007.

6. Ben Casselman, "Animal House Meets Empty Nest," *Wall Street Journal,* May 11, 2007.

7. See J. Walker Smith and Ann Clurman, *Generation Ageless,* Collins, 2007.

Chapter 16

1. See Sperling's Web site: www.bestplaces.net/fybp/quiz.aspx.

2. The BLS has detailed and easy-to-use data on occupations and earnings on its Web site: www.bls.gov.

3. See the following Web sites: www.fbi.gov/ucr/ucr.htm has location-specific data on especially serious crimes. Detailed data for metropolitan

regions can be found at www.fbi.gov/ucr/cius_04/offenses_reported/ offense_tabulations/table_06.html. Information for towns and communities is at www.fbi.gov/ucr/cius_04/offenses_reported/offense_tabulations/ table_08.html.

4. Available at www.census.gov/acs/www/le.

5. Daniel Kahneman, Alan B. Krueger, David A. Schkade, Norbert Schwarz, and Arthur A. Stone, "Survey Method for Characterizing Daily Life Experience: The Day Reconstruction Method," *Science* 306, 5702, December 3, 2004, pp. 1776–80.

6. The Segmentation Company, a division of Yankelovich, *Attracting the Young College-Educated to Cities*, CEOs for Cities, May 11, 2006. Available at http://www.ceosforcities.org/rethink/research/files/CEOs forCitiesAttractingYoungEducatedPres2006.pdf.

Index